ALSO BY ELIZABETH KENDALL

Where She Danced

The Runaway Bride

The Runaway Bride

Hollywood Romantic Comedy
of the 1930's

Elizabeth Kendall

ALFRED A. KNOPF  NEW YORK 1990

Grateful acknowledgment is made to the following for permission
to reprint previously published material:

PolyGram International Publishing, Inc.: Excerpts from "Never Gonna Dance" and
"The Way You Look Tonight," music by Jerome Kern and lyrics by Dorothy Fields.
Copyright 1936 by PolyGram International Publishing, Inc., 3500 West Olive Avenue,
Suite 200, Burbank, CA 91505. Copyright renewed. International
copyright secured. All rights reserved. Used by permission.

Warner/Chappell Music, Inc.: Excerpt from "Remember My Forgotten Man"
by Harry Warren and Al Dubin. Copyright 1933 by Warner Bros. Inc.
(Renewed). All rights reserved. Used by permission.

The photographs reproduced in this book were provided with the cooperation and kind
permission of the following: Los Angeles County Art Museum Film Department: ii, 234–5,
261; Los Angeles County Museum of Art: 134–5, 147; Movie Stills Archive, Santa Fe:
201; Museum of Modern Art, New York: 66–7, 156–7, 157, 182–3, 222;
Photofest: v, 23, 26–7, 43, 50–1, 59, 79, 90–1, 105, 114–15,
127, 169, 210–11, 249; Wesleyan Cinema Archives: 2–3.

Library of Congress Cataloging-in-Publication Data
Kendall, Elizabeth.
The runaway bride.
1. Comedy films—United States—History and criticism.
I. Title.
ISBN 0-394-51187-5
PN1995.9.C55K38 1990   791.43'617'0973   90-53164

Manufactured in the United States of America

FIRST EDITION

Photograph facing title page: Claudette Colbert at the altar, looking dismayed.

FOR M. L. J.

and in memory of my grandmother
with the Irene Dunne wardrobe,
Rebecca Steites Kendall

Clara Bow

CONTENTS

DEDICATION

This page must invoke the name of an actress who anticipated the genre of romantic comedy—Clara Bow. Bow's career doesn't fall within the parameters of this book. Bow, in fact, was retiring from the screen in despair, just as the Depression was bringing the radical shift of ideology that allowed romantic comedy to emerge and great-hearted heroines to flourish. A beauty contest in Brooklyn had first brought her into the movies. She had arrived in Hollywood in 1923, a vibrant, gum-chewing, slightly tattered, and emotionally vulnerable eighteen-year-old. The pretentious social hierarchy of twenties Hollywood, embodied by her "discoverer" and producer, B. P. Schulberg, had slotted her into semipornographic flapper and Cinderella stories, where she would remain until the end of her career in 1933.

But now that Bow's movies are emerging from vaults, it is possible to see how original was the talent she brought to those cheap twenties formulae, and how critical is her place in the whole history of female screen acting in America. Bow not only summed up the techniques of her predecessors Mary Pickford, Lillian Gish, and Mae Marsh—the D. W. Griffith pioneers—she suggested those of her "descendants." She brought to the screen an openness that hadn't been seen before, an elemental good nature, a wish to please that read as a healthy sexuality, and an unstudied naturalness about the extremes of grief and joy—qualities that Mae West took from her and caricatured, and which the romantic comedy heroines then took over, via West, and turned into virtues. Yet Clara had done it all herself: no director, producer, or screenwriter ever tried to build a movie around her unstinting generosity. She constructed her own roles. Romantic comedy was obliged on the surface to repudiate her example, since she was associated with the wild jazz years thought responsible for the Crash. But this most exploited of actresses haunts the genre. Her trustingness lives in its heroines; her magnificent vulnerability prepared the way for them.

ACKNOWLEDGMENTS

I would like to thank the following:

The people who made the movies, and who graciously gave me their time and their memories, on the telephone, in letters, in person: Pandro Berman; Frank Capra; Viña Delmar; Irene Dunne; the late Cary Grant; the late Andrea Leeds Howard; Joel McCrea; the late Walter Plunkett; the late Morrie Ryskind; the late Hal Roach; the late Barbara Stanwyck—and, especially, Katharine Hepburn, who informed herself about the exact nature of my interview and precisely addressed the questions, and Claudette Colbert, who gave me extra time (and drove me to the other side of Barbados to make sure I saw it).

Relatives of people who made the movies, who were generous and trusting with materials and insights: Forrester Greene; Jean Owens Hayworth; Patricia Kirkland; Mr. and Mrs. William La Cava; Mrs. Leo McCarey; Mrs. Yvonne Stevens; George Stevens, Jr.; Jo Swerling, Jr.; Gertrude McCarey Tietzel; Mary Virginia McCarey Washburn.

Scholars, critics, administrators who helped with details and encouragement: Jeanine Basinger and Candace Bothwell of the Wesleyan Cinema Archives; David Chierichetti; Ned Comstock of the University of Southern California; James Curtis; Sam Gill of the Academy of Motion Picture Arts and Sciences Library; the late Jon Hall; the late Vincent Harbin (founder and tireless curator of the great RKO Archives, now dispersed); Richard Jewell; Larry Kleno; Joseph McBride; John Mueller; Emily Sieger, formerly of the Library of Congress; and Charles Silver and Ron Magliozzi at the Museum of Modern Art.

The Ford Foundation and the Guggenheim Foundation, for generous grants to research this book.

Pauline Kael, who offered encouragement at a crucial point.

Gregory Portley, artist-gardener of Manhattan Plaza, who created places of refuge outside my back door.

My copyeditor, Patrick Dillon, for his attention to spirit as well as detail.

My subeditor, Mary Maguire, for her diligence.

My agent, Maxine Groffsky, for her enthusiasm.

Friends who listened and had ideas: Tom Bender; Gail Conrad; Don Daniels; Ann Douglas; Adam Gopnik; Anne Hollander; Harry Kendall;

Joan Krevlin; Phillip Lopate; Y.P.; Carl Schorske; Elliott Sirkin; Laurie
Stone; and, especially, Arlene Croce and Margo Jefferson, mainstays each
in her own way throughout.

And my editor, Robert Gottlieb, who has seen millions more movies than
I will ever see, who remembers them in uncanny detail, and who responded
generously and cheerfully to all stages of this book.

PREFACE

James Stewart and Ginger Rogers are riding at night on top of a double-decker bus. The year is 1937. The movie is George Stevens' lyrical, though impacted, romantic comedy, *Vivacious Lady.* The two characters have just met, in the nightclub where she works as a singer. He's seen her putting over her song, in a playful fashion that mocks all the techniques of a big-band singer of the era but also conveys her own lilting autonomy.

Now Stewart's character is trying to explain what he does—why he likes being an associate professor at Old Sharon University. (Stevens has lit them softly, so that their faces seem to glow in the dark, with that rich light of black-and-white celluloid.)

"So when I see something like that university, it gives me quite a thrill, because . . ." Stewart says.

"Because why?" Rogers says.

"I'd like to tell you," he says, "but I'm afraid you'd just think I was bragging."

Here we would expect her, a mere entertainer, lacking anything like his prestige in the world, to look up at him sweetly and tell him it's all right with her if he brags. Instead, she responds with a statement that shows the same amused certainty about herself and her judgments that we've seen her bring to her rendition of her song. "No," she says thoughtfully, "I like people who think they're good."

THIS IS A MOMENT that can sum up what's rarest and most unexpected about the romantic comedies of the 1930s. Two people have fallen for each other, and they're trying to communicate across all that new and confusing emotion. Both of them are struggling to be honest; but it's the woman who presides over the tone of their exchange, who lays out the psychic space they will dare to occupy and gives them both permission to open up and trust each other.

Picturing a woman with this kind of easy emotional authority was not habitual to Hollywood. Throughout most of its history, the American movie industry did not allow actresses to carry themselves on the screen as self-knowingly as Rogers does here. If we think back over some of the great

Hollywood stars of serious drama—Garbo, Dietrich, Swanson, Crawford, Davis—we might suppose that femininity consisted of a surface glamour mixed with a fatal languor or an obsessive ferocity. The women portrayed by those stars were usually bent on some kind of self-destruction, even when they allowed themselves, at the end of a movie, to be rescued by romance. But the thirties romantic comedy stars—Barbara Stanwyck, Claudette Colbert, Myrna Loy, Katharine Hepburn, Ginger Rogers, Jean Arthur, Carole Lombard, Irene Dunne—stood for, and still stand for, something different: a vibrant strength of character. They look as stylish on the screen as the other movie stars, but they act more untragically sure of themselves. Their thirties roles assigned them this assurance, along with eccentricity, stubbornness, and wit. And having these women in our movie history along with the more fatalistic and doom-eager stars means that we possess an inherited idea of a spacious and prideful femininity.

Such an idea could not have surfaced in the movies without the economic chaos of the thirties, during which the whole country fell into the grip of the Great Depression. Poverty and uncertainty played havoc with people's assumptions about themselves. If the economic promises of American life could be reversed so suddenly, what was to prevent emotional promises from breaking down as well? Faced with the specter of total dissolution, Hollywood in the early thirties, the pre-Roosevelt, Herbert Hoover years, was obliged to change its stock character configurations. Rich people could not be shown as virtuous on the screen without an explanation, and poor people could not be made villainous. And for a while, male actors could no longer stand, as they had in twenties comedies, for some kind of decency at the heart of American life. A rash of violent and dispirited males (Warner Bros.'s and MGM's gangsters and drifters) cropped up—almost involuntarily, it seems—in early-thirties movies, and they posed a challenge to Hollywood's habitual social optimism. The wholesome, sensitive young heroes of Gary Cooper, James Stewart, and Henry Fonda were yet to surface: during the first years of the Depression, it proved almost impossible for the movies to articulate an ideal American man. So by process of elimination, the function of protagonist devolved upon the actresses.

That's why romantic comedy became so important in those years—and not just any romantic comedy, but a special kind that was first worked out by Frank Capra in his landmark 1934 movie, *It Happened One Night,* and which might be called "Depression romantic comedy." This genre used the heroine to articulate the good impulses at the bottom of the American soul, and it used the heroine's romance with a charming but psychologically underdeveloped young man to dramatize a rapprochement between the good and the more negligent impulses. Put another way, Depression romantic comedies responded to their audiences' loss of faith by making a virtue of personality traits usually thought of as feminine—a moral subtlety, an unashamed belief in the validity of emotions. And they did this with a light touch, in a spirit of good-natured, comradely, and even comical wisdom. This seriocomic ritual, this taking the side of a feisty but also vulnerable heroine, both comforted and amused audiences, which made it immensely valuable to the movie industry. But the formula for the ritual didn't originate with the official masterminds at the big studios; it came from Capra, and some other younger directors—George Stevens, Gregory La Cava, Leo McCarey, and Preston Sturges—who, like him, started out on the margins of the movie industry.

Many directors and writers made romantic comedies during the thirties, and many producers oversaw them. But the few directors named above, together with some writer-collaborators, were the ones who shaped the genre, who worked out its methodology, defined its philosophy, kept it responsive to the volatile course of the Depression, became its "auteurs." Capra and his confreres were also the ones who protected romantic comedy's semimaverick status in its heyday (between the stock-market crash and the onset of World War II) so that the genre didn't glaze over with official Hollywood approval. Strangely enough, their humble origins within the industry helped them to wield power in the thirties. All of them had learned movie-making on the silent-comedy lots of the twenties—all but Preston Sturges, and he worshiped silent comedy. They brought the slapstick humor of the silents into mainstream genres such as melodrama. (Romantic comedy, in fact, can be defined as a cross between silent comedy and melodrama.) But they also took care to keep their methods a secret from the producers and moguls: they let it be known that their improvisatory touch with a script could not be duplicated by authorial teams in assembly lines—and that's what made them so awesome to the Hollywood establishment.

More than skill at outwitting the bosses, though, it was these directors' genuine interest in women, and in romance imagined from a woman's point of view, that ensured their prestige in the thirties. These were men who found it easy to collaborate with their leading ladies, to scrutinize them and take narrative cues from them. Of course, Hollywood was full of directors who "specialized" in actresses. Even as romantic comedy emerged, Clarence Brown and Greta Garbo were creating a string of erotic melodramas together at MGM, as were Josef von Sternberg and Marlene Dietrich at Paramount. But teams such as Garbo-Brown or Dietrich-Sternberg were collaborators in the old-fashioned manner: they were ringing variations on the pop-culture theme of the rogue male making love to the despoiled and fatalistic female. The romantic-comedy directors, on the other hand, brought a style of male-female collaboration into the movies that hadn't yet been seen (except, perhaps, on the earliest movie sets where D. W. Griffith and his young actresses invented the whole art of screen acting). Capra and company treated their leading ladies not as icons of femininity but as companions. This choice wasn't so much a question of methodology as of psychology: these were men who didn't shrink from imagining what it might feel like to be a woman. Their portraits of romance, therefore, turned out wittier and fairer than Brown's or Sternberg's, and just as lyrical.

Lyricism in romantic comedy was mostly rejected by another group of directors who fell in, temporarily, with the thirties vogue for romantic comedy—the "action" men. John Ford, for instance, left westerns in 1935 to try romance, and therein lost all the lyric talent that galloping horses and dusty deserts had inspired in him. Howard Hawks also crossed over from action to romance and did somewhat better than Ford, making some fiendishly clever romances. W. S. Van Dyke came to romance from Great Adventure in the early thirties and brought a goofily understated style to the genre, especially in his *Thin Man* series. These action directors managed to treat their leading ladies as companions—but they had no need of them as muses. Nor did they need romantic comedy to delve into the very nature of movie-making, or the nature of love. Their specialty was exploring the mechanics, the nuts and bolts, the rapid-fire pace, of comedy-cum-romance. Temperamentally, they were at the opposite end of the Hollywood spectrum from the melodramatic directors—Brown, Sternberg, Frank Borzage—who explored the mechanics of sentiment. In the middle stand Capra and his confreres, who took something from each end of the spectrum in order to create, and then re-create, all through the thirties, this new, hybrid genre that spoke to the Depression.

THESE ORIGINATORS of romantic comedy, along with their leading ladies, are the subject of this book. In the era after the Crash—after Herbert Hoover, after the national trauma of nearly losing a whole way of life—some men and women in the movie industry collaborated with an extraordinary ease and sophistication. They worked in an arena only haphazardly protected from Hollywood's usually compulsive sentimentality; but in it, they made movies that contained real wisdom about the relations between the classes and the sexes—and real wit about the persistently hopeful naiveté of us, the Americans.

The Runaway Bride

1

CAPRA AND STANWYCK:

LADIES OF LEISURE

Frank Capra,
Barbara
Stanwyck, and
Adolphe Menjou
on the set of
Forbidden.

I N JANUARY OF 1930, Frank Capra was assigned to his first "woman's picture"—in other words, his first melodrama about romance. Capra was only thirty-one and was still unknown to most of Hollywood, but inside the small studio he worked for, Columbia Pictures, he was considered a phenomenon. He had shown up at Columbia in 1928, an unemployed director with a couple of feature-length silent comedies to his name—a nobody. He had offered to direct a script of his own for a very small fee. In an impulsive moment Columbia's boss, Harry Cohn, let him do it. And then, against all expectations, Capra's picture, *That Certain Thing,* took off at the box office. The picture deserved its acclaim. Though it was a typical twenties "business fantasy"—about the son of a restaurant mogul who marries an Irish tenement girl against his father's will, then wins back his father's favor in a business venture—it was presented with breezy, good-natured charm.

Capra followed his surprise hit with four more Columbia light romances in animated, late-twenties style (*So This Is Love, The Matinee Idol, The Way of the Strong,* and *Say It with Sables,* all 1928). He also saved one of Columbia's prestige productions which was in trouble, a naval adventure story, *Submarine.* In 1929, he took on the still-crude technology of putting soundtracks to pictures and turned out three part-talkie B pictures, *The Power of the Press, The Younger Generation,* and *The Donovan Affair,* and one A picture with a complete soundtrack, another naval adventure, called *Flight.* It was at the end of this string of achievements that Capra started on his woman's picture, *Ladies of Leisure.* Cohn had offered it to him as a sort of reward for service well done. MGM, the biggest studio in Hollywood, had just ventured into woman's melodramas, and Cohn wanted to emulate the big guys in any way he could. By giving Columbia's MGM imitation to Capra, Cohn was letting him know that the studio valued him.

In the course of making it, Capra would turn *Ladies of Leisure* into something much more complicated than a stock woman's picture. It would become an odd, rich movie, in which the documentary mode mingled with the fantasy mode; in which improvised humor vied with stock pathos. *Ladies of Leisure,* moreover, would serve as the sketchbook for the next, most important phase of Capra's career. It was in *Ladies* that he first tried out the strategies, the methods, the pictorial ideas he would bring to fruition four years later in the landmark picture *It Happened One Night,* the first Depression romantic comedy.

· · ·

THE ''GOLDEN ERA'' of Hollywood—the period in which everything
about the movies, from the manufacturing to the distributing, was controlled by the corporate studios—stretched from the mid-teens to the late
forties. In settled times in that era, movies were informally ordered by
genres, a system that was understood by everyone. Producers, directors,
writers, stars, cameramen knew what genre they were working on—a comedy, a melodrama, a western, a costume drama—and what its conventions
were. From a movie's billing at the local theater, the public usually got an
idea of what sort of story to expect. But in early 1930, the conventional
arrangement of movie genres was in serious disarray.

Sound had entered feature films in October 1927, when Warner Bros.
unveiled its first part-talking picture, *The Jazz Singer*. Warner Bros. was the
pioneer. The other studios were not convinced in 1927 that they would be
obliged to follow Warners. None of them rushed to abandon silent movies
and install the technology to make pictures with recorded sound—until
they saw, early in 1928, that the public would accept nothing less. Only
then did they embark on the complicated and costly changeover from silents
to talkies. On the movie lots, the old open-air stages of wood and cloth were
gradually replaced with sealed cement stages; the cameras were enclosed in
soundproof sheds; new, ultra-bright lights and microphones were installed
on the sets; and the machinery for editing soundtracks onto celluloid was
brought in and given room. At the same time, the rewiring of the approxi-
mately twenty-two thousand movie theaters across the country got under
way, directed, for the most part, by the movie studios, which owned many
of them. From 1927 to 1929 the question of movie genres barely concerned
the studios. Audiences would go to see anything that talked. Because of the
novelty of the talkies, in 1929 movie attendance reached an all-time high.
It was assumed in most studios that making a talkie simply meant adding
talk, music, and background noise to the scenario for a silent movie.

And that scenario, in the late twenties, would probably have been a
comedy. The bulk of Hollywood movies in those years, both silents and
part-talkies, concentrated on lightweight love—on youth, temptation, and
upward mobility. Big stars—Clara Bow, Colleen Moore, Richard Dix, Joan
Crawford, Marion Davies, William Haines, Janet Gaynor, even the comedi-
ans Buster Keaton and Harold Lloyd—played stock characters from popular
culture: flappers, college boys, young businessmen, and bosses' daughters.
These characters indulged in predictably animated behavior all over the
screen. Late-twenties movies displayed a veritable obsession with jokes, and
with jazzy gestures, spontaneous Charlestons, and general "good-time

spirit." A perfunctory touch of populism could usually be found in them: the hero or the heroine was often a social underdog who rose up in the world through luck, love, and some kind of wholesome merit. But rising in the world was viewed as absurdly easy. Wishes came true in late-twenties movies at every turn. Tenement heroines were handed new wardrobes and whisked off to nightclubs; earnest heroes got business breaks and made a million—all this without more than minor, temporary setbacks. The hijinks of the stars—their constant expressions of elation or of short-lived disappointment—covered up, in most mainstream movies, for a pervasive carelessness about dramatic structure.

The formula had worked even in mediocre silent films, though, because of the nature of the medium. Audiences in silent movies sat and received the innermost, wordless thoughts and feelings of the figures on the screen by means of pure gesture and close-up emotion, heightened by the titles. (The screen would go black and show the words the characters were saying.) In the silents, the most ordinary characters—the girl or boy next door— could become compelling protagonists, because their inner lives were revealed in mime by actors and actresses, to poignant musical accompaniment. Wordless, "choreographed" looks and gestures constituted a secret language in the silents, shared by the audience and the players—and this wordless drama could be generated from the slightest of situations.

But the proportion of emotion to action changed when audible dialogue was added. When the flappers and Arrow-collar men opened their mouths and *spoke* the lines audiences had once read in titles, the very sound of speech destroyed the intimacy of the silents. Talking pictures put a sort of scrim between players and audience, which blocked off that trusting and private communication in the dark. This wasn't much of a problem before 1929, when the novelty of the talkies carried all before it. But in that year, audiences began to tire of the floods of jazzy singing, dancing, and slanging that had poured into the talkies. *Variety,* that unfailingly quick barometer of enlightened public opinion, started to complain about shoddy workmanship and loss of quality.

THE MOVIES NEEDED a new tone, one tailored to the talkies instead of borrowed from the silents. Each of the studios in that crucial year 1929 tried to find that tone in a different way. Paramount concentrated on frothy musicals, bringing in a slew of stars who could sing and dance and speak with charming foreign accents. Fox developed outdoor westerns, borrowing from its own open-air newsreel technology, and making important contributions to the mobility of sound recording. Warner Bros., the studio that had pioneered sound in 1926 and '27, merely coasted, adding more slang and tough talk to its already slight stories. RKO simply hired more radio personalities. (Warner Bros. and RKO had recently thrust themselves into the Hollywood mainstream by their hook-ups with the dynamic new radio industry of the twenties; both lacked the other studios' experience with storytelling genres.) MGM, the biggest and richest studio in Hollywood, chose to concentrate on what must have seemed at first a simplistic, even old-fashioned movie genre—melodrama. But MGM's melodrama, it turned out, was the key that opened the way to the first real advances in talking drama.

Irving Thalberg, MGM's head of production, was interested above all in protecting his silent stars, especially his actresses, during the studio's changeover to sound. He was married to one of them, Norma Shearer. His tactic was to delay the talking debut of each actress, until he had crafted a movie, usually a melodrama, to suit her, even if it meant contradicting her persona from the silents. For Shearer's talking-picture debut, for instance, Thalberg rejected the fast and jazzy stories she had specialized in as a silent star and chose the courtroom soap, *The Trial of Mary Dugan,* about a Follies girl mistakenly accused of murder. (*The Trial of Mary Dugan* had opened on Broadway as recently as 1927, but it was written in scenery-chewing style by Bayard Veiller, a veteran of teens melodrama, who also directed the movie.) The box-office response told Thalberg he was on the right track. In May 1929, a month after the release of *Mary Dugan,* Thalberg consolidated MGM's investment in talking melodrama by releasing another influential example of the genre, a new version of the 1910 theatrical warhorse *Madame X,* about a wealthy woman's downward slide, starring the high-toned ex–stage actress Ruth Chatterton. Thalberg also held off Greta Garbo's talking debut even longer than Shearer's—until 1930. Then he put her into the Eugene O'Neill play *Anna Christie,* which was distinctly melodramatic.

Thalberg's "fallen-woman melodrama" was the first "new" genre to be generated (aside from the musicals) by the movies' conversion to sound. Naturally, the movies had seen fallen-woman tales before: in the teens and early twenties, Mary Pickford, Lillian Gish, and Mae Marsh had all undergone the loss of babies and reputations. Thalberg's policy, though, represented not only a recycling and updating of this older genre but also a shrewd deployment of it in a troubled time. The new-old melodrama, with its exaggerated pathos and its air of crisis, was calibrated to provide the intimate link with the audience that jazz talk and slang had removed from the movies. The main character in these melodramas—a wronged woman—

always had occasion to plead her cause (often to a judge and jury in a courtroom). And in pleading, the actresses could appeal to the audience's emotions with words, the way silent actresses had done with mime.

Thalberg couldn't have known in 1929 just how popular and resonant his new genre would become in the wake of the stock-market crash. Nor could Harry Cohn have guessed this. Cohn was simply intent on imitating the big studios, so that Columbia could acquire some class: if Thalberg made a weeper, Harry Cohn would make one too. Columbia was a small studio, founded by Cohn with his older brother, Jack, and their friend Joe Brandt. The Cohns and Brandt incorporated in 1924, and in 1926 they bought a California studio to operate in—a rattletrap place on Gower Street, Hollywood's Poverty Row. In 1927 Columbia got its first big break: its silent adventure movie *Blood Ship* was chosen to open the new Roxy Theater in New York. This rise in Columbia's status was prompted by the temperament of Harry, who in the late twenties was gradually wresting control of the studio from his partners. Harry was the one who lusted after prestige (and who in 1932 would appoint himself simultaneously president and chief of production of his studio—the only mogul in Hollywood holding both titles).

Three weeks after the April 3, 1929, release of *The Trial of Mary Dugan,* Harry bought a stage melodrama to match Thalberg's, the 1923 Broadway play *Ladies of the Evening,* which would become the movie *Ladies of Leisure.* The play, written by Milton Herbert Gropper (although it bore the stamp of its flamboyant and frequently maudlin producer, David Belasco), was a limp reworking of George Bernard Shaw's London hit of 1903, *Pygmalion.* It was about a young gentleman in a New York club who sees a prostitute outside the club window and bets two of his friends that he can reform her. Of course he ends up marrying her. Cohn must have thought his new property conveyed even more excitement over female transgression than *The Trial of Mary Dugan* or *Madame X:* a prostitute was lower in Hollywood's class hierarchy than a murderess or an aging derelict. (And *Ladies of the Evening* boasted a scandal in its history: it was one of four plays censored in 1924 by an overzealous New York district attorney.) Cohn probably thought he could accomplish two things at once: attract the swells by imitating Thalberg's high-class theatrical genre; draw the masses by throwing in some low-class pornography.

LADIES, however, went off in a direction that was neither pretentious nor pornographic. Cohn assigned the script to a young writer he had just imported from New York, a thirty-one-year-old newsman-turned-playwright named Jo Swerling. Swerling was a childhood immigrant, like Capra, though from Russia instead of Italy; a self-educated man who was passionate about culture. He loved the plays of Shaw and recognized, as Harry Cohn probably did not, the resemblance of Columbia's new property to its more robust (and unacknowledged) model, *Pygmalion*. To improve Gropper's play, which he scorned as claptrap, Swerling simply reinfused it with some of the witty, crypto-feminist spirit of Shaw. Specifically, he transformed *Ladies*'s limp and masochistic prostitute, Kay Arnold, into a late-twenties, New York–flavored update of Shaw's London flower girl, Eliza Doolittle. Swerling's Kay Arnold became a professional escort, a "party girl," who boasted as much Broadway vernacular in her repertoire as Liza had boasted Haymarket slang. Her gentleman protector, Jerry Arnold, became not just a colorless socialite, as in the play, but a painter. Swerling gave him this "hobby," to match Henry Higgins's linguistics, and then assigned him a vaguely bohemian place of residence, a Fifth Avenue penthouse.

Ladies, therefore, was altered even before Capra got to it. Swerling's script had removed it from the condition of sentimental melodramas like *Mary Dugan* or *Madame X.* But *Ladies* hadn't become merely a good-time Cinderella tale in early-talkie Hollywood style; it had turned into a mock-Shavian, slice-of-life drama. Swerling had colored it with Broadway's worship of the latest slang and appetite for vulgarity. Starting in the mid-twenties, the Broadway theater had experienced a fascination with modern-day underworlds—with their texture of life and their wildly inventive and tough-posturing languages. A slew of hit plays (*Broadway,* 1926, *Burlesque,* 1927, *The Barker,* 1927, *The Front Page,* 1928, Swerling's own *The Kibitzer,* 1929) celebrated those vibrant local milieux—vaudeville shows, circuses, newspapers, nightclubs, and corner stores—where the new slang was hatched. Swerling's real contribution to *Ladies of Leisure* lay in connecting that literary enthusiasm about low life to a movie plot about a girl on the make, bringing her language alive in risqué New York style.

It wasn't Swerling's script alone, though, that gave Capra his scheme for revising the play in the movie: the actress whom he cast as Kay Arnold proved even more crucial to him. But before Capra even met Barbara Stanwyck, a catastrophic event occurred that was to change the nature of life in America and, along the way, to transform the very intention behind ˙the making of *Ladies of Leisure.*

BETWEEN FRIDAY, OCTOBER 25, and Tuesday, October 29, 1929, the New York stock market fell sixty-nine points—a rout in those days—and in the succeeding week it lost an estimated thirty billion dollars of its value.

At every level, from corporate investments to family installment buying, the economy had been propped up by unsubstantiated credit, so when the market went, so did banks, companies, jobs, mortgages, savings. In the big cities, the signs of disaster grew obvious to anyone watching: homeless people congregated, and breadlines formed. In the country, conditions were even worse, because the farmers had been in a depression for most of the twenties.

The movie industry didn't feel the effects of the Crash right away, except as a damper on some of the studio merger plans that had been burgeoning in the financial euphoria. Fox in the end didn't annex MGM, as it had intended, nor did any of the Big Three studios—Fox, MGM, Paramount—buy Warner Bros. But movie attendance around the country stayed high, because soundtracks remained a novelty; and the conversion of theaters from silence to sound continued after the Crash. Still, some individuals in Hollywood were harmed by the Crash, and Capra was one of them. In early October 1929 Capra, according to his autobiography, had been persuaded by Harry Cohn to put his savings—the money he had made from his rise at Columbia—into the stock market; before that he had kept it in safe-deposit boxes. Of course he lost everything when the market fell. And to someone who had grown up with Capra's chronic bad luck and poverty, the loss was bitter.

Capra had come to this country with his family from Sicily when he was six years old. The sixth of seven children, while growing up he had been deprived of contact with the theater or the movies by the demands his family made on even its youngest members. As a little kid Frank sold newspapers in downtown Los Angeles. He was obliged to work twice as hard as most other boys putting themselves through school, since he was supposed to contribute to the family till as well as earn the money he needed for himself. His mother worked in a factory; his father picked oranges. The family finally scraped together the money to buy an orange grove of its own, but Capra's father died in an accident with a well pump soon after they had bought the farm, so they had to give it up. Fatherless, Frank put himself through high school and then college by working in factories and in a newspaper plant. He graduated from Cal Tech with a degree in chemical engineering, just as the U.S. was entering World War I. Like many other proud college graduates, he enlisted.

He wanted to go back to Europe, where he had come from, to fight for his new country; instead, the Army sent him up the coast to San Francisco to teach engineering. That was the beginning of a new streak of bad luck. In 1919, he caught influenza during the dread flu epidemic, which meant he went back into the postwar job market late and lost out to other vets.

From about 1919 to 1921 Capra held no steady job. Neither did many other young war veterans—a situation whose repercussions would be felt nearly ten years later in the Great Depression. (The Depression's "forgotten man" was, technically, a World War I veteran. "Remember my forgotten man," went Harry Warren and Al Dubin's famous song in *Gold Diggers of 1933;* "You put a rifle in his hand / You sent him far away / You shouted hip hooray / Now look at him today!") In Capra's unemployed years, he went out on the road; he bummed through the West, peddled various products, hustled poker, hopped freights. At one point he worked as a private tutor to a son of old gold-mining wealth, an experience that, if his autobiography can be trusted, opened his eyes to how rich the American rich could be.

Capra stumbled onto movies by accident in 1921, accepting an odd job from a seedy ex-actor making poetic movie shorts. The actor let Capra direct one of them himself, the Kipling-inspired *Fultah Fisher's Boardinghouse.* This experience prompted Capra to begin a serious apprenticeship in movie-making. He worked his way up from film editor in San Francisco, to comedy gag writer in Hollywood on the Hal Roach and Mack Sennett lots, to writer and then director for the Sennett star Harry Langdon. The high point of Capra's silent comedy career was directing two Langdon features for Sennett—1926's *The Strong Man* and 1927's *Long Pants* (movies that are funny in some parts but uneven overall). But Capra quarreled with Langdon on the set of *Long Pants.* Langdon wanted to be his own director, like Chaplin; Capra walked out on him just before the end of the movie, so Langdon shut him out of Hollywood by spreading the rumor that it was he, not Capra, who had done the directing.

This dispute plunged Capra back into the nightmare of unemployment and vagrancy he had known after the war—a nightmare compounded by his Italian family's disapproval of his apparently unstable career. He was married by then to his first wife, Helen, and he was supporting his mother and sister as well. Late in 1927 he managed to make one small-time movie, *For the Love of Mike,* at William Randolph Hearst's New York studio, but he was never paid and the movie bombed. By the time Capra got to Columbia in 1928, he was desperate. He made good there beyond his wildest dreams, but the loss of his savings in the winter of 1929 stirred up all his old feelings of inferiority and helplessness, along with his old intuitive mistrust of the rich and reverence for the poor. The Crash, in other words, brought an emotional populism, half bitter resentment and half despair, back to him in full force. We know that because we can read it in the movie. We can also read in the movie how, amid the tangled emotions of the Crash, Barbara Stanwyck came to represent, for Capra, a symbol of his resentment and an antidote to his despair.

HARRY COHN had seen the young Barbara Stanwyck in a Hollywood charity show with her husband, the famous vaudevillian Frank Fay. Hollywood considered Stanwyck a minor Broadway star. She had played the lead in *Burlesque,* the long-running Broadway hit of 1927; but it was her husband's movie contract with Warner Bros. that had brought her to California. Once there, she appeared in one low-budget United Artists talkie, *The Locked Door* (1929), which flopped, and did one screen test for Warners, which was ignored. Cohn, who was as crass as any Hollywood mogul and yet shrewd about predicting talent, decided to take a chance on her. He took out an option on her services, put her in a Columbia throwaway, *Mexicali Rose* (1929), and then urged her on Capra for *Ladies*—a substantial gamble, since *Ladies* was expensive by Columbia standards. Capra didn't want Stanwyck at first; he was thinking of someone else for Kay Arnold, and resisted her—until he saw her screen test. It was a scene from the Broadway play *The Noose,* in which her character, a chorus girl, pleads tearfully to the governor to let her bury the body of the man she loves. Capra "got a lump in his throat as big as an egg," he says in his book, and he hired Stanwyck on the spot.

His impulse served him well. In Stanwyck, Capra found not only a screen actress who was supple and unstilted but also someone like himself, a city kid whose life had been as full of struggles and deferred hopes as his. Born Ruby Stevens, she was orphaned at two and grew up in foster homes in Brooklyn. She got her first job at thirteen, wrapping bundles in a Brooklyn department store. At fifteen, with the help of a vaudevillian older sister, she broke into the chorus line at the Strand nightclub, then moved up to the touring company of the Ziegfeld Follies. She might never have made it out of the chorus line though, if it hadn't been for Broadway's infatuation with late-twenties underworlds, which provided material for theater-verité-style plays. *The Noose* (1926), written and produced by Willard Mack, was a gangland melodrama that called for a chorus girl in a bit part. Stanwyck at nineteen got the part and became a minor celebrity for her big pleading scene. The next year she opened opposite the dancer and comedian Hal Skelly in *Burlesque,* a backstage tale about a husband-and-wife song-and-dance team. It was again a role that imitated her life, and it made her a star.

In the course of being "discovered," Stanwyck was put through rigorous training in repertory, speech, and manners by her two producers, *The Noose*'s Willard Mack and *Burlesque*'s Arthur Hopkins. But she wasn't over-trained. She left Broadway before she had a chance to glaze over in stage-star manner. When Capra met her in Hollywood, she still had her Brooklyn accent, her street-tough façade, and a palpable aura of hurt hopefulness right behind the façade. She did not have an established persona: she didn't yet know who she was on the screen. Nor did Capra know whether he could handle a melodramatic woman's picture—especially one with an untried actress in the starring role. But Capra and Stanwyck inspired each other to a new level of skill. Their effect on each other electrified the movie and gave it, from its first scene, a social slant that hadn't been spelled out in a Hollywood production since before the twenties boom.

THE OPENING SHOT of *Ladies of Leisure* shows a dark street in midtown Manhattan, with pedestrians hurrying by on the sidewalk. Suddenly they are shocked by some objects falling out of the sky. A crowd gathers. The camera quickly moves where passers-by would look—up the windowed façade of a swank apartment building, to the illuminated penthouse on top, where some drunken young ladies are gleefully throwing liquor bottles into the street. Here is a visual allegory, presented in mock-newsreel style, of what was happening in the aftermath of the Crash: something dangerous was falling on the ordinary people in the street, something that came from the careless doings of the idle rich above them. This sequence not only describes the twenties turning catastrophically into the thirties; it reconstitutes the movie audience as a body with a new, post-Crash social perspective. We are the ones in the street, looking up, not the ones in the penthouse, looking down. We don't automatically want to live in that penthouse, the way we would if a more complacent director had made this movie. We are wary of penthouse life, and we resent the power that penthouse people have over us. The goings-on up there seem to us like a reminder of the mad decade just past—the twenties, one long party on top of a skyscraper.

This reorienting of the audience determines the movie's perspective on its central characters. Jerry, the rich hero (played by the stolid and affable twenties actor Ralph Graves), is discovered brooding at the window in the midst of the revels. We approve of him, not because he is rich and eligible, but because he is out of sync with the party, alienated from his own class. That in itself was not so new: Hollywood protagonists were supposed to be more sensitive than the rest of their group. But the way he meets his leading lady breaks wholly with Hollywood precedent. Jerry abandons his snooty fiancée and her guests and goes out in his car, by himself, into the country.

On a hill above a shoreline, his tire blows. At that moment, Barbara Stanwyck in a white gown is docking at the shore in a rowboat. She calls out
to him, scrambles up the hill, and comes into close-up—her long, wavy hair
disheveled, her mascara smudged.

This is not one of those class-bound settings that were habitual to late-
twenties movies—the department store in *It* (1927), where Clara Bow, a
salesgirl, met Antonio Moreno, the boss; the hotel in *Orchids and Ermine*
(1927), where Colleen Moore, a telephone girl, flirted with millionaire
guest Jack Mulhall; the office building in Capra's own *That Certain Thing*
(1928), where Viola Dana's candy seller bumped into Ralph Graves's young
swell. This hill above the shore is a neutral place, empty of people and of
social codes. Here Kay and Jerry are not "party girl" and "rich guy," as they
are in the city; they're momentary equals. They have something in common:
they've both fled from twenties-style orgies. Kay has used the rowboat to
escape from a wild party on a boat; Jerry has escaped another in his car. This
idea of a neutral, classless meeting place was probably more Capra's than
Swerling's. In *Ten Cents a Dance,* which Swerling wrote for Stanwyck the
year after *Ladies,* he arranged for her taxi dancer to meet the wealthy lover,
Ricardo Cortez, right in the socially stratified dance hall, whereas Capra,
after *Ladies of Leisure,* always had his cross-class lovers meet somewhere out
of the way for both of them—a ship, a bus, a rainy sidewalk.

It's not just Jerry who sees Kay differently here than he would see her in
the city. We, the movie audience, incorporate her setting into our first
impression of her, and so avoid classifying her with the cute Cinderellas of
the late twenties—Colleen Moore, Louise Brooks, Viola Dana, and the
others. That kind of heroine always embodied a paradox: her setting
branded her "lower-class," but she was also supposed to possess a kind of
moral refinement that would make her worthy of the "prince" she was to
marry. (Twenties movies even condescended to the great Clara Bow,
through her clothes, her kewpie dolls, her spit curls, and her slang, even
as they telegraphed that she was a swell, principled kid inside.) But this Kay
Arnold comes with no such coded assurances. By the time we have figured
out who she is and where she belongs, we have also realized that she violates
the convention that assigned blamelessness to the Cinderellas. Kay is no
slum flower: she's an opportunist. Living off men is her job. Swerling's
script has given her a cynicism that is surprisingly gritty even to us today.
"Do you tote a flask—you know, first aid to the nearly injured?" is the first
thing she says to Ralph Graves in her untutored yet suave Brooklynese. And
then we watch her go to work. She prompts Jerry to offer her a ride back
to the city; she convinces him to put his polo coat around her while they're
riding; she steals the wallet out of the coat pocket (though she later returns

it), and she covers for her actions with a stream of clever patter. "That's my racket. I'm a party girl. I'm the filler-in," she says sardonically. And when she takes the wallet, she says "Isn't it a lovely night?" to distract him with poetics.

This is an almost documentary attempt at presenting a "real" type on the screen. People knew about this type from newspaper scandals—she was a version of the "Follies girl," who danced in the chorus of Ziegfeld shows and lived in apartments paid for by older gentlemen. But they hadn't seen her in Hollywood movies—or at least not as the heroine. Kept girls usually showed up in bit parts, representing the path to degradation. Making a type like Kay the heroine constituted a breakthrough in itself. And because of Stanwyck's acting, Kay Arnold emerged even more lifelike than Swerling's script had imagined her. Stanwyck plays her tough, as the script indicates. But as she reads the lines, she also presents us with the spectacle of a young woman on her own, improvising a living. She gives Kay a kind of lonely cheerfulness. And Stanwyck's persona, as it was emerging in this film, absorbs and neutralizes the tawdriness of Swerling's portrait. The young Stanwyck projected an austere beauty onto the screen—the wide, thin mouth, straight brows, and classically straight nose—softened by a creamy youthfulness of skin. The purity of her face contrasts wonderfully with the risqué talk that comes out of her mouth. Altogether, she possesses a personality more complicated than either the cute and reckless kid of late-twenties movies or the pathetic, persecuted woman of the nascent MGM weepers. We accept that she's a prostitute, but we understand that her instincts for independence run against the grain of her profession. She's like us, the newly impoverished audience—not too proud to work at a low job, but meant for finer things.

BACK IN HER APARTMENT after meeting Jerry, Kay tells her roommate, Dot (played by Marie Prévost), that she's met a society guy, and he has asked her to pose for a painting. It's a sunny, easy scene, yet as revisionist as Kay and Jerry's meeting. Before 1930, movie heroines usually had lived with their families: the Cinderellas in tenements, the flappers in mansions. It was the second-lead "bad girls" who lived by themselves, with lingerie spilling out of drawers and bonbons out of boxes. (Only in semiexperimental films like Paul Fejos's *Lonesome* [1928] and King Vidor's *The Crowd* [1928] did respectable heroines have apartments they paid for themselves.) But Capra and Swerling didn't make the *Ladies of Leisure* apartment a naughty place, filled with signs of dissipation. They made it wholesomely untidy. There are kimonos, not "step-ins," on the chairs. And Kay and Dot seem easily, not unctuously, at home in it. They wash the dishes; they perch on chairs; they lean on doorways to talk to each other. Even when Kay sits on Dot's bed, it looks natural and matter-of-course.

This was a new approach to the very fact of being "lower class." Capra, Swerling, and Stanwyck all had worked their way up in the world—and on some level, their own experiences informed this Kay Arnold and made her more "real" than her movie forebears. But even more important than experience were the generic conventions they brought to the character. None of the three belonged to mainstream Hollywood. Swerling and Stanwyck had learned their crafts on Broadway. Capra had learned his in a corner of Hollywood that was separate from the big studios—the silent-comedy lots: they taught him to animate the underdog.

The teams on the silent lots had worked by trial and error to create a comic persona. They would study what a leading comic had done in shows or earlier movies; they would observe him on the set; they would try out gags, settings, and situations; and they would gradually construct a fictitious character who was related by metaphor to the qualities the comic projected on the screen. The comedy teams went after "character" instead of "story line," psychic insight instead of moral lesson. On the set of *Ladies of Leisure,* Capra did exactly that with his actresses. Swerling had written a clever Kay Arnold into the script. Capra fleshed out Kay's personality—tough, direct, yet always mournful—by observing what Stanwyck could do in front of a camera.

And Capra created the character of the roommate, Dot, which had barely existed in Gropper's play, by means of this impromptu, take-from-what's-at-hand method. Marie Prévost was a frizzy-haired, saucer-eyed comedienne who had emerged a star in the mid-twenties, working with Ernst Lubitsch in his "sex comedies" at Warner Bros. By the late twenties she had sunk back to the second-lead slot. Columbia hired her for *Ladies*—the studio saved money on stars who had lost prestige—but she showed up at the studio with an unexpected weight problem. So Capra and Swerling wrote it into the movie. "You're talkin' to a lady that's gonna eat caviar," says Prévost, preparing to go out to "work" at another party. "Don't eat too much, just 'cause it's free," Stanwyck rejoins. Several gags improvised from Dot's plumpness—her love of food, her motorized fan belt to jiggle off the fat, the song she sings while she stands on this machine, "Frankie and Johnny"—created a memorable character, a good-natured foil for Stanwyck's melancholy Kay.

So long as the characters were being introduced, Swerling and Capra's different methods complemented each other. But as the drama deepened, Capra's impromptu directing began to vie with Swerling's theatrical script. Kay goes several times to Jerry's penthouse to pose for his painting, which he wants to call *Hope*. She bristles at Jerry's milieu, but she bristles too cleverly, like Eliza Doolittle wisecracking at Henry Higgins's experiments with her gutter speech. "Look up!" Ralph Graves keeps telling Stanwyck as he tries to sketch her, and Stanwyck retorts that the picture ought to be called *The Lost Zeppelin*. We suffer through a series of gags in which Lowell Sherman, as Jerry's best friend, tries to keep himself drunk. He goes after Jerry's Napoleon brandy, proposing "a little nippy with Nappy." Swerling has packed the script with far too many bromides and epigrams.

But little by little the movie intensifies its focus on Stanwyck. It's as if the camera had acquired a will of its own. Instead of filming the characters from middle distance in early-talkie theatrical style, it shows us Stanwyck's face again and again in close-up. There is an excuse for this: the artist within the movie is painting her. But sometimes the camera even peers at Stanwyck over Ralph Graves's shoulder, as if annoyed that Graves has interposed himself in front of her. There is one remarkable moment when Graves's Jerry, in an effort to see Kay better, goes over to her modeling chair and proceeds to wipe off her lipstick, roughly, with a handkerchief, and peel off her false eyelashes. Swerling wrote this as another Henry Higgins–like act of mild sadism. Capra transformed it into a comment on the purity of Kay Arnold—and of Stanwyck herself. The camera goes right in on Stanwyck's clear, calm young face, beautifully pale without cinematic makeup. It looks as if Capra were trying to get under the surface of Stanwyck's Kay, to assign her an interior self that was deeper and more compelling than Swerling's clever wisecracker.

Almost involuntarily, Capra was rewriting the conventions of movie romance, even though the script was against him at this point. It tries to convey Jerry's and Kay's attraction to each other by means of Jerry's increasing brusqueness and Kay's nascent melancholy. (Swerling wrote a scene in a Chinese restaurant for instance, which Capra shot, in which Kay confesses angrily to Dot that she's fallen for Jerry.) But in general, Capra and Stanwyck had so softened and intensified Kay Arnold that she no longer fit into Swerling's hard-boiled Broadway drama. The new Kay was so emotional she was bound to lose control in some way. So Capra drastically altered the script to dramatize her breakdown.

Jerry brusquely invites "Miss Arnold" out to the penthouse terrace one night to take a rest from the work of the painting. Stanwyck, in a beautiful close-up, puts a record on the phonograph, so that soft music drifts out to the terrace. But once outside and sitting down, she finds herself so hurt by Jerry's detachment that she blurts out her pain. "Can't you call me Kay? I'm a human being!" Stanwyck invests her cry with the mournful desperation that was her special note. Swerling had written this line to sound at the end of the scene, almost as a wisecracking aside. Capra moved it up to the front of the scene, and improvised most of the dialogue that follows. (It's penciled into the margins of his working script.) Kay's outburst resolves itself in a "Capraesque" rather than a "Swerlingesque" situation. Jerry begins to tell Kay about Arizona, "where you can reach up and touch the stars." She looks up at the stars and dutifully thinks about Arizona (although she misunderstands at first and thinks he's telling her to watch the twinkle of the streets down below—her world). The evocation of Arizona puts the two back into an imaginary "wide-open space," just like the hill above the shore where they first met. In Arizona it wouldn't matter who they are in the social hierarchy, just who they are on the inside.

THIS IDEA that the woman needs respect from the man before love can happen—that love may depend on a climate of respect between a man and a woman—was entirely new to Hollywood. The late-twenties Cinderellas had wanted romance and wealth, not recognition of their personhood: they were content to be the pets of the men they fell in love with. The new weeper ladies despaired of getting respect, because they'd sinned; so they accepted romance as a narcotic. But Kay Arnold's very identity in the movie is based on her constant sensation of deserving respect. Capra has endowed her with something more complex than the Shavian spunk that Swerling put into her vocabulary: he has allowed her a private, thoughtful core of *self* that relates more to the movies than to the stage, but which had not yet been spelled out in a movie heroine's nature.

Capra got the qualities of this Kay Arnold more from a type of movie hero—the twenties comic—than from a heroine. The great silent comics had played clowns who longed for the stuff of respectability—warmth, comfort, nice clothes, and maybe love—which they never got, except by accident, at the end. But their movies weren't about getting those nice things; they were about *not* getting them. Twenties comedies had celebrated personalities formed in adversity yet clinging to self-respect—the dandified Charlie Chaplin, the sadly sweet Buster Keaton, the eager Harold Lloyd, the dimly embarrassed Harry Langdon. Their piquant performing had allowed people in the twenties audience to acknowledge the part of themselves that was funny-looking, or poor, or awkward, and yet still stubbornly proud. *Ladies of Leisure*'s Kay Arnold doesn't look anything like a comic caricature: her clothes, her apartment, her city know-how all mark her as a melodrama heroine, cut to a more "realistic" cloth. She's a grown-up, cynical young woman on the surface, not an oversized child like the silent comics. And yet she contains a stubborn *self* like them, comprised of her longing, her resentment, and her improvised dignity.

Swerling's sophistication, Stanwyck's naturalness, and Capra's impromptu methods, functioning inside of a melodrama, had begun to suggest a new dynamic for movie romance. It was the dynamic of silent comedies, but with the genders reversed. In the silents, the male comics had struggled for self-respect along with love. In *Ladies* it's the young woman who is struggling. Moreover, switching the gender allowed Capra to encounter the subject of sexuality, which the silents had excluded. There is a "sex scene" of sorts in this movie. Kay faints in her chair after posing till 1:00 A.M., and Jerry arranges for her to stay the night on the studio divan. He lends her a pair of his pajamas and then retires to his room. It's raining heavily outside. We see several chiaroscuro tableaux of Stanwyck preparing for the night: Stanwyck's torso silhouetted against the glowing fireplace; her darkened figure undressing before the tall studio windows awash with rain; the same figure in her lingerie viewed from the rainy outside into the lit salon; then the young, calm face of Stanwyck in close-up, lying on the studio couch. Harry Cohn must have told Capra to put some sex in the movie: these images bear some resemblance to the conventional soft-porn of the time (twenties heroines were always stripping down to their lingerie).

And yet the scene isn't placed here just for titillation. There's another kind of awareness in it—a sensual feel for the qualities of light on celluloid, for the different ways to illuminate a face, for the look of firelight in a room and the sheen of rain on a window with the light shining through it. This sequence reveals that Capra's sensuality was connected, not just to eros, but to the whole set of vivid sensations belonging to Kay's plight, her infatuation with Jerry, her fear of revealing this. Capra had already shown a special sensitivity to the socially inferior lover in his first Columbia movie, *That Certain Thing,* in the scene where the newly married heroine, informed of her father-in-law's displeasure, walks forlornly home in the rain to her family's tenement at night, wearing her wedding dress. Here was a memorably bedraggled image. But the hasty, overanimated atmosphere of late-twenties movie-making hadn't permitted Capra to explore such lyric impulses. Fortunately for Capra, *Ladies of Leisure* was intended as a high-class picture; it was supposed to include lyricism. Moreover, Capra had employed Joseph Walker, Columbia's sensuous "pictorial" cinematographer, for *Ladies.* And there was Stanwyck herself, who stirred up Capra's imagination as no movie actress had done before. The result of all this was a "sex" scene that belongs to the deepest kind of storytelling rather than to pornography. It is a lyric visualization of Kay's wish to be accepted into the home and the affections of a wealthy protector. The scene becomes more gorgeous—the wish more erotic—because it's filtered through Kay's skepticism, her impoverished expectations.

These subjective currents washing through Capra's movie make it much more powerful than a twenties wish-fulfillment about cross-class romance. In the twenties, such romances had occurred in the twinkling of an eye. In *Ladies,* romance becomes a near-hopeless proposition, threatened by dangers and obstructions. And it is obstructed most by Kay's own melancholy. This "sex scene" says something, by inference, about the mood of the movie audience in early 1930. That audience hadn't yet had time to give up its automatic, twenties-style wish to be wealthy, to be united with wealth. But it must have begun to feel, in the aftermath of the Crash, a melancholy dimming of the prospects. Capra put a little tag onto the end of the scene, as if to tease the audience for even thinking about that old twenties combination of sex and quick wealth. We see Jerry's doorknob turning, a close-up of Jerry's slippers padding across the floor toward Stanwyck—is he going to molest her?—then a blanket being laid on the supposedly sleeping Stanwyck by the hands of an invisible Ralph Graves. Jerry has proved himself once and for all a gentleman, who can respect even a "party girl" like Kay. The scene fades out on a close-up of Stanwyck's face, shining with gratitude.

STANWYCK AT THIS POINT has become the movie's instrument: it vibrates to her feelings, and its climax comes at the apogee of the furious internal struggle between her hopes and her melancholy. Capra dramatizes this in tour-de-force manner, drawing on all the resources the movie has been experimenting with—Swerling's smart dialogue, Stanwyck's wounded pride, his own strategies for producing spontaneity, and even his new sensitivity to the qualities of light and air. This climactic scene opens on a close-up of eggs frying in a skillet—a witty contrast to the rain and firelight of the previous scene. Kay in an apron is making Jerry's breakfast. She goes out to the terrace—now flooded with sunlight—and picks some flowers for the table. Jerry sits down at the table and, in another Henry Higgins–like move, puts a newspaper in front of his face. Kay, with a little smile of dazed adoration, sits down in the other chair at the table, and moves aside a vase so she can see Jerry better. The vase falls (a mishap on the set); Kay bursts into tears.

So charged has the scene grown that euphoria can change to disaster in an instant; and still Capra prolongs the tension. Stanwyck has Kay try a gag to stop herself from crying: she throws a morsel of toast into the air and attempts to catch it in her mouth, saying in a wavery voice, "Can you do this?" Just as we feel Kay can't hold herself in check any more, Capra brings on Jerry's father, who barges in to announce that Kay is nothing but a gold digger, and pulls out his checkbook to buy her off. Now Kay does break down, and retreats to her modeling chair, twisting a handkerchief, sobbing, "Oh, gee . . . oh, gee." His father gone, Jerry takes out his confusion in his usual brusque manner, yelling that he knew all along she was a gold digger. Kay puts her hand over Jerry's mouth to protect her dignity, and all the pain flows into her touch. She comes into his arms.

It's a wonderful love scene, and a triumph for Capra and Stanwyck's Kay. She is the one who has made the decisive gesture to bring them together. She has overcome her melancholy and reached for Jerry, claiming him. But the movie can't sustain this level of experimentation, this stunning mix of humor and melancholy that gives it such a lifelike texture. In trying to resolve the story, Capra falls into cliché. Kay and Jerry's plans—to marry and go to Arizona—go awry when Jerry's grand and pompous mother visits Kay and begs her to give Jerry up "for his own good." Kay agrees, in a scene that Stanwyck plays with an affecting listlessness that keeps turning to tears. "You won—you won a long time ago," she tells Jerry's mother, and the "you" means everybody wealthy and well-born. She starts off on a cruise to Havana with Jerry's dissolute best friend but decides to throw herself overboard instead. Kay's moment of decision is deadly serious: Capra superimposes Stanwyck's face onto the waves. Then he shows her hitting the water below—a frightening shot. But the movie, in spite of itself, has nose-dived into weeper territory: from an expanded *Pygmalion* it's turned into a listless *Camille*. Kay doesn't die: she's rescued in time. The movie fades out, though, on the weakest of happy endings, with Stanwyck lying in a hospital bed and Graves sitting stolidly at her side.

NEVERTHELESS, Capra and Stanwyck had created a radically complex Kay Arnold—the lower-class girl who longs to be loved and protected but is too proud to believe that could happen. And what a tide of emotion sweeps through the movie when she gives up that pride to confess her love! But Jerry hasn't undergone a similar boiling-over of his personality, and herein lies the movie's weakness. Jerry has played one downbeat scene with his parents in which they disown him for intending to marry Kay. At the end, though, he remains what he was at the beginning, a Henry Higgins mock-up, a cipher for bringing out Kay's passion and pride. Capra's imagination wasn't fired up by Graves. The movie had expended all its imaginative energy on Stanwyck's struggle, leaving Graves to be wooden and rich.

And once Kay and Jerry have acknowledged their romance, there is no

Ralph Graves and Barbara Stanwyck in *Ladies of Leisure*.

psychological suspense left between them to dramatize. Capra was almost forced to end the movie on a defeatist note. In weepers, the female—poor, parentless, and immoral—had all the worldly counts against her, while the male—wealthy, respectable, backed by his family—had power on his side. A few years of crisis (and the accession of FDR) would alter these kinds of assumptions, but in 1930 the Depression had barely made a dent in Hollywood ideas of class structure. Even Capra, Swerling, and Stanwyck, with all their populist instincts, couldn't, or wouldn't, figure out how to change the ending of the story they had inherited. Besides, there was an overwhelming precedent for the cathartic rescuing of the fallen or almost-fallen woman. Cinderella tales featured upbeat rescues; the new weepers relied on near-tragic ones. Both genres assigned the rescuing role to a figure who was male and upper-class, as did Capra in *Ladies.* If Capra was forging a new view of the lower classes via Kay Arnold, he wasn't able yet, at this point in his career, to use the figure of Jerry to change Hollywood's traditional views of the upper classes.

It's clear as early as this movie that Capra's feelings about rich people were complicated, intense, and not particularly clear to himself. On the one hand, he harbored a fierce populist streak. On the other, he was thrilled to his aesthetic core by the mere idea that safety, luxury, and power existed somewhere in the world. Later in Capra's career, his impulse to celebrate the underdog would turn treacly and automatic, and his addiction to rich and powerful benevolence would take on gigantically improbable proportions. This backsliding didn't begin to happen, though, until the second half of the thirties. Early in the decade, Capra was bold, fresh, and gifted—and newly awakened by the catastrophe of the Depression. *Ladies of Leisure* was the beginning of his attempt to shake up Hollywood's attitudes, partly toward wealth, more toward gender. Those lackluster scenes at the end revealed Capra's own desire to be rebellious, just as much as the more vital scenes in the beginning and the middle. By their plainness he all but confessed that he couldn't yet calibrate the old story of the poor girl rescued by the rich guy to make it feel new.

The romantic comedy that Capra finally developed by 1934 would find the right proportions for the rescue drama. It would correct the imbalance between the cross-class lovers, so they could rescue each other. It would strengthen the defiant girl of the masses that he and Stanwyck had invented in *Ladies,* and it would fill out the blank figure of her co-star. It would explore this idea, which Capra had all but stumbled on here, of the "neutral" setting, where the hero and heroine could escape their class and see each other's "true" selves. But in 1930, when the Depression was just settling in, conventions were pushing the movies toward melodramatic shame and despair instead of toward irony. These were the Hoover years, when it seemed that nothing was being done to change the downward slide of the economy. Hollywood was turning to the maudlin genre of the woman's weeper and the sensationalist genre of the male crime story.

Capra, though, had brought the germ of a new genre into being. He would keep it alive over the next few years, in a cycle of movies starring his muse and collaborator, Barbara Stanwyck.

2

CAPRA AND COLBERT:

It Happened One Night

Claudette Colbert, Clark Gable, and Frank Capra on the set of *It Happened One Night*.

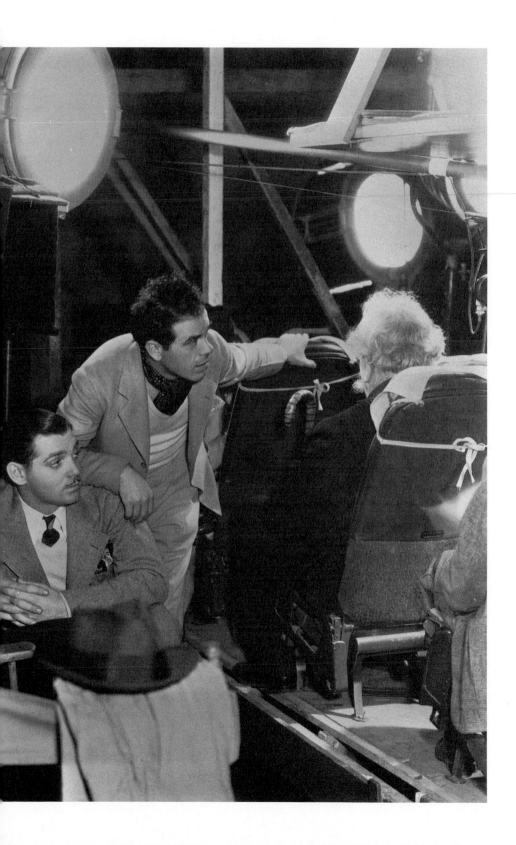

THE EARLY-THIRTIES gangster movies of MGM and Warner Bros.—*Little Caesar* (1930), *The Secret Six* (1931), *The Public Enemy* (1931)—represent Hollywood's most vigorous response to the Depression. One can almost feel, in the suppressed energy of a Wallace Beery, a James Cagney, or an Edward G. Robinson, the movies' helpless admiration of the banditry that had caused the Crash, which shifts, as the gangster goes down at the end, into a collective urge for self-immolation. But the weepers of those years addressed the Depression, too, though less defiantly: they were about the more insidious emotions that came with disaster—fear and remorse. The basic weeper heroine, beautiful, smart, and no longer young, had once given into a reckless impulse and was now paying for her mistake with a maimed life, a life without dignity or security. Pitying her and condescending to her, the audience could atone for its sins of fast living in the twenties: the weeper heroine was, in short, a Depression scapegoat.

And in 1931 she was everywhere in the movies. There was the upper-class edition at MGM, RKO, and Universal—the woman entrapped in the genteel poverty of her apartment, raising the illicit child of the married man she loved. There was the lower-class version at Warner Bros. and Columbia—the city girl who was framed and sent to prison, where she scrubbed floors and exchanged bitter wisecracks with fellow prisoners. At Fox, the rural waif-woman emerged, compromised by a man and misunderstood by narrow-minded townsfolk—a descendant of Lillian Gish in Griffith's 1921 *Way Down East*. The sheer volume of these 1931 love-and-sin titles was awesome: *Transgression* (Kay Francis), *There's No Limit* (Clara Bow), *The Common Law* (Constance Bennett), *Woman of Experience* (Helen Twelvetrees), *The Woman Between* (Lily Damita), *Devotion* (Ann Harding), *Consolation Marriage* (Irene Dunne), *Susan Lenox: Her Fall and Rise* (Greta Garbo), *The Easiest Way* (Bennett), *A Free Soul* (Norma Shearer), *The Sin of Madelon Claudet* (Helen Hayes), *Possessed* (Joan Crawford), *Once a Lady* (Ruth Chatterton), *City Streets* (Sylvia Sidney), *Dishonored* (Marlene Dietrich), *The Night Angel* (Nancy Carroll), *His Woman* (Claudette Colbert), *Illicit* (Barbara Stanwyck), *Bought* (Bennett), *Safe in Hell* (Dorothy Mackaill), *Daughter of the Dragon* (Anna May Wong)—and there were many more. "Sinful girls lead in 1931," said *Variety* at the end of that year. "The Great God Public fully endorsed the heroines of easy virtue. . . . More babes were wrenched from mothers' arms; more tears shed over unofficial mother-hood, than in any previous film year . . ."

But by the beginning of 1932, this outpouring of anger and remorse in the gangsters and weepers had subsided. The box office could never sustain unregulated emotion—or Hollywood didn't think it could—so the "pure" genres of 1931 gave way to the hybrids of 1932. The gangsters started turning into newsmen and criminal lawyers; the weeper ladies remained prideful and flawed but descended to the level of second leads in more panoramic genres, such as the urban "all-star" melodrama (MGM's *Grand Hotel;* RKO's *Symphony of Six Million*), the colonial romance (MGM's *Red Dust*), the shipboard affair (Paramount's *One-Way Passage*), or the baronial family melodrama (RKO's *A Bill of Divorcement*). In its heyday, however, the weeper, like every genre in Hollywood history, had attracted several directors who found it congenial to their temperaments and who stayed to become long-term masters of it. John Stahl developed a deceptively simple pseudodocumentary style with melodrama. His 1932 *Back Street,* based on the popular Fanny Hurst novel, in which middle-class Irene Dunne carries on a lifelong affair with upper-class, married John Boles, stands today as the classic Depression weeper. Those final close-ups of the stoic and graying Irene Dunne, as she boards the ocean liner to accompany Boles's family "anonymously" to Europe, seem to sum up Stahl's vision of the weeper heroine: so much handsomeness exchanged for so much hollowness.

Meanwhile, Josef von Sternberg at Paramount had inaugurated a weeper style of his own, using the actress he had "discovered" in Germany in 1930, Marlene Dietrich. The movies usually began after the Dietrich figure had passed beyond the pale of respectability and was wandering about the world in a "fallen" state. Sternberg created a texture of languid voluptuousness to complement her: the movies were full of shadows, wooden slats, palm fronds, military uniforms, *moderne* demimondaine fashions, and a hothouse conception of a kind of stultifying romance that visits only jaded personali-ties. The peak of the Sternberg-Dietrich oeuvre was the 1932 *Shanghai Express,* which placed the blond Dietrich, dripping with black feathers, in the landscape of fascist Shanghai.

FRANK CAPRA, too, in the early thirties became a weeper specialist, of sorts. After *Ladies of Leisure* he made three other pictures with Barbara Stanwyck that contain partial weeper plots and an intermittent weeper air of tragic desperation: *The Miracle Woman* (1931), *Forbidden* (1932), and *The Bitter Tea of General Yen* (1933). All of these movies feature indepen-dent women who suffer for their ambition. In *The Miracle Woman* Stanwyck plays a lady preacher modeled on Aimee Semple McPherson; in *Forbidden* she's a newspaper woman cynically involved in the affairs of the big city; in *The Bitter Tea of General Yen* she's the fiancée of a missionary to China, who intends to share his work with him. Two of these movies, moreover, were modeled explicitly on big-studio weepers: *Forbidden* recalls *Back Street; The Bitter Tea of General Yen* refers to *Shanghai Express.*

But the Capra-Stanwycks display a different emphasis from the mainstream weepers. First and foremost, they avoid the smug aura of condemnation that hovered around the images of the other weeper heroines. Stanwyck pictured alone is always pictured vital, not resigned and stoic like the Dunne of *Back Street* or the Dietrich of *Shanghai Express.* Her beauty is located in her intensity, not in her pathos. In other words, these movies don't fetishize female loneliness; they come close to admiring it. All three start off with strong scenes, unimaginable in conventional weepers, in which the Stanwyck character declares her autonomy: in *The Miracle Woman* she mounts the pulpit and excoriates her dead father's congregation for neglecting him; in *Forbidden* she abandons the small-town library where she works, withdraws her savings, and books herself on a cruise to Havana; in *General Yen* she travels alone to war-torn China to meet her fiancé and, on the night of her arrival, urges him to let her help save some orphans. At bottom, the Stanwyck character is not a weeper heroine, lacking the fortitude to be virtuous: she's a figure on the opposite end of the spectrum, strong-willed and ready to acquire virtue from experience.

And that experience concerns a kind of disaster that was related to the disaster in the country at large. Conventional weepers almost never alluded directly to the Depression—their settings give off an upper-and-middle-class flavor. But Capra in these four movies links the self-awareness of the Stanwyck figures specifically to poverty. We saw how Stanwyck in *Ladies of Leisure* embodied the defiant spirit of the little people. In *The Miracle Woman* Stanwyck's lady preacher owes her rise to the miseries of poor rural Americans. In *Forbidden* the secretary she plays is poor herself, and raising a child out of wedlock. And in *General Yen* her New England girl, Megan Davis, awakens to human suffering when she finds herself alone in the streets of Shanghai, surrounded by the Chinese masses. *The Miracle Woman* is especially important for its visualization of suffering. The images that we associate today with the Depression—the worn, homely faces of rural people—had begun to appear in newsreels some time around 1931. But *The Miracle Woman* was one of the first feature films to photograph these faces, along with the surroundings that match them—the bare wooden tabernacle-church where Stanwyck preaches, the rutted dirt road leading to it.

Besides capturing the surface look of war and poverty, Capra also explored the psychological ramifications of such disasters in the lives of his protagonists. The love affairs in these movies, unlike the passive, hopeless kind of love in the weepers, incorporate a struggle for power between the lovers, arising from the social upheaval surrounding them. Sometimes Capra makes the Stanwyck figure more powerful than her leading man, as in *The Miracle Woman,* where she's the popular lady preacher and her lover is a blind ex-aviator from her congregation. Sometimes he puts her back in a subservient position, as in *Forbidden,* where she's a newswoman and her lover is a prestigious married politician. In *General Yen* he has her New England girl fall in love with a Chinese warlord who is her equal, emotionally and intellectually, but who is bound to be her antagonist as well, since he comes from another race.

In all these movies, the power struggle between the lovers gradually transforms itself into an acknowledgment by both of them of mutual need and respect. The challenge Capra set himself was to show these private rituals of romance evolving within the most chaotic of social situations. And this dynamic is what definitively distances the Capra-Stanwycks from the early-thirties mainstream weepers. The weepers had exaggerated the social differences among the characters: the tarnished ladies could never become untarnished, even if some gentleman took pity on them and married them. Capra in his Stanwyck movies broke down the differences: love, for his characters, served to transcend social boundaries in the past and the present.

THERE'S AN INTENSITY about these movies, awkward though they are at times, that Capra never really recaptured. It's not the conventional intensity of the weeper; it's a more genuine urgency about emotions, which doesn't resemble anything else described on the screen at this time. Where Capra got his ideas about this kind of emotion is revealed in the movies themselves, especially in the second of them, *The Miracle Woman.* Capra wrote or co-wrote all these scripts (*The Miracle Woman* and *Forbidden* with Swerling; *The Bitter Tea* with Edward Paramore); and so he helped create the characters. In this, his second "Stanwyck," he drew the hero as an exaggerated version of himself ten years back, the wounded war veteran as blind aviator, who persists in wearing his army uniform way past the war, as Capra says he did himself.

Such an unmistakable Capra stand-in in *Miracle Woman* suggests that the whole Capra-Stanwyck oeuvre can be looked at as a sort of personal journal, worked out in narrative form, about the emotions of Capra's real-life love affair with Stanwyck. In *Ladies of Leisure* Capra "discovered" Stanwyck, and the movie became the story of that discovery—an artist painting a portrait of his model, with whom he then falls in love. The success of *Ladies of Leisure* did not give Capra the personal reputation he had hoped for, but it made Stanwyck a star. And in *The Miracle Woman,* Capra cast Stanwyck as a star figure—as the lady preacher beloved of the masses, with her lover an abject, impaired version of himself. Following *The Miracle Woman,* Stanwyck apparently decided to save her failing marriage with Frank Fay, even though she was scheduled to do another movie with Capra, *Forbidden.* According to the trade papers, Stanwyck left the set during the filming of *Forbidden* to appear in a show with Fay in New York. *Forbidden* is an angry movie about a romance poisoned by middle-class conventions. Capra wrote the story himself (though not the dialogue), and it's the nearest he ever came to a mainstream weeper—with one violent twist at the end. The Stanwyck figure shoots and kills the man she has finally married, when he threatens harm to her lover.

Forbidden marked the end of whatever offscreen involvement Capra and Stanwyck had permitted themselves. After the movie, Stanwyck returned to Frank Fay (though she would divorce him a few years later), and Capra, who had divorced his first wife, married his second wife, Lucille. The final Capra-Stanwyck movie, *The Bitter Tea of General Yen,* concerns a pair of lovers, the American maiden and the warlord, who never can find a way to declare their love, no matter how much they may desire to—and it projects all the tenderness and aching regret of such a situation. Love's claims are frail indeed, the story implies, in a world where there is missionary work to be done. The movie doesn't pretend, like the weepers, that the affair ends because of something so sentimental as fate. The lovers in *General Yen* make clear choices at every turn. Stanwyck, the American, chooses to offer herself to Yen, the Chinese, even without marrying him. It's an extraordinary moment when she appears at his door, wearing the Chinese courtesan costume he has lent her, and then kneels, weeping, before him—it seems to break all of Hollywood's (then) unwritten codes: an unmarried woman actually gives in to her sexual longing for a man of another race. In response to her gesture, Yen chooses love too, but his love takes the form of protecting her, of refusing to stigmatize her among her own people. He has lost his war; his soldiers have all deserted him. She is at his feet. But instead of seeking solace with her, he sips the poison tea with which defeated generals are supposed to end their lives, and dies.

With *The Bitter Tea of General Yen* Capra and Stanwyck's professional collaboration, with its intimations of homespun poet and muse, came to an end (although they would work together later in one more movie, the confused *Meet John Doe,* 1940). Besides the real-life barriers between the two

of them, there were commercial disappointments to contend with: none of
the later Capra-Stanwycks had done as well as the first one, *Ladies of Leisure.*
The movies Capra had made in-between or just after the Stanwycks—*Dirigi-
ble* (1931), *Platinum Blonde* (1931), *American Madness* (1932), and *Lady for
a Day* (1933)—were the ones that scored at the box office, even though
they were not centered on romance. Moreover, by 1933 Stanwyck's own
box-office appeal had fallen way off. That was natural enough: she was a
weeper star. That genre declined so precipitously from 1932 to 1933 that
the popularity of virtually all the weeper actresses—Garbo, Dietrich, Constance Bennett, Kay Francis, Ann Harding, Ruth Chatterton—plummeted.

Today, though, we can see that the persona Capra had created with
Stanwyck in the course of those four movies was a stunning achievement.
What Capra had gotten from Stanwyck was what a serious person gets from
falling in love—a vivid sense of another psyche in the world, an effortless
transference of one's own sensuality into that person's perceptions. Out of
their collaboration had come a movie heroine who was not a scapegoat like
a weeper heroine; she was a full protagonist. Things didn't happen *to* her,
they happened *within* her. She was the one through whom the audience
experienced the movie. And when romance came along and threatened to
engulf her deepest self, she bravely let it in. *General Yen* is a parable whose
subject is emotional bravery. How different was its Stanwyck from that
other weeper heroine in China, the Dietrich of *Shanghai Express*! "It took
more than one man to change my name to . . . Shanghai Lily," Dietrich
tells her lost love, Clive Brook, when he reappears by chance on the Shang-
hai-bound train. *Shanghai Express* brings its ostensibly independent heroine
back into marriage with the starched and stoic Brook. *The Bitter Tea of
General Yen* allows its heroine to seriously contemplate an affair with a
Chinese bandit. Sternberg's movie fades out on the reactionary weeper pair
reviving their old love; Capra's movie closes on the face of Stanwyck headed
toward an unknown, solitary future.

Although the Capra-Stanwyck muse-protagonist ostensibly disappeared
from the movies (until *Meet John Doe,* and in that movie she was an impersonal, un-erotic version of her former self) she would live on in spirit in the
role that brought the romantic-comedy heroine to vivid life, Claudette
Colbert's Ellie Andrews in *It Happened One Night.* Capra, in working so
consistently and intensely with Stanwyck, had developed the interior dynamic he needed to make the classic thirties heroine he created for Colbert.
But it wasn't only Stanwyck who served as the model for Colbert's part. A
new and unlikely movie star hit the scene just as Capra was ending his
collaboration with Stanwyck, a star who challenged all kinds of popular
assumptions about what a heroine should be.

. . .

IN FEBRUARY 1933, a month after the release of *The Bitter Tea of General Yen,* Paramount unveiled Mae West's first starring vehicle for herself, *She Done Him Wrong,* about a lady saloon keeper in the gay nineties. The movie struck a fatal blow to the weeper and everything it stood for. In October 1933 Mae West's second original effort (actually, her third movie) emerged, *I'm No Angel,* about a lady lion tamer who makes it big on Broadway. Both movies were written and partially directed by Mae. And both movies, to the astonishment of Hollywood, swept all before them at the box office and made her the biggest star of the year.

Everything about Mae West spelled the opposite of doom. She was a synthesis of brash female vaudeville headliners like Eva Tanguay and Sophie Tucker, with a dimension borrowed from the great black blues singers of the twenties like Ida Cox and Bessie Smith (Mae admits in her autobiography to spending long hours in Chicago blues clubs), and a liberal dose of mannerisms lifted directly from Clara Bow. Bow played a snake dancer in a carnival in her last movie, *Hoopla* (1933), just as Mae did in *I'm No Angel* later that same year. In her own screen persona, Mae amplified these paradoxes: she directed the camera to emphasize her porcelain plumpness and her Nordic platinum hair, while she swaggered, smirked, and rolled her eyes like a Negro blues singer or an overripe flapper. Here was a hybrid that mixed the outlaw qualities of black women and wild women with the delicate complexion of the old-time melodrama heroine. What's astonishing is how much, in the context of mainstream Hollywood, this somewhat camouflaged but potentially disruptive creature got away with, in both *She Done Him Wrong* and *I'm No Angel.* Her lady bartender in *Wrong* and her lady lion tamer in *Angel* did what they wanted, dressed as they pleased, made overtures to whomever they wished, exposed all the other characters as hypocrites, prudes, snobs, and fops—and still found true, if tongue-in-cheek, romance with Cary Grant.

The narrative triumphs of Mae West's characters were especially resonant in 1933, when the Senate had begun its investigations of Wall Street malpractices and Prohibition, with its attendant hypocrisy, was about to be repealed. Mae obviously meant *She Done Him Wrong* to be anti-Prohibition and *I'm No Angel* to be antiwealth. (She came from a Brooklyn family with a traditional allegiance to Tammany Hall's "wet" working-class neighborhoods.) But Mae West wasn't the only unlikely social critic to emerge in the movies at this time. In early 1933 Warner Bros. revived the movie musical, which had all but disappeared in 1931 and '32, restyling it for Depression audiences with new topical content and new character types. The most vital figure in *42nd Street* (March) and *Gold Diggers of 1933* (June) was the precocious gold digger–chorine, impersonated by ingenues Ginger Rogers, Una Merkel, Joan Blondell, or Aline MacMahon with some junior Mae West touches.

The gold digger–chorine was cynical by nature. She lived in what she saw as a rotten world. But she mocked and resisted the rottenness all the time with wisecracks, and she kept her own decent values squarely in place. This character wasn't supposed to be realistic. She was a composite. She contained some 1920s Ziegfeld girl, a lot of Clara Bow, some weeper-tough-girl in the Warner Bros. mode; but, even more important, she shared—she recreated—Mae West's taste for irreverence in formal situations. Ginger Rogers's Fay Fortune of *Gold Diggers of 1933,* for instance, sang the movie's opening song, "We're in the Money," in pig Latin; this went with her monocle and her goofy pretensions. (And Ginger herself invented the gag on the set.) Such a devil-may-care juvenile heroine signaled the absorption into the movies of a younger and tougher generation of actresses who had survived the Depression slump in the entertainment business. It seemed right that she should be more knowing and scornful than most other leading ladies who had preceded her. Even the weeper heroines seemed innocent beside her. And in 1933, the Depression's lowest point, a dose of defiant female scorn seemed to be the catharsis the public wanted most. At the end of the year, not only had it put Mae West's *She Done Him Wrong* into first place among box-office draws, it had made MGM's *Tugboat Annie,* starring the large and raucous Marie Dressler, the second-largest-grossing movie; *Gold Diggers of 1933* and *42nd Street* the third and fourth, respectively; and RKO's *Little Women,* featuring, in the role of the obstreperous Jo, that studio's newest young star, Katharine Hepburn, the fifth.

IN 1933, two short stories about young women on Greyhound buses, both by the pulp fiction writer, Samuel Hopkins Adams, appeared in magazines. The first, in the March *Collier's,* was a one-page piece called "Last Trip": it featured a forlorn and suicidal secretary cheered by an encounter on a bus with an equally despairing young man. The second, "Night Bus," which appeared in the August *Cosmopolitan,* was a much longer, less melancholy story about a runaway heiress and an inventor. Both stories can be considered sources for *It Happened One Night.* Capra mentions only one story in his autobiography, but says he came upon it in the *spring* of '33 while in Palm Springs working on the script for *Lady for a Day.* That was the date of the first story—and that first story would have suggested Barbara Stanwyck to him. It had the brave "woman traveling alone" theme he associated with her.

The story on which he actually based the movie, however, was the second one, whose heroine is not a Stanwyck type at all, but a robust and haughty heiress, deigning to travel on a plebeian long-distance bus to spite her overpossessive father. Her lover in the story is a penniless inventor, though of blueblood origins. Once again, Capra's instinct was working in top form. There was a new spirit in the air in the fall of 1933. Between spring and fall of that year—between these two bus stories by the same author—the public had absorbed not only Roosevelt's fireside chats and his relief plans for the jobless, but also Mae West and the gold-digger musicals. Capra obviously recognized that a new heroine, more hardy than his Stanwyck character, was needed in the movies, along with a new devil-may-care spirit. Accordingly, Capra found a new collaborator, the former Broadway playwright Robert Riskin (the author of the play Capra had based *The Miracle Woman* on) and set to work tailoring this second bus story for the movies.

But he didn't forget his watching and listening Stanwyck heroine. The Ellie Andrews of the movie is more tentative than the haughty Elspeth of the second story. Moreover, Capra and Riskin set it up so that she's more uprooted than Elspeth too. In Capra and Riskin's script, the heiress doesn't only play at evading her father, she actually escapes from a Florida yacht where he's imprisoned her for marrying the wrong man, and starts back to New York, incognito, on the Greyhound. Meanwhile, Capra and Riskin changed the inventor Peter Warne from a blueblood in disguise to an honest-to-goodness working person, a newspaper reporter. (For a while Capra had wanted his hero to be a painter like Ralph Graves in *Ladies of Leisure* but was persuaded by the more worldly Riskin, and by an ex-newspaperman friend, Myles Connolly, to toughen up his profession.)

Therefore, whether by instinct or intent, Capra created his new leading characters to correspond uncannily to the spirit of the moment. The man wouldn't be a sissy but a cynic. The woman wouldn't be too forlorn either. In fact, she would be partly unsympathic, at least at first. As the pure panic of the Depression leveled off to resentment, the extravagances of several ultrarich young debutantes made bitter reading for the masses—especially those of Woolworth granddaughter Barbara Hutton, who had married the shady Prince Alexis Mdivani against her father's will in June 1933, a few months before Riskin and Capra wrote their script. Miss Hutton had never subjected herself to the fears and discomforts of a Greyhound bus, but it was cathartic to wish that she might have to. Combining a Depression scapegoat with a Depression victim in one character proved a brilliant stroke of plot invention.

It created a problem in casting, however. Where was the actress with both the wit and the pathos to switch back and forth between imperious heiress and diffident waif? Almost no female stars in Hollywood in 1933 called themselves comediennes. The young gold-digger chorines—Rogers, Blondell, Merkel—were listed only as featured players. Stars in 1933 had for two years played mostly weeper roles, which called for anything but irony. Some of the younger weeper heroines had shown flashes of mischief here and there. To them, one after another, Capra submitted his script, still with the unglamorous working title *Night Bus.* First he tried MGM's young veteran of exotic vamp roles, Myrna Loy; then Paramount's only comic ingenue, Miriam Hopkins; then Universal's recent Broadway import Margaret Sullavan; finally he approached RKO-Pathé's former top weeper star, Constance Bennett. All of them turned him down. (RKO's Irene Dunne wasn't considered because she hadn't yet done anything labeled as comedy; neither were Paramount's Carole Lombard—she was still too small-time.) No actress outside of Columbia could have known what freshness and care Capra, a Poverty Row director, would bring to the task of directing a woman, because no one in Hollywood had paid much attention to the unprofitable Capra-Stanwyck movies that had followed *Ladies of Leisure.* Consequently, the *Night Bus* script looked to its readers much too thin: nothing happened in it except that a woman met a man on a bus—and the woman changed costume only once in the whole picture. A self-respecting actress did not make a picture in just two costumes. The project might have died on the spot if Louis B. Mayer of MGM hadn't sent his recalcitrant young star Clark Gable over to do the male part in the picture, as a punishment for Gable's request for a raise.

Gable's immediate effect on the movie was to sweeten it for the last actress Capra approached, a Paramount featured player, Claudette Colbert. Though Colbert still blamed Capra for the flop of her first movie, the 1927 silent *For the Love of Mike,* which he had directed, she had shrewdly assessed her middling position among her peers at Paramount—Miriam Hopkins, Carole Lombard, Nancy Carroll, not to speak of Dietrich and West. She had also noticed her studio's weak roster of male stars: Gary Cooper was its only bright spot amid such aging figures as Maurice Chevalier, Harold Lloyd, and George Bancroft. In addition to whatever financial arrangement Capra offered her, Colbert realized that doing a movie with a strong young male co-star might make Paramount notice her. She accepted Capra's movie because Gable was in it.

Colbert was a dramatically different kind of actress from Barbara Stanwyck. Born Lily Claudette Chauchoin in France in 1905, she had come to New York at the age of six when her banker father failed in his Paris business and decided to try America; he died soon after. Finishing high school, Colbert needed a career to help support her mother and brother. She was studying to be a fashion designer when she met the playwright Anne Nichols at a party in 1923. Nichols, author of the cross-religion Broadway blockbuster *Abie's Irish Rose,* gave her a bit part in her new play, *White Collars,* and Colbert went from there into a long apprenticeship in the old-fashioned farces of producer Al Woods, working her way back, by the end of the twenties, to contemporary comic roles on Broadway. She sported a witty, polished technique instead of the "natural" intensity of a Stanwyck. Soubrette roles such as the ingenue snake charmer in her 1927 Broadway hit, *The Barker,* became her specialty. (Colbert once gave an interview proclaiming her preference for Sarah Bernhardt over Eleonora Duse—this in the days when Duse's naturalism had supplanted Bernhardt's high-toned artifice as the height of Broadway chic.) Having given up movies after the 1927 lemon, *For the Love of Mike,* she made a smooth transition back into them in 1929, becoming the main star of Paramount's East Coast studio in Astoria, Queens, and playing Astoria's specialty: Depression debutantes thrown out on the job market.

In 1932, when Paramount shut down its East Coast facilities, Colbert moved to the Hollywood lot, only to find herself shunted aside by the up-and-coming starlets already positioned on the Paramount roster. Colbert, with her round face, wide smile, and mischievous eyes, was not considered a beauty; she was a wit. Wits, though, were not in demand in weeper-dominated Hollywood. Cecil B. DeMille rescued her in 1933 by "discovering" her on the Paramount lot and starring her in his lascivious ancient epics *The Sign of the Cross* (1933) and *Cleopatra* (1934); but by doing so he almost consigned her permanently to the domain of "camp." *It Happened One Night* would rescue her in turn from DeMille's orbit. Sooner or later, though, Colbert would have rescued herself. Behind her charming exterior there lurked a shrewd and self-promoting mind. In signing with Capra she was simply seizing an opportunity that other actresses failed to recognize. Still, she was lucky that Capra saw through her charm to the intelligence that controlled it. He would make full use of Colbert's "hidden" willfulness in the role of the heiress-waif that he tailored, in his customary way, to fit her.

· · ·

THE MOVIE OPENS aboard a yacht, lying in a sunny sea. But this idyllic yacht is anything but peaceful. The tycoon's rebellious daughter, Ellie Andrews, has locked herself in her stateroom, refusing to eat. We first see Colbert backed against the stateroom wall, her heart-shaped face with the pencil-thin eyebrows expressing dismay, as her worried, portly father (played by character actor Walter Connolly) brings in a tray of food. We scarcely have time to follow the argument between father and daughter about her new husband before Colbert upsets the food tray. Her father slaps her. A swift cut to Colbert's surprised face tells us it's the first time this father has ever slapped this daughter. In the heat of the moment she bolts through the door, onto the deck, up onto the railing—and with a beautiful, high athletic dive she's into the sea and swimming away. The sunlit close-ups of her climbing onto the railing fill the foreground of the screen, while the quick cuts to her father reveal him behind her on the shaded deck, helpless, calling his staff to watch for her in train stations and airports. The wit of this scene (which was created by Capra and Riskin, not Adams) reverts back to the mechanisms of silent comedy, where the action emanated from a stylized central character. Perhaps it was the rise of Mae West that allowed Capra to rediscover the comedy dynamic in a woman. But it was also Claudette Colbert herself.

Barbara Stanwyck would never have inspired such an opening scene. Stanwyck's effectiveness in Capra's work had depended on the visible inwardness of her reactions, on a stubbornness that proved ultimately mournful. Colbert offered Capra an imperious energy and a comically opaque characterization. And yet the Stanwyck and the Colbert characters are related. Compare Stanwyck's Kay Arnold at the end of *Ladies of Leisure,* jumping into the sea to drown, with Colbert's Ellie Andrews at the start of *It Happened One Night,* diving into the sea to escape. Capra must have been struck by what Colbert, with her wealth of pre-Hollywood stage work, could do that Stanwyck couldn't: mock herself. She could sketch in a presence with a few swift, stylized strokes—the wide eyes, the asymmetrical slouches, the pouting, honeyed voice that turned a simple line about her marriage like "I'm over twenty-one and so is he" into a slightly risqué song. She could put a Mae Westian spirit into a domestic quarrel.

Colbert's artificiality allowed Capra to treat his essential theme, Depression rootlessness, in a less serious manner than he would have needed for Stanwyck. When the scene switches to the bus station, introduced by a humble little sign, NIGHT BUS TO NEW YORK, and discovers Colbert mute and wide-eyed, wedged into a corner of the screen, the audience has been invited to contemplate the artificiality of the movie itself. We can see that Colbert is acting a part-within-a-part, a waif imagined by an heiress imagined by an actress. But we recognize as well that this ironic figure of the heiress has been superimposed on, almost pasted over, a kind of image that didn't usually go with her—a pseudodocumentary evocation of a shabby Depression bus station. The playfulness of such a juxtaposition allows the movie to float free of weeper sentimentality. A situation from the Capra-Stanwyck weepers with an infusion of Mae Westian artifice: this was the romantic-comedy formula that coalesced in this movie.

Having brought the heiress to the bus, the movie temporarily deserts her. The camera, as if distracted by a ruckus, does one of Capra's dizzying strides across space to discover a crowd collected around a phone booth, watching a tall man conducting a drunken argument into the telephone. Here is Colbert's opposite number, Clark Gable, wedged into the booth, a soft felt hat on his head and his eyebrows hopping up and down as he talks to his editor in New York. Audiences of 1934 would have recognized this type from Hollywood's 1932–33 newspaper comedies (relatives of the gangster pictures) as well as from tales of legendary journalists like Richard Harding Davis, H. L. Mencken, Ben Hecht, Gene Fowler, and Ernest Hemingway: the rogue newsman who was as rascally, soused, and undependable as he was talented. The script needed only to include a few lines of his invective to his editor—"That was free verse, you gashouse palooka!"—to peg him as an American caricature even more familiar than the heiress.

But Capra also drew on real-life material to shape Gable's role, as he had done for Colbert's. According to Capra, when Gable first reported to Columbia on Louis B. Mayer's orders, he came drunk—a kind of compliance that also signals rebellion. That's how he is portrayed in his movie entrance (which doesn't appear in the magazine story), locked in a tipsy telephone battle with a fatherlike newspaper editor. Both main characters, introduced symmetrically in opposite corners of the bus station, have embarked on fatherless escapades, just as Gable and Colbert in real life had ventured out of their paternalistic studios to make a movie with a "small-time" director on Poverty Row. Capra blends these cinema-verité details into the scripted story, as he had done in the Stanwyck movies. The new dimension in *It Happened One Night* came from the cultural resonance of the types Gable and Colbert were playing, the heiress and the reporter.

SINCE IT WAS the Depression, the more plebeian reporter had an edge over the heiress. Capra had worked with these two types already in one of his lighter early-thirties movies, *Platinum Blonde* (1931), in which he had married an heiress (Jean Harlow) to a reporter (Robert Williams), then turned their relationship into a coy class war fixed in favor of the reporter. But *It Happened One Night* proved much more complex in treating the same two figures. It distributed attributes of power more evenly between them, as the Capra-Stanwyck films had done with their co-stars. Colbert's heiress possesses social power as her father's daughter but becomes just a solitary, vulnerable woman on the bus trip. Gable's reporter stands socially "beneath" an heiress in the regular world but becomes her manly protector on the bus trip. The bus's milieu turns Colbert's class ascendancy into Gable's gender ascendancy, then reverses that configuration too, as the woman shows herself more resourceful than the man and the man grows more tender than the woman. For all its intricacies, the movie displays a breezy, offhand air. Capra made it, as he said, like "a throwaway game of golf," right after he finished what he thought was a masterpiece, *Lady for a Day,* about the fantasies of an old-lady apple seller. (Actually, *Lady for a Day* is a heavy-handed movie, in part because Capra thought it was important while he was shooting it. The projects he thought unimportant were the ones that usually turned out to be better movies.)

Even before Gable and Colbert meet, Capra gives us a taste of how their temperaments will square off, in an incident cleverly reproduced from the story. Gable enters the bus and finds only one seat free in the back, though newspapers are piled on it. He throws the papers out the window, an act that embroils him in an altercation with the bus driver. That's when Colbert slips behind them through the frame and takes the seat. This moment registers like a jazz duet, with Gable as saxophone and Colbert as clarinet: it prefigures the way his blustering will later succumb to her quick efficiency. Face to face, though, in this early scene, Gable and Colbert veer back and forth between class friction and sexual attraction. Gable chastises Colbert for her squeamishness about bus crowding. He turns gentleman to chase a thief who steals Colbert's suitcase. Colbert turns lady and offers Gable money. Provoked, he sheds his manners and calls her a brat. Back in the bus, Gable chivalrously rescues Colbert from a vulgar seatmate, but he does so in working-class style by claiming her as his wife.

In 1934, the audience's own confusions would have made Gable's and Colbert's role-switching seem familiar. Men in the audience had lost their jobs; women had gone to work. What's striking today is to see how the characters' shifts of status, especially the heiress's, determine the movie's very structure. Capra all but shaped the movie around Ellie Andrews's duality, making her stand, in sleight-of-hand fashion, for privilege and helplessness at the same time. Even as the plot is humbling the heiress, the visual underpinning of the movie is evoking sympathy for the woman, telling us through pictures about the loneliness, the vastness, the underclass

Clark Gable
and Claudette
Colbert in *It
Happened One
Night*.

pathos of her first Depression bus trip. The shiny black chrome of the bus at the gate, with its several licenses piled at off angles on its right fender, its lit headlights, the labels NEW YORK and ATLANTIC GREETINGS arching over its front windows—all recall the piled-up, handmade signs in the documentary photographs of the Depression by artist-photographers like Walker Evans and Dorothea Lange. Capra could not have copied these photographers, though, since their pictures weren't widely visible until the Farm Security Administration began to commission and distribute them in 1935, nearly two years after *It Happened One Night*.

Capra seems to have made up his Depression aesthetic by himself, from newsreels, from the images of poverty in the Stanwyck movies, from memories of his own wanderings in the twenties. Samuel Hopkins Adams had set up the situation of the bus trip, but he hadn't lingered on the visual background of his story. Capra clothed Hopkins's story in pictures that were responsive to the bleakness of the times. Unlike the rhapsodically modern blimps and airplanes of his earlier naval epics, the bus in *It Happened One Night* appears makeshift and anthropomorphized, as do its surroundings. When Capra shows a nighttime rest stop—a trailer with a neon HOT DOGS written on it—he takes care to picture it small, floating in a vast space of dark highway. And he follows this with a shot of Colbert at the rest stop, leaning against the bus, smoking, with the listless, suspended quality of any Depression photographer's subject. Here is where Capra links the Colbert figure to social upheaval, as he had done with Stanwyck's characters. She's traveling alone through Depression America, finding out who she is under her heiress façade, coming to a sense of her personal autonomy through her uncertainty.

Ellie Andrews's isolation from her usual surroundings leads her, as isolation led the Stanwyck heroines, to love—in a pair of scenes that relate directly to Capra's Stanwyck movies. The passengers are forced by a storm to spend the night in an auto court. Gable, again playing the reluctant gentleman, takes Colbert in charge and rents a cabin for both of them. Colbert runs through the downpour into the cabin. We see her in profile against the door; we register its glass knob and chintz half-curtains even as we note her mute dismay at having to spend the night with a strange man. This moment recalls the scene in *Ladies of Leisure* when Stanwyck agrees to spend the night in Ralph Graves's penthouse—and the connection was intended by Capra. According to Colbert, this was the only time in the rapid shooting schedule that he redid something, because he had decided she didn't look "scared enough." She had played the scene, she says, "with bravado, as if she [Ellie Andrews] still knew what time it was." What Capra wanted was the vulnerability of a Stanwyck when Ralph Graves places a blanket on her.

He got this in the printed retake—Colbert's wary surveying of the setup with the twin beds, her uncertain wisecrack to Gable, "Darn clever, those Armenians." Colbert looks so wary, in fact, that Capra broke the pathos with some comic relief. He had Gable hang a blanket between their beds and start taking off his clothes, to get her to go to her side of the room. But the comedy doesn't obscure the familiar Capraesque poetry of what follows—a shot-by-shot reprise of the lightly pornographic "night" poem to Barbara Stanwyck in *Ladies of Leisure:* the same backlit rainy window, the female's torso silhouetted against it, the pensive undressing, the reverse view of the woman through the window, the close-up of her face and hands as she lies in bed—even the pajamas the man lends the woman to sleep in (a detail from Adams's story that matched Capra's own narrative conventions). Here Colbert's Ellie Andrews becomes practically a reincarnation of *Ladies of Leisure*'s Kay Arnold.

THE CONTRADICTIONS INSIDE ELLIE, her heiress's courage alternating with her waif's fear, make her "realer" than other Hollywood heroines of her day. But the Gable character also breaks with the stock leading-man image. The morning that follows the night in the auto court of *It Happened One Night* echoes the morning in the *Ladies of Leisure* penthouse four years earlier, but with a substantial shift: it's not the woman who's cooking the eggs in this scene—it's the man. One could say that this moment, with Colbert still in bed and Gable at the stove, marks the long-delayed birth of a hero suitable for the Depression. Capra didn't plan it this way: he merely played Gable against the grain of his semisadistic MGM image, to show him cooking eggs, laying the table, buying the groceries while Ellie slept (as Adams had indicated). But a domestically inclined man offered an alternative to the misogynous gangster-newsman who was hanging on at Warner Bros. and the fastidious Arrow-collar man who lingered at MGM. Gable's Peter Warne, unlike those outdated stereotypes, has no pretenses to social power. He's broke; he's out of a job; he can't even run fast enough to catch the guy who stole Ellie's suitcase. He's a surprisingly frank embodiment of the ineffectuality of the American male in the face of the Depression. He can do only one thing well: take care of someone who's lost.

They're a curious couple—he keeping house, she appreciating it like a lost kid. Capra has mixed up their class and gender traits to make a new model of the American couple. The man isn't always supermanly; the woman isn't

always ultrafemale. Each possesses qualities that should by convention belong to the other. This movie was Capra's last entry in his Capra-Stanwyck
diary, completing the revision of "male" and "female" he had started in the
Stanwyck movies, a revision that allows for frequent role reversals and class
trade-offs. Colbert's waif-heiress becomes the finished cartoon of the figure
who haunted him in the Stanwyck movies—the big star who is also a
woman. Gable's reporter becomes the cartoon of the Capra figure in the
Stanwyck movies—the man who has both more and less power than the
heroine. Gable brought an easy erotic charisma to his part that smoothed
out the habitual nervousness of those earlier Capra stand-ins, Stanwyck's
co-stars. As Gable portrayed him, this gruff-tender man in *It Happened One
Night,* without money or position of his own but with the natural authority
to put the heiress on a budget, tell her what to eat, have her clothes ironed,
and coax a story out of her for his newspaper, is an allegorical simplification
of what Capra actually was, a director of movie stars.

Peter Warne even coaches Ellie in a mock movie scene, when her fathers'
detectives come looking for her in the auto court. He musses her hair,
undoes her collar, and cues her in a loud, bullying voice. She catches on
and pretends to be a rowdy wife arguing with her Cracker husband. Such
a moment invites the audience backstage to witness Hollywood's mystical
secrets. These are actors playing roles—sometimes even roles within roles.
And Capra's use of documentary-style backgrounds further heightens his
characters' artificiality. When Colbert hippity-hops to the shower through
a set that looks like a newsreel of a Hooverville, with cabins, refuse, children, dogs, women lined up in bathrobes, we see two worlds juxtaposed on
the screen, privilege and poverty. And we have the illusion, which must have
thrilled the 1934 movie audience, that poverty is instructing privilege.

One could say that *It Happened One Night* amounts to an ingenious effort
by Capra to get privileged people (including movie stars and directors) taken
back into the plebeian American heart. That impulse was present in the
Capra-Stanwycks too, in that one of the two leads always represented the
People, as a missionary or a politician—a reminder to the audience that
power could be benign. But *It Happened One Night* rounds out the fable.
The hardship of the bus trip abolishes social classes and turns everyone into
members of a giant, "economy class" community. In what can be seen as
the heart of the movie (a scene not present in the story), the bus's congregation erupts in a spontaneous rendition of "The Man on the Flying Trapeze." Different passengers sing different verses, but everybody, including
Gable and Colbert in their double seat, joins in happily. It would read as
a terminally corny image of disparates united by pop culture except that it,

too, is undercut by irony: just as the driver joins in the chorus, he loses control of the wheel and the bus veers off the road into the mud.

IT SEEMS HERE as if a foundering ship of state had spilled Gable and Colbert into the landscape to fend for themselves. Actually, they leave the bus because one of the passengers has found out that Colbert is the heiress Ellie Andrews. But once they strike out on foot with no money, the movie enters a new phase (indicated in the story, but not developed)—a lyrical extension of the narrative, a kind of interlude that would turn up in the best romantic comedies throughout the decade, which might be called a Depression pastorale. They cross a moonlit stream; they sleep—apart—in a haystack; they hitchhike on a rural highway; they get picked up in an old Model T and taken to a Walker Evans café. Narratively the sequence explores the territory beyond the Capra-Stanwyck equation, beyond falling in love. It's like practice for marriage—Capra's Depression-style marriage—with the woman learning to do unladylike things and the man learning to appreciate some competition from a raffish mate. Gable isn't the one who gets them a ride, despite his professorial demonstration of the three methods of hitchhiking; Colbert does. Tossing off one of Mae West's many mottos, "I've got a system all my own," she ambles nonchalantly onto the road, slides up her skirt to show some leg—and stops a car.

By now, the two actors seem to be soaring on inventiveness: Colbert almost goofy, nibbling raw carrots, limping down the road beside Gable, letting him pick a piece of hay out of her teeth; Gable ruefully macho, shooting seductive looks at passing autos and pulling up dumbfounded as the cars pass him. This is where the surreal, buoyant, all-but-improvised couple-acting that would attach itself to romantic comedy was born. How fresh it must have looked to audiences who had been fed, weeper-style, lovemaking-in-the-mist of trench-coated stars! And the visually shrewd, weather-sensitive Capra, who shrouded his movie's beginnings in darkness and rain, threw open this part of it to unpretentious daylight.

IF THE STORY had ended here, if Peter and Ellie had simply run off and gotten married, *It Happened One Night* would be a charming little movie, not a prototype for a new genre. Capra and Riskin, prompted by Adams, added an ordeal for their couple that turned it into a parable about Americans both high- and middle-class growing up. Gable and Colbert, as they near the end of their journey in a commandeered Model T, cannot find a way to declare their feelings. It's the woman who breaks the deadlock, as in the Capra-Stanwyck stories. Colbert creeps around the blanket "walls of Jericho" in another auto court and offers herself, sobbing, to Gable—like Stanwyck throwing herself at the feet of General Yen. Gable says nothing but sneaks away to write up their journey for his newspaper, so he can earn the money to propose to Colbert. This part of the movie is more melodrama than comedy, returning each character temporarily to the fate of an earlier genre. The proprietress of the auto court finds the deserted Colbert and supposes her compromised—the scourge of the weepers. Gable, hurrying back in the jalopy to claim her, sees the motorcade sent by her father to fetch her and returns to his old life—newspaperman barbarism. Each thinks the other a traitor to the experience they've just shared, and each keeps on thinking this until the last possible moment, which is the famous scene, made up for the movie, of Ellie's formal remarriage to her original playboy husband, King Westley.

Capra staged this in a documentary-style return to Barbara Hutton turf, a full-dress society wedding on the lawn of the Andrews mansion, complete with bridesmaids, ushers, flower girls, and—Capra's sly salute to a visual source—two newsreel cameramen cranking away on the roof. We see the long, slow procession cross the grass toward the altar. Capra draws it out, teasing the thirties audience, which would have blanched at the idea of interrupting such a costly ceremony. But there's a chance she can be saved, we see. Old Mr. Andrews, escorting his daughter toward the altar, tells her that Peter Warne is an okay guy—he's only asked for $39.60 in expenses, instead of a big reward. Still, Colbert does nothing, until the minister has addressed the groom and had his answer, then turned to the bride with the question "Wilt thou take this man to be thy wedded husband, as long as ye both shall live?" At this moment, Colbert heaves her chest, bites her lip, shakes her head, and breaks away across the sloping lawn, her long white veil streaming behind her, running down to a car waiting at the gate (presumably with Gable in it). Scenes of her flight are interspersed with cuts to the newsreel photographers, madly rotating their cameras to catch her moving image. The sequence provides an ingenious climax—a reprise of Colbert's initial escape from the yacht, but with a new dimension represented by the newsreel cameras. The first escape was an impulsive, "private" act, witnessed only by the movie audience; the second one, no matter how split-second and dramatic, is a "public" decision recorded on a newsreel-within-the-film. Colbert has grown up from heiress to citizen.

· · ·

THE RUNAWAY BRIDE is one of the most joyous, kinetic, and rebellious images produced by mass culture in the Depression. What she signifies is the end of the extravagant, wasteful, snobbish life of the upper classes of the twenties. In rushing away from her wedding, she is unclassing herself to join with Peter Warne in a new kind of unit held together by something besides class. The last image of the movie, the "walls of Jericho" falling down, refers to the real meaning of their marriage—not social but erotic, private. Here is one of the only moments in Hollywood's history when a proper wedding stood for something undesirable: six or seven years later, when war threatened, on-camera weddings would regain their sentimental power. Though Capra diluted the impact of this moment by making old man Andrews of Wall Street instrumental in his daughter's escape, he still put a vital populist message into a Hollywood artifact. *It Happened One Night* makes a cross-class love affair between two consenting adults, begun on a bus, stand for a renewal of democracy.

The strong-willed lovers that peopled Capra's neo-weepers with Barbara Stanwyck had survived, comicalized, as the leading characters of a movie fable that was custom-made, through trial and error and brilliant cinematic instinct, to speak to the anxieties of the Depression audience. *It Happened One Night* contained profound cultural resonances at the time it was made. As the lovers negotiate equality across the gulf of class and gender, they are metaphorically healing the painful divisions in American society. But, though they match each other by the end in self-knowledge and goodwill, it is still the woman who controls the action. She is the one who had set the plot in motion at the beginning and the one who saves the romance at the end. It is true that the male protagonist, Gable's Peter Warne, is asked to take a stand at a crucial point in the movie: he must choose between the heiress and a life of debauchery. His choosing the heiress, however, doesn't generate the movie's climax. That comes when Colbert's Ellie Andrews realizes that she too has a choice. One of her suitors offers her upper-class status; the other offers her sex—and companionship, adventure, and good, cheap fun. She chooses sex, which all Americans had potentially in common, over class, which they didn't.

3

ROMANTIC COMEDY SETTLES IN

Myrna Loy, William Powell, and W. S. Van Dyke on the set of *The Thin Man*.

THE PUBLIC EMBRACED *It Happened One Night* as it has embraced few movies in Hollywood history. The picture did normal business after its February 1934 opening; then gradually, by word of mouth, it took off. Some theaters that had replaced it after the regular two weeks called it back; other theaters just let it play on and on, to become a grass-roots hit of huge proportions. By the end of the year, Columbia's "little" comedy ranked fifth among the top box-office hits of 1934. This was a near-miracle, since Columbia didn't own any theater chains and, unlike the bigger studios, couldn't exercise much control over how and where its movies were shown. "Had Columbia possessed the booking lineup of other major companies," *Variety* remarked in its summary of 1934, *"It Happened One Night* would have been at the top of the big grossers." Faced with this overwhelming expression of the public's enthusiasm, the movie industry responded at the end of the year with a lavish tribute. It presented Capra's bus-trip romance with a straight flush of Academy Awards (Best Picture, Best Director, Best Actor, Best Actress, and Best Script), marking the first time since the awards began in 1927–28 that one picture had won so many, and the first time a comedy had shown such prominence. (In the first year of the awards, comedy was so little respected, so little connected to "art," that Best Comedy Director was a separate category from Best Director.)

Capra didn't invent Hollywood's comic love story. Twenties movies had depended on light, joking romance; and even in the melodrama-prone early thirties, light love stories were still being made. Charlie Chaplin cast himself as a tramp in love with a blind girl in *City Lights* (1931); Warner Bros. generated a series of urban working-class romances starring Jimmy Cagney in the early thirties; Paramount turned out some sophisticated, *haut monde* romantic comedies in those years—the best are Ernst Lubitsch's *Trouble in Paradise* (1932) and *Design for Living* (1933). Most of these early-thirties comedies contain a Depression-inspired class-consciousness something like Capra's: Lubitsch was especially good at having his elegant, amoral leading characters mock the pretensions of the rich.

The new element Capra brought to movie comedy was his leading lady, who seemed to sum up and resolve the audience's conflicting feelings about the Depression. She had come out of the weepers; she was solitary like the weeper heroines. At the same time, she held within herself an antidote to weeper despair—her stubborn irony. She was an ingenious symbol of both the audience's fear and its wish to defy the fear. But the best thing about her from Hollywood's point of view—and probably from the audience's as well—was that she didn't need to punch anybody, break the law, or change basic social rules to get away from her panic, the way a man would have had to do. A movie *hero* in the early Depression was almost obliged to be violent, to register the wave of anger and frustration that had swept through the populace as the very meaning of money turned chaotic. But a woman could work out her resentments in a combative love affair instead of in the more problematic arena of business deals and social status.

The combat within the love affair—the lovers' attempts to control their status in each other's eyes—provided the drama. The literal class identity of this new heroine didn't affect the movie as much as where she stood in the eyes of the hero. True, Ellie Andrews's privileged background was never lost sight of. It removed her from the danger of real poverty and hunger on the bus trip. But being on the bus also put her, at least temporarily, into a semihelpless underclass. Her struggle, as she falls in love, is to win the respect from her lover that any member of the Depression-created under-class—that is, the audience—thought he or she deserved. Her lover's strug-gle, keyed to hers, is to learn to love her for her self-reliance, her stubborn presence, instead of looking for a more pliant femininity. Capra's movie was a political fable as well as a romance, with the politics buried far beneath the surface. The Capraesque woman stood for a Depression mentality, fearful but resolute; the Capraesque man was America before the Depres-sion, heedless, boisterous, headed toward catastrophe. The task of the two characters was to come to understand and love each other by the end.

Capra wasn't interested in literal class conflict. If he had been, he would have made movies like William Wellman's *Heroes for Sale,* at Warner Bros., about a down-and-out World War I veteran; or King Vidor's *Our Daily Bread* at Paramount, about migrant farmers and irrigation. (Warner Bros. still encouraged marginal subject matter in 1933, and Paramount allowed Vidor this one literal Depression experiment in 1934.) Instead, Capra was drawn to reconciliation, any kind of reconciliation—between the classes, the genders, the generations; between Depression anxiety and happy-go-lucky optimism. And he dramatized reconciliation, even in the thick of the Depression, by means of romance. As a result, romance in romantic comedy came to stand for more than just love or sex; it signified the actual reunion of disaffected Americans. No wonder *It Happened One Night* proved to be a huge hit. It pictured the Depression as an event that taught a lesson about love. It portrayed that love as self-redefinition, coming out of hardship, leading to reconciliation. It implied, by metaphoric association, that the recent, nightmarish Hoover years had been good for the national character. And it gave people license to enjoy the catharsis of a love story, because the love story was intimately bound up with their own recent communal trauma.

WHILE CAPRA WAS DEVELOPING his romantic-comedy formula, a slightly older director at MGM was working out some similar hunches about the character of leading ladies and the nature of romance in the Depression. W. S. Van Dyke, a veteran of westerns and safari stories, moved over to crime and gangsters in 1932 with a sleeper called *Night Court.* In the genre sequel to *Night Court,* which was called *Penthouse,* Van Dyke got assigned an MGM starlet, Myrna Loy, to play the part of a good-hearted chorine who ends up marrying the society lawyer. Myrna Loy's early career had been a particularly comical example of Hollywood's persisting in a wrong-headed image of an actress. This tall, freckled redhead from Montana had started out, like many aspiring starlets, as an interpretive dancer. But then, perhaps because dance seemed exotic to Hollywood, she spent from 1925 through the early thirties entrapped in a female-predatory hall of mirrors. She was given mostly B pictures, in which she played a series of Indian half-castes, Mexican wenches, Oriental seductresses, slovenly gyp-sies, and other kinds of "bad" women, with occasional appearances as a normal flapper. As the thirties got under way, she was cast in some bigger supporting roles as a worldly young woman, in better pictures—*The Animal Kingdom* (1932), *Topaze* (1933), *When Ladies Meet* (1933).

But her definitive rescue came in *Penthouse,* when Van Dyke consciously matched her breezy, witty offscreen personality with her on-screen persona. There's a moment in the movie when Loy's down-to-earth Gertie gets rebuffed at an elevator door by a society dame. As if to imply how queer and ill-mannered some people are, she gives a private shrug, a gesture that points up the subtle eccentricity of the star she was about to become. In his next two Myrna Loy movies after *Penthouse—The Prizefighter and the Lady* (1933) and *Manhattan Melodrama* (1934)—Van Dyke coaxed out more of Loy's laconic, prairie-style wit, which combined so interestingly with the seductive, too-available woman MGM still insisted Loy was. By the time of Van Dyke's fourth movie with Myrna Loy, the murder-mystery-cum-marital-comedy *The Thin Man,* which came out in July 1934, Loy had become sure of her new self. She played Nora Charles, wife of William Powell's Nick Charles, and she showed Powell a mildly obstreperous independence of mind—not unlike the quality with which Colbert's Ellie Andrews confronted Gable's Peter Warne in *It Happened One Night.*

The fact that Capra and Van Dyke, working independently under very different conditions, had designed similar dynamics for their lead couples reveals the pervasiveness of the desire for change. Not just movie directors but the movie public wanted to see new kinds of relations between men and women on the screen; they wanted to watch the woman, who was supposed to be weak, become strong, and the man, who was traditionally strong, become vulnerable. Like *It Happened One Night, The Thin Man* became a surprise hit, a supposedly modest film that registered a resounding success at the box office, though it didn't show up in the 1934 Academy Awards. (Since it came out in July, it didn't have time to make its full impact by the year's end.) MGM, on the strength of these two movies—one that had starred its own actor, Gable, and one that had emerged unexpectedly from its own lot—immediately adopted romantic comedy for itself, remaking the genre to suit the studio's high-toned self-image. In late 1934, it put Gable into a seriocomic love triangle in the upper-crust mode, *Forsaking All Others,* along with Joan Crawford and Robert Montgomery. In the 1935 *After Office Hours,* the studio gave him another newspaperman role, opposite another heiress, played by Constance Bennett. And Loy, too, after a hiatus in her career (which she spent on strike, demanding the money and status she was entitled to after *The Thin Man*), started on what would be a long string of star romantic-comedy roles. In 1936 alone she appeared in four romantic comedies: *Libeled Lady, Wife Versus Secretary, Petticoat Fever,* and a sequel to her original hit, *After the Thin Man.*

IN TERMS OF PLAYERS, MGM was the best equipped of any studio to develop romantic comedy. It held three promising young leading ladies under contract, Myrna Loy, Jean Harlow, and Joan Crawford. Each of these actresses projected the willfulness of the romantic-comedy heroine in a different mode: Loy was ladylike and sensible; Harlow was brassy and good-natured; Crawford was tremulous and defiant. The studio also employed a whole host of sophisticated leading men, from the gentlemen roués William Powell and Robert Montgomery, to the tough guys Clark Gable and Spencer Tracy, to the beautiful but overrefined Robert Taylor, who became a big star in 1935. MGM commanded the biggest budgets, the finest theaters, and the largest profits of any movie company in thirties Hollywood.

But MGM never put the energy into romantic comedy that its resources would have allowed it to. For one thing, its bureaucracy lacked flexibility. MGM didn't possess the administrative structures to let directors initiate and control projects the way Capra had done with *It Happened One Night*. Producers were in charge. Directors, writers, and actors at MGM were paid by the week rather than by the movie. They were kept on tight schedules by the front office and told what to do and when. Very rarely did any of them have a chance to claim a movie, to shape it and take responsibility for it. (Woody Van Dyke, for instance, who had shown such flair for free-form invention in parts of *The Thin Man*, never managed to develop the flair into a methodology.) Accordingly, the studio's many romantic comedies of the thirties, though clever in spots, display an assembly-line air. Story lines and scenes were recycled from picture to picture. And once the actors and actresses had been typed in the genre, they rarely got the chance to vary their personae or enrich their acting on the screen. Myrna Loy, for instance, who projected as much luminous eccentricity in romantic comedy as any of the actresses in this book, never encountered a director at MGM other than the gifted but slapdash Van Dyke who took the care to build a movie around her. As a result, she turned in increasingly underanimated performances as the decade wore on.

Paramount, the other big studio in the thirties that embraced romantic comedy, did better with it than MGM. (Neither Warner Bros. nor Fox was showing much interest then in comic romance—Warners abandoned humor almost entirely after Darryl F. Zanuck left in 1933, and Fox, where Zanuck landed, was concentrating its efforts on musicals.) Paramount's older tradition of sophisticated comedy provided the new genre with a fund of in-house knowledge. Moreover, the studio possessed a looser administrative framework than MGM, a condition that always favored humor. When its featured player Claudette Colbert came back a star from *It Happened One Night*, Paramount instituted a small and inventive Colbert "industry." In 1935 that "industry" turned out two strong romantic comedies, *The Gilded Lily* and *The Bride Comes Home*, and loaned Colbert to Columbia for a third, *She Married Her Boss*. After that, Paramount took up the genre with a vengeance, creating romantic comedies not just for Colbert but for Carole Lombard and, a little later, for Jean Arthur, accompanied by leading men Fred MacMurray, Gary Cooper, and Ray Milland. Paramount cannot take the credit in the mid-thirties for discovering any of its actors' potential for seriocomic playing, but if one of its players made good in another studio's movie, Paramount registered the achievement and recast accordingly. The studio also gave directors and writers more leeway on the lot than MGM. The director-writer team of Wesley Ruggles and Claude Binyon, the directors Mitchell Leisen and Preston Sturges, and the writers Charles Brackett and Billy Wilder—all of these men found a way to create romantic comedies from scratch on the Paramount lot. And they rewarded the studio's trust by inventing the Paramount "style"—by infusing Capra's original home-spun genre with the delicious double entendres and gleeful sophistication that fit with Paramount's reputation for worldliness.

Though MGM and Paramount didn't actually control the nature of romantic comedy in the thirties, they helped to invent its basic texture. MGM's contribution lay in the field of costumes. It would have been unthinkable for such a big, plush studio to embrace a movie genre, such as Capra's, in a format that called for only one costume change in the course of a movie. So MGM slanted its romantic comedies to allow its characters to change clothes more often. Basically, it introduced more high-class types into its stories, characters whose lives held more clothes-oriented occasions. The quietly flashy furs, hats, and evening gowns of Myrna Loy's heroines denoted an imaginary, MGM kind of "high life," whereas the Jean Harlow characters' more tawdry, sensational attempts at finery conveyed the studio's quaint idea of "low life." And male tailoring, whether for the impeccably turned-out William Powell or for the rough-edged Clark Gable, was always envisioned in sharp, class-specific detail. But if MGM amplified the costume palette of the genre, it did not explore its geography. Mid-to-late-thirties MGM (held firmly in hand by Louis B. Mayer) concentrated on plush interiors rather than on the atmosphere of locations. The rooms where MGM's action took place usually projected a glassy look of deadly bour-geoisification. Mayer's MGM, in fact, all but suppressed the flavor of the city, which Thalberg, the studio's early-thirties head of production, had so carefully evoked in films such as the Wallace Beery gangster thriller *The Secret Six* (1931) or the Jean Harlow–Clark Gable prison movie, *Hold Your Man* (1933).

It was Paramount rather than MGM that led the way with scenery, and with city scenery in particular. *It Happened One Night* had vouchsafed even fewer signals about scenery than about clothing, since it took place almost entirely along a rural southern highway. So Paramount on its back lot began to work out an urban geography to indicate where on the social scale its movie characters figured. As early as 1935, the skyscrapers, nightclubs, and fancy hotels favored by the rich materialized in Paramount movies, as well as the homely apartments, front stoops, spaghetti joints, park benches, and city buses frequented by the not-so-rich. Paramount essentially invented these locations, which became primal within the genre. *The Gilded Lily,* the first of the "Colberts," began with secretary Claudette Colbert and reporter Fred MacMurray eating popcorn (Depression style, kernel by kernel) on a

Carole Lombard
and Fred
MacMurray
encounter each
other in *Hands
Across the Table*.

bench in front of the New York Public Library. It proceeded through scenes set in the New York subway, on the front stoop of a brownstone, on a Coney Island beach, in a fancy New York nightclub, and in a plush English hotel—all marking the heroine's picaresque path up the social scale—before it returned to sanity and the library bench for its low-keyed happy ending.

But besides urbanizing the genre's setting, Paramount also performed the crucial task of urbanizing Capra's heroine. In *It Happened One Night,* Colbert, the heiress, got pushed temporarily into the rural underclass. Paramount turned Colbert into a city girl with a job, who hovered just above the working classes of the big city. It's possible that someone at Paramount simply realized that the sad professional woman from the weepers could be lightened up and moved over, scenery and all, to romantic comedy. At any rate, the units that produced romantic comedies at Paramount showed more interest than Capra, and certainly more than MGM, in the textures of the urban working world—and in the place of "work" in a woman's psychology. Where Capra had attributed Colbert's stubbornness to a surfeit of privilege, director Wesley Ruggles and writer Claude Binyon, of *The Gilded Lily,* related it to a working girl's pride. Thanks to Ruggles and Binyon's pioneering notion in *Lily* of Depression dignity, all of Colbert's subsequent 1935 movie characters held jobs. Having played a secretary in *The Gilded Lily,* she played a magazine editor in *The Bride Comes Home;* a department-store manager in her Columbia loan-out, *She Married Her Boss;* and a hospital psychiatrist in Paramount's odd and interesting weeper *Private Worlds.* In all these movies, the Colbert figure projected scorn for anyone, such as her co-star, who appeared to belittle her work. And this insistence on work-related values extended to other Paramount heroines. *Hands Across the Table* (1935) was written by Norman Krasna for Colbert but then assigned to Carole Lombard. It portrays a scrupulous and ambitious hotel manicurist (Lombard) who falls in love with a penniless ex-playboy (Fred MacMurray)—she's mortified when she messes up his manicure—even as she's being courted by the crippled and wealthy Ralph Bellamy. At the climax of the movie, MacMurray decides that he might be capable of getting a job if it means he can settle down with Lombard. It was not Capra, in fact, but Paramount's writers and directors who placed hard work at the center of romantic comedy's priorities.

BUT IF THE BIG STUDIOS turned out romantic comedies that were clever, funny, and occasionally surprising, the little studios or the struggling studios—Columbia, RKO, and, on one occasion, Universal—were the ones that hosted the real breakthrough movies, the movies that kept the whole genre fresh and alive to the course of the Depression. The little studios could afford, where the big ones could not, to maintain relatively loose contractual relations with the romantic-comedy directors. Those studios were set up, administratively and financially, to give the directors more control of their movies—Columbia because of Harry Cohn, who had learned through Capra that profits could be made in this fashion; RKO because of the vacuum that persisted, throughout most of the thirties, in its top-boss slot; and Universal because it was simply the most bankrupt of the studios and would try anything once. It was in the little studios or the bankrupt ones where gifted directors were able to choose their writers, co-write their stories, select their casts and collaborate with them (and take their leading ladies as their muses)—were able, in fact, to personalize their movies. And because of this more direct relationship between directors and their movies at Columbia and RKO (and once in a while at Universal and Paramount), those movies can be looked at as emanations of a director's personality.

The vast majority of movies from Hollywood's "golden era" cannot be analyzed this way. Too many people's ideas went into them; too many hands signed them. They are products of work collectives, of factories—and their ultimate authors must be counted the studio heads, who determined their values and their overall "look" through a kind of loose but unmistakable censorship. But the landmark romantic comedies, which kept turning up to mark the orientation of the whole genre throughout the decade—these were "authored" by one man, usually a director. They can be examined the way we examine the work of artists who shape their art "on" or with people as their "matériel"—the plays of a playwright with a stock company, the songs of a jazz composer with his big band, the ballets of a ballet master with a dance company. The intuitive authorship of these movies allows us to read in them something about the shape of a director's emotional life and his attitude toward women. And when we put a few directors' romantic comedies side by side, we can see the concerns of a whole generation.

Capra and his colleagues were born around the turn of the century. That makes them contemporaries of the famous literary generation of the 1920s, which Gertrude Stein called "lost." Even before Capra became a director in Hollywood, young writers such as F. Scott Fitzgerald, Ernest Hemingway, John Dos Passos, and Philip Barry, who were his age, had made a sophisticated and semi-erotic camaraderie between men and women a rallying point of the generation. Such knowledge, Fitzgerald recalled later in *The*

Crack-up, was absorbed in the very process of reaching adolescence during the twenties, through the books that shocked the country, that were talked about in every drawing room. Books, said Fitzgerald, brought yearly "revelations" to the adolescents of his era—revelations vivid enough that even in 1931 he recalled them in the present tense:

> We begin with the suggestion that Don Juan leads an interesting life (*Jurgen,* 1919); then we learn that there's a lot of sex around if we only knew it (*Winesburg, Ohio,* 1920), that adolescents lead very amorous lives (*This Side of Paradise,* 1920), that there are a lot of neglected Anglo-Saxon words (*Ulysses,* 1921), that older people don't always resist sudden temptations (*Cytherea,* 1922), that girls are sometimes seduced without being ruined (*Flaming Youth,* 1922), that even rape often turns out well (*The Sheik,* 1922), that glamorous English ladies are often promiscuous (*The Green Hat,* 1924), that in fact they devote most of their time to it (*The Vortex,* 1926), that it's a damn good thing too (*Lady Chatterley's Lover,* 1928), and finally that there are abnormal variations (*The Well of Loneliness,* 1928, and *Sodom and Gomorrah,* 1929).

Even if Capra, Stevens, La Cava, McCarey, and Sturges had escaped such a sensationalist literary baptism in their youth, they needed only to look around them in Hollywood to get an idea of the atmosphere Fitzgerald was talking about. The writers from New York who poured into Hollywood at the onset of the talkies—Jo Swerling, Robert Riskin, Morrie Ryskind, Viña Delmar, Dorothy Parker, Fitzgerald himself, and a host of others—brought it with them. This "new" (or, by the thirties, once-new) attitude came down in daily life to a way of speaking, a way of telling anecdotes, a way of talking at parties—and a way of inventing movie stories. By the time the writers brought it to Hollywood, however, such an attitude was no longer unqualifiably desirable. The Depression had skewed the country's once-easy tolerance for promiscuity. In the thirties, therefore, the task of any serious member of the lost generation—a task that very few of the New York writers in Hollywood could summon the gravity to take on by themselves—was to put this high-flying sexual modernity into the context of the Depression. (Fitzgerald himself managed to do this, not in the movies but on the page—in the unforgettably brave essays of *The Crack-up.*) In Hollywood, the people who first took on this task were not the writers but the maverick romantic-comedy directors. Whether they intended to or not, these directors confronted, even in comedies—*especially* in comedies, because these provided a smoke screen for seriousness—the entire question of modernity versus responsibility in the relations between the sexes.

What led them to do this we can only speculate. Their motivations lay in their inner lives, their family histories, their psychologies; and such motivations can be pieced together only case by case, in a full-scale biography of each man. What concerns us here is what is visible and readable in the movies themselves. And the movies tell us that these directors were willing to deal with what the climate of the twenties had implied, not just about men and women but about the tricky question of women's status. Hovering in the consciousness of any male contemporary of the lost generation were invariably the twenties "women of achievement," those famous or notorious figures tossed up on the roiling sea of the jazz age's encounter with the Puritan ethic—figures such as the wicked literary critic Dorothy Parker; the bold foreign correspondent Dorothy Thompson; the ultramannered bohemian poetess "Vincent" Millay; the tall, silent female aviatrix Amelia Earhart; the renegade debutante who defied her father to wed Irving Berlin, Ellin Mackay; the wildly rebellious Zelda, Fitzgerald's writer wife— not to speak of performers-cum-public-figures such as Mae West and Clara Bow. The public knew about these female icons from the tabloids, the newsreels, and the gossip magazines.

However, the Depression all but buried this twenties reexamination of women's parameters, or transformed it into the literal topic of class in America—at least in the intellectual centers of the country. Politics, communism, socialism, capitalism, and the like, replaced sex as the burning discussion topic among writers in New York and even among some writers in Hollywood. But among directors, at least within romantic comedy, that twenties puzzle, the proper status of women, remained a concern, and got mixed in with the plebeian idioms of storytelling. And so those notorious twenties feminine icons lived on fitfully in the imaginations of the directors and their actresses and thus were incorporated, via the romantic comedies, into the pop culture of the Depression.

IN OTHER WORDS, Depression romantic comedy belonged to a charged and distinct moment in the nation's history and in Hollywood's evolution. The talkies had matured. There were a few studios that were functioning with loose, trial-and-error leadership. There were some young directors baptized in the saloon-and-livery-stable atmosphere of the comedy studios but drawn to the complex subject of modern romance and its role in the

Depression. There were writers here and there interested in real collabora-
tions with directors. There was a group of vivid female actresses willing to
lend themselves in a sporting manner to the directors' experiments in
romantic-comedy style—and a group of good-natured leading men who
took the experiments, for the most part, in stride.

And there was a fast-breaking political climate that had superseded the
frustration of the Hoover years. In Washington, Franklin D. Roosevelt was
mobilizing the government to address the gargantuan problems of the
Great Depression. Roosevelt, in tones much more august than Capra's, had
also put forth Capra's intuitive idea that some sort of virtue could be
extracted from so much suffering. "We must move as a trained and loyal
army willing to sacrifice for the good of a common discipline," Roosevelt
had said on assuming the presidency, "because without such discipline no
progress is made, no leadership becomes effective." Capra's brand of romantic comedy, despite its sly slapstick diversions, concerned itself with nothing
less than the transfer of discipline to the field of human relations—the
taking of that free-and-easy behavior of the twenties and turning it to the
service of commitment and loyalty and meaningful marriages.

It's not a coincidence that in July 1934, a few months after *It Happened
One Night* brought the new notes of discipline and clearheadedness into
movie romance, the industry encountered the threat of a nationwide boy-
cott of the movies by Roman Catholics. The church objected to the scanty
clothes and low-life talk that hung on in the wake of the weepers and
gangster pictures. In response, the Motion Picture Producers and Distribu-
tors of America, who regulated the industry from the inside, formed the
Production Code Administration Office, put a Roman Catholic ex-news-
man named Joseph Breen in command, and empowered it to impose a fine
of $25,000 on any studio that released a movie without its seal of approval.
The establishing of the Breen office, which censored anything too smutty
or too violent in the movies, cannot be called a major factor in the rise of
Depression romantic comedy, as some critics have claimed. Romantic comedy was already launched before the Breen office came into existence. Moreover, the genre came with a mandate that was subjective, personal to the
directors and the leading ladies. They had decided intuitively that it was
right to abolish the sexual misery of the weepers and replace it with a vision
of sex that was more wholesome, witty, and comradely. This was the feeling
of their generation: no censor had to tell them to do it.

The Breen office's appearance, however, provided another sign of the
timeliness of Depression romantic comedy. Capra had brought a clean
adventurousness into movie romance, which the public found entertaining

and meaningful. He had used his silent-comedy-inspired point of view and his own wishes and longings to change the nature of movie romance and the status of the romantic-comedy heroine. Capra had made this heroine a symbol of the nation's Depression wish to grow beyond snobbery and bitterness. Now other directors and actresses would reinvent her.

4

STEVENS AND HEPBURN:

ALICE ADAMS

Katharine Hepburn
with (on her
left) Fred
MacMurray and
George Stevens,
during the
filming of *Alice
Adams*.

IN THE SPRING OF 1932, David O. Selznick, head of production at RKO, heard about an intriguing young actress on Broadway named Katharine Hepburn. Hepburn was then playing her first starring role, in a farce about the ancient Amazons, *The Warrior's Husband*. Arrayed in her tights and tunic, she displayed an awkward yet somehow refined grace. It happened that Selznick was looking for a young stage actress to star in his pet project of the year, a movie of the 1921 Broadway play *A Bill of Divorcement*, and he thought she might do. She would be playing an aristocratic daughter who confronts her long-lost father (John Barrymore) after he has escaped from a lunatic asylum. There was prestige attached to the role: it had made the great twenties actress Katharine Cornell a Broadway star.

Selznick approached Hepburn. She demanded the astonishing sum of $1,500 a week. He hired her anyway—and his gamble paid off. *A Bill of Divorcement* did exceptionally well at the box office and gave Hepburn a personal hit. Her strange, half-awkward intensity on the screen, visible in spite of the sultry Joan Crawford makeup the studio put on her, caught the notice of the public and the fan magazines. She was hailed, a little prematurely, as "the American Garbo." And after one setback (the Anglophiliac weeper *Christopher Strong* of 1933, which followed *A Bill of Divorcement*), Hepburn's career took off. By the end of 1933, with Selznick's guidance, she had reached the top rung of Hollywood. She had won an Oscar— almost never awarded to a neophyte—for her role as the ruthless young actress in *Morning Glory*. And she had won the public's heart for her portrayal of Jo March, the heroine of RKO's 1933 blockbuster *Little Women*. Hepburn was so popular at the box office in 1933 that *Variety* put her second to the biggest star of that year, Mae West, and on a par with Paramount's major new heartthrob, Bing Crosby.

Hepburn's sudden superstardom proved a godsend to her studio, which resembled no other studio in Hollywood. RKO, or Radio-Keith-Orpheum, had not been carefully built up by a business wizard such as Fox's William B. Fox, Paramount's Adolph Zukor, or Columbia's Harry Cohn. It had been born of an arbitrary stock-market maneuver in the boom year of 1928—the merger, under the auspices of the giant Radio Corporation of America, of a little studio named Film Booking Offices with the Keith-Albee-Orpheum vaudeville chain. Because of the greed involved in its beginnings, it suffered from the start from insufficient capital and lack of direction.* Furthermore, its nervous management in the early thirties had no idea how to improve matters. By 1933, RKO had made so many wrong business decisions (such as taking over the two mammoth theaters in New York's Radio City) that Hepburn's box-office receipts were practically floating the studio.

But in early 1934 there occurred a seemingly inexplicable reversal of Hepburn's success. Her first movie of that year, *Spitfire,* a local-color yarn about an Ozark mountain girl, turned out to be a box-office disaster. And then Hepburn herself compounded the crisis by leaving Hollywood in the spring of 1934 to return to Broadway in a play called *The Lake,* a delicate drawing-room tragedy about a neurasthenic English girl at odds with her parents. The play enjoyed an extra notoriety because its author, the English actress Dorothy Massing, had committed suicide soon after she wrote it in 1933. But Hepburn failed to take advantage of this special aura of disaster. With her cerebral mode of approaching roles, she couldn't bring *The Lake*'s sweet and morbid heroine to life. And her movie stardom proved a magnet for Broadway's spleen about actors who had deserted the theater to go to Hollywood. (This is the play that prompted Dorothy Parker to chide her for "running the gamut of emotions from A to B.") Then, when Hepburn finally returned to Hollywood after her Broadway fiasco, RKO jinxed her further by putting her into two overprecious movies about eccentric, "artistic" women—*The Little Minister* (1934), a tale of nineteenth-century Scotland based on a J. M. Barrie novel, and *Break of Hearts* (1935), a romantic melodrama about a famous conductor's marriage to an unknown composer (Hepburn played the composer)—neither of which did well at the box office.

FROM THE MOMENT Hepburn's career started to sag, RKO became completely bewildered about what to do with her. Part of the problem was a confusion of leadership in the studio itself. Selznick, that partisan of tastefully heavy drama, had quit RKO in a dispute with the studio's parent company, RCA, and had been replaced by Merian C. Cooper, gentleman adventurer and producer of RKO's 1933 hit *King Kong.* But Cooper suffered from heart trouble, so he spent most of 1933 and early 1934 away from the studio. Hepburn's career and screen image therefore passed to the

---

*Joseph P. Kennedy, father of the late President, was the villain here: he was the one who made the deal; he skimmed off huge profits for himself, and then abandoned the little institution he had fathered with nothing in its coffers.

care of twenty-eight-year-old Pandro S. Berman, Selznick's former assistant, who was just stepping into the role of RKO's production head (a role he would take on reluctantly at various points throughout the thirties: he preferred actual hands-on producing). It was Berman who put Hepburn into the ill-fated *Spitfire* and who later chose *The Little Minister* and *Break of Hearts* for her.

The mishandling of Hepburn, though, cannot be blamed on Berman alone. It must be blamed on the studio as a whole. Nineteen thirty-four was the watershed year for female stars, the year in which comediennes replaced tragediennes in the popular taste. But no one at RKO saw that the shift applied to Hepburn. Even audiences knew that Hepburn must move out of the weeper category if she was to survive as a star: they made this clear when they categorically rejected each of her coy and precious screen heroines in 1934 and early '35—whether they wore Ozark rags, gypsy gowns, or modern frocks. But in this case, the studio wasn't listening to the public.

Just how confused RKO was can be seen in the suggestions for future movie roles Pandro Berman sent Hepburn while she was in New York doing *The Lake,* which read like an anthology of Hollywood's ideas of the high-toned and high-class: theatrical classics like Shaw's *Saint Joan;* historical biographies of imposing women from Napoleon's Josephine to Florence Nightingale; a few more women-artist tragedies and World War I shell-shock weepers. Amid all this pretentiousness was one lone comedy script, Norman Krasna's *The Richest Girl in the World,* about an heiress who changes places with a secretary. When Berman sent the comedy, he apologized: "It might seem lighter to you than the material you expected to see," he wrote. And since he was not serious about the suggestion, Hepburn didn't respond to it. (*The Richest Girl in the World* was done in 1934 with Miriam Hopkins, who was then the only ingenue besides Colbert advertising herself as a comedienne.)

The mistake Berman and the rest of the bosses made was to mix up the Hepburn they knew offscreen with the movie roles they were designing for her. Hepburn came from a family that seemed to the movie world—a world of self-made people—like the essence of old, settled Anglo-Saxon respectability. Her parents weren't divorced, like the parents of many of the actors and actresses who found their way to the movies. Hepburn's father was a prosperous Connecticut doctor; her mother was a well-born campaigner for women's rights. Both mother and daughter had gone to Bryn Mawr. Moreover, even after their daughter became a movie star, her parents didn't move to Hollywood: neither of them was visible in that socially vulnerable position of the star's manager and beneficiary. Hepburn was therefore an anomaly among Hollywood divas, a fact that she played up in her own way. She made a point of speaking with an upper-crust Boston drawl; she dressed in boys' clothes; she wore no makeup off the screen; she appeared to disdain the press. She behaved, in short, as if she were oblivious to all of Hollywood's customs, practices, signs, and signals. And this show of supreme nonchalance caused her studio to treat her in a way it treated no other actress: RKO acted intimidated.

The RKO bosses' intimidation can be recognized in an incident that happened on the set of *Spitfire*. The film finished on schedule, but its director, John Cromwell, decided he needed a day's worth of additional scenes to round out the movie. Hepburn, who was supposed to leave for New York, demanded $10,000 for the extra day of shooting. The studio decided not to shoot the extra scenes. But then Hepburn about-faced and said that it ought to shoot the scenes for the sake of the movie, and if it didn't, she would leave Hollywood forever. When RKO reminded her that this would be a breach of her contract, she said she would be satisfied to "give this all up, go home and raise a couple of kids." "It was like having a gun held to your head," said production chief B. B. Kahane in a letter to RKO's New York office. "She was in her dressing room at noon awaiting an answer from us as to whether she should remove her make-up and go East never to return, or stay on to do the extra scenes." The studio gave her all that she wanted: it shot the scenes and paid her the money.

Hepburn was probably acting here more on whim than with foresight: wanting to be recompensed for the inconvenience yet wanting the movie to be good. But in the bosses' eyes, it looked as if she had had the nerve to tell them how to run the studio. Nor was this the only occasion when Hepburn behaved, or seemed to behave, as if she were superior to the status and money Hollywood could confer on her—and then managed to get them anyway. To Hollywood minds such an attitude translated as an uncanny business acumen, rarely encountered in a woman. (Mary Pickford was the other legendary manager of her own career.) Hepburn wasn't even susceptible, or she seemed not to be, to the flatteries and attentions that usually brought female stars around. The studio's astonishment in the face of such a character was as responsible as anything for her career going awry. What's clear to us now—that Hepburn desperately needed a comedy to make her sympathetic to the socially sensitive Depression audience—was unimaginable to them.

IT WASN'T UNTIL early 1935 that Berman arranged for a modern movie for Hepburn. And even then he didn't choose a story with Capraesque humor; he chose another "great book" (like *Little Women*)—Booth Tarkington's classic 1921 novel *Alice Adams,* about a girl in a middle-sized Indiana city, trying to struggle up the social scale through a romance with a wealthy young man, even as the rest of her family was slipping further down it. *Alice* was one of the properties that had been in preparation for Hepburn for some time. To offset what were considered the "slow and old-fashioned" qualities of the novel, Berman had given the job of scripting it, in the winter of 1933–34, to the studio's weeper specialists, Jane Murfin and Dorothy Yost, who had tried to streamline and update *Alice,* adding modern touches such as Alice tap-dancing and her brother playing the radio. But Murfin, who had written some of Constance Bennett's riper early-thirties tragedies, as well as *Spitfire* and *The Little Minister* for Hepburn, couldn't avoid giving the *Alice* script her favorite aura of literary melodrama, and in the process she and Yost drained away all vestiges of Tarkington's own wry humor.

As late as the spring of 1935, *Alice Adams* was on its way to becoming another pseudoweeper, which might have finished Hepburn's career once and for all. Pandro Berman was giving the movie a lot of attention, but he didn't know exactly what he wanted to do with it—that is, he didn't know which director to assign it to. Berman and Hepburn considered nearly thirty candidates, including King Vidor, John Ford, Frank Borzage, Gregory La Cava, Leo McCarey, William Wyler, and George Stevens. Hepburn and her agent, Leland Hayward, were enthusiastic about McCarey, but Berman persuaded them that he was too much of a comedy specialist to handle her. Berman himself thought John Ford should do the movie; but Ford wasn't free. At the end of March 1935, scheduling and bargaining had narrowed the choice to William Wyler and George Stevens.

Wyler was the safer choice. He was thirty-four; he had made feature films at Universal for ten years; and he had directed the 1933 highbrow hit with John Barrymore, *Counsellor at Law,* from the Elmer Rice play. Stevens, thirty-one, was not a safe choice at all. He was known at RKO as a slapstick man; his credits were the kind of broad comedies Berman had objected to when McCarey's name had come up.

Stevens, though, had just made his first straight feature film under Berman—*Laddie,* the idyllic autobiography of the Indiana writer Gene Stratton Porter. It wasn't released yet, but Berman must have known it was good. (It did well at the box office when it came out.) Maybe Berman thought that *Laddie* had made Stevens an Indiana expert, which would help with *Alice.* Maybe he just wanted to give Stevens his big chance. Maybe he had a hunch he couldn't even admit to himself—that Stevens's comedy experience was just what Hepburn needed. Or it could be that Hepburn herself decided on Stevens, since her friend Eddie Killey, an assistant director, had told her he was a good-looking man. (That's what the rumors say.) There is an apocryphal story, which Berman tells and Hepburn denies, that she and Berman flipped a coin and came up with Wyler but decided to flip it again and got Stevens. At any rate, Stevens was made director of *Alice Adams*—a decision that would save Hepburn's stardom, at least for the moment. It would also launch Stevens's own impressive feature-film career and inaugurate RKO's particular mode of Depression romantic comedy.

GEORGE STEVENS had drifted into the movies while still in his teens. As a kid he had practiced photography, and at age fifteen, with a friend, he had started a little business taking pictures of companies in Glendale, where his family lived, and selling them to their owners. Parlaying his "business" connections into a movie-studio entree, Stevens got work at two studios in the town of Culver City—first at Metro Pictures (soon to be MGM), then at the Hal Roach studio. Fred Jackman, a Roach western director, took him on as his assistant, and they went up to Utah to do "Rex the Wild Horse" pictures. After a while Stevens moved over from westerns to the Roach studio's specialty, comedy, joining the team of the Roach headliners, Laurel and Hardy. In the beginning, Stevens kept his allegiance to westerns, but Laurel and Hardy's skill soon convinced him that comedy could be "graceful and human." By 1927, at the age of twenty-three, Stevens had become chief cameraman and sometime gag man on the Laurel and Hardy pictures; by 1929 he was a two-reel director on the lot; by 1932 he had gone to Universal and was directing comedy features; and when Universal shut down briefly in 1933 during the Depression bank crisis, Stevens at twenty-nine became a comedy director at RKO.

This was a prodigiously fast rise. But Stevens had drama in his blood. His maternal grandmother, Georgia Woodthorpe, had been a classical actress in San Francisco in the Gold Rush days. His uncle, Ashton Stevens, was a prominent theater critic in Chicago. His parents, Landers and Georgie (Cooper) Stevens, were actor-directors, who at the time their son was born in 1904 managed a stock company that toured all over the West Coast.

According to George, his parents were interested in modern acting, in the new naturalism that was filtering into American theater from Europe. But their repertory contained no Ibsen or Strindberg: it consisted, rather, of that grand old mix of highbrow and popular, of Shakespeare, Dickens, and melodrama, that had fed the American stage for at least three decades. What Stevens got from his family was saturation in a kind of theater that was nearly obsolete. He had made his debut at age five at San Francisco's Alcazar Theater in an old Sarah Bernhardt vehicle, Daudet's *Sapho,* starring the great western actress-manager Nance O'Neill. But it wasn't just his own

acting experience that shaped his temperament; it was the whole atmosphere, the feel and sound and smell of the kind of theater his parents were
immersed in. Stevens later told about sitting backstage in the dark when he
was little, during *A Tale of Two Cities,* listening for the moment when
Sidney Carton would make his final speech at the gallows: "It is a far, far
better thing that I do than I have ever done. . . ." He remembered hearing
the audience grow especially quiet, and almost breathless before the thump
of the guillotine. Then he would hear the wooden board of the curtain
coming down, and a wave of applause. Such moments gave him a primal
grasp of the rhythms of theatrical storytelling.

Later, those rhythms would inform his movies. But Stevens used the
movies at first to rebel against his family's brand of theater culture, and to
explore the life the theater had kept him from. Such a rebellion might have
begun even before he went to work in Hollywood, in his childhood, with
his hobby of taking photographs. As the Stevens family traveled all over the
West, performing in towns like Vancouver, Denver, Portland, and
Ogden—places still smallish and neighborly in those days—George took
pictures of local life with his Kodak. These pictures, of streets and stores and
people with children, betray a certain wistfulness about what he couldn't
experience himself. Then, around 1920, the Stevenses' stock company
closed, a victim of the big shows touring from Broadway and of the prolifer-
ation of movie theaters. Stevens recalled peeping through the curtains at the
empty seats, left vacant by people who had switched their allegiance to other
kinds of entertainment. This debacle afforded George an actual experience
of small-town life, brief though it was.

The family had been performing in the summers in the little town of
Boyes Springs in the Sonoma Valley. Young Stevens stayed behind when
his family went on to do a tent show in San Francisco—a humiliating drop
in theatrical status—and he attended at least part of the ninth grade at the
Sonoma Valley Union High School. This was real rural America: the population of Sonoma was only six hundred in those days. Here Stevens did the
things small-town American young people did: he walked to school; he
went to a dance with his classmates. But all too soon the elder Stevenses
decided to swallow their thespian pride and remove to Los Angeles in order
to "repair the family fortune" in the moving-picture business. They landed
in the Glendale section of L.A., next to Culver City, where they stayed for
a while with relatives before renting a small house of their own nearby.
George at fourteen was taken permanently out of school so that he could
drive his father to auditions at the movie studios spread all over the then-
empty Hollywood landscape.

If his later movies are any guide, the young Stevens formed an intense attachment at this time to the ordinariness of places like Sonoma and the still-small Glendale; he rejoiced in suddenly being a normal kid instead of a child actor—and he appreciated the chance the movies gave him to escape from his parents' shabby genteel attitudes. ("No kid of mine is going to be a stagehand," his father supposedly remarked on learning that his son was photographing for the movies.) The slapstick of Laurel and Hardy also provided relief from the high-toned swashbuckling of his parents' plays. And Laurel and Hardy's cinema-verité settings—the streets of sleepy little Culver City outside of the lot, the local parks, the Southern California countryside that was Stevens's new home—took him far away from the world of greasepaint and cardboard. There is a surreal edge to some of Stevens's photography for these late-twenties Laurel and Hardy shorts that betrays his excitement. In *Two Tars* (1928), settings such as the shady sidewalk under the drugstore awning where the "tars" pick up two girls, or the scruffy, sun-flooded country where Laurel and Hardy take the girls for a ride in their rented jalopy, are so fixedly banal they're exotic.

This hypernormalcy is even more noticeable in the short-lived two-reel series Stevens got Roach to let him write and direct, *The Boy Friends* (1930). Stevens invented a group of high-school boys working as soda jerks and messengers, and their girls—a teenaged *Our Gang*. There's a breezy contemporary air of boy-girl camaraderie in the few episodes that got made, and a precocious alertness to the shadings of class within the bourgeois newness of California suburbia, where they were photographed. The directorial tempo, moreover, is slowed-down and pseudonaive, as if Stevens were both charmed and repelled by the self-importance of small-town life.

IN 1930 Stevens was probably too new a director to realize that in *The Boy Friends* he'd hit upon his great subject—adolescence in provincial America. But even if he did know, he couldn't use the knowledge yet. Anybody would have had trouble crossing over from comedy to straight feature films in the panicked early-Depression movie industry. Stevens had gotten himself to RKO, but only as a comedy director. He made three RKO feature-length comedies in 1934—*Bachelor Bait*, a farce on the order of *The Boy Friends*, and two pictures starring the accident-prone and pun-addicted comedy duo Wheeler and Woolsey—before he was given the Indiana idyll *Laddie* to direct in 1935. With *Laddie*, Stevens began to move out of the world of straight comedy. But to go from the children's environment of *Laddie* to the milieu of a Katharine Hepburn picture meant another huge leap. Of the first *Alice* meeting at Hepburn's house, Stevens recalled, "She was a young but grand lady in this studio, and I was shooting this stuff with guys falling into mortar and things. . . . I thought, 'If Katharine Hepburn sees this she'll want to air the house out.'" Of her first impression of Stevens, Hepburn has said, "I thought he was the dumbest man I ever met. He just stood there with that solemn face, those pop eyes."

It's true that Stevens already had a reputation for being poker-faced and reticent on the set. It was also believed in Hollywood circles that his reticence came from American Indian ancestry—a rumor he enjoyed too much to discount. But Hepburn's and Stevens's jokes about his Laurel and Hardy manner are anecdotal exaggerations. Stevens and Hepburn actually got along very well. Hepburn was fascinated by this western man of strong will and few words, who also knew "the theatah," and Stevens quickly saw through Hepburn's grand exterior to the excruciatingly nervous but stimulating person underneath.* And somewhere in the preparation of *Alice Adams* Stevens began to construct the movie around Hepburn's personality, as Capra had done in his movies with Stanwyck and Colbert.

No property could have been better suited to this young director's skills than *Alice*. It offered him a setting of small-town Americana, which he had used in the *Boy Friends* series. It was geared to a complicated star who already interested him. And it came with ideal working conditions: Berman had agreed to let Stevens have more than the customary authority over the picture. Stevens began to use this authority right away, by throwing out the Murfin–Yost script and assembling a team to reconstruct the movie. It consisted of Stevens himself; a writer friend of Hepburn's from Universal, Mortimer Offner; a gagman named Harry Edwards; and Hepburn—who had a full voice in the story conferences. In fact, Hepburn acted as co-author of the heroine from the beginning. She even shopped for some of Alice's clothes at the Hollywood Woolworth's: one of the dresses, she now says with professional pride, cost $2.98.

In the absence of a script, they shot the book. "We'd dictate dialogue from the book for three or four pages, and do that scene," Stevens told Leonard Maltin in 1970. "We finally got a few pages ahead of ourselves." (They had a final script twelve days before the end of the thirty-six-day shooting schedule.) What emerged from this potluck collaboration was not just a good screen version of Tarkington's novel but a live, unpredictable movie that responded, in a seriocomic idiom Stevens invented on the spot, to the hopes and fears of the country in the Depression, played out in the

*For years Hepburn and Stevens kept alive the idea of collaborating on a movie of that landmark American play of 1904 *The Great Divide,* about romance between a cowboy and an eastern woman.

life of a young woman. In short, in the midst of its creation, *Alice Adams* became a romantic comedy.

FROM *ALICE*'S OPENING SCENE Stevens made a point of demonstrating how unimpressed he was by the class associations of Hepburn's earlier screen persona. 75TH JUBILEE YEAR; SOUTH RENFORD, says a cheerful billboard in the first shot of the movie. (Tarkington's middle-sized midwestern metropolis has shrunk to the size of Culver City.) The camera strolls slowly along the tops of stores, reading their names: SOUTH RENFORD NEWS—CIRCULATION FIVE THOUSAND, VOGUE SMART SHOP, SAMUELS 5-10-15¢ STORE. At Samuels, it descends to street level to observe a large black matron and her two children coming out, followed by a slim Katharine Hepburn as Alice Adams, dressed in a neat dark summer dress and a little hat with a veil, and peering around nervously. Here she's not the grand and adorable Hepburn of her recent movies; she's a self-conscious shopper, worried that someone will see her in the dime store. She walks quickly back (where the camera was coming from) to the doorway of the Smart Shop, then pauses, in close-up, to take out the compact she's just bought at Samuels. She indulges in a little show, biting her lip and hiking her shoulder, to convince potential passers-by that she actually bought the compact at the Smart Shop. It's a sequence of Lillian Gish expressions Hepburn reproduces here, and their antiquated associations make her look youthful and delicate and foolish. Still posing, she enters the flower shop to ask grandly about bouquets for that evening's party at the Palmers'. She wants the florist to be impressed that she's been invited to the Palmers. But, cut short by the actual prices (five dollars for orchids, two dollars for violets), she backs hastily out. "I *hardly* see anything that will do, thank you just the same," she says with affected disdain. The next thing we see is Hepburn picking violets in the park.

This opening scene upends the social geometry of Hepburn's previous screen persona. Instead of some kind of privileged person (a countess, a composer) who falls into "real-life" emotions, here she's an ordinary girl straining to appear privileged, and using mannerisms learned from the movies. This scene not only exposes Alice's playacting, it shows why she has to do it—because prosperous people in the town, like the kindly florist, have no idea about the struggles of people like Alice. She is a victim of that painful middle-class half-poverty which Tarkington had been moved to expose in 1921, but which the Depression had magnified since then. The surprise of the scene is how wholeheartedly Hepburn throws herself into this portrayal of shame about poverty, this assuming of mannerisms to project prosperity. She seems almost relieved to be playing someone ill at

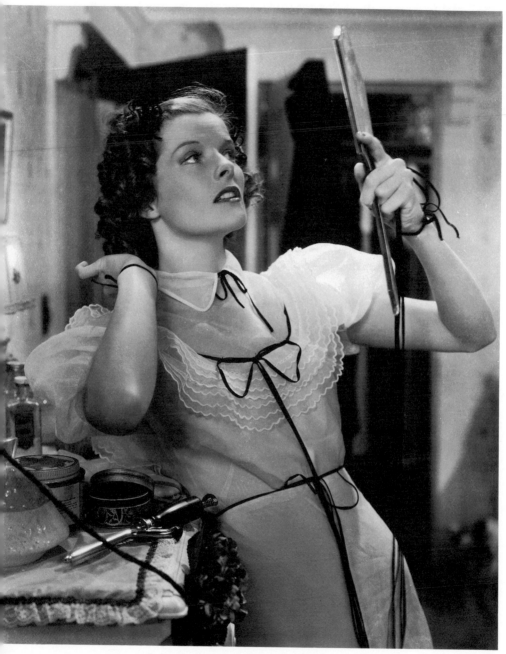

Katharine Hepburn in *Alice Adams*.

ease rather than someone grand and precious. And the clear, Laurel and Hardy–style sunlight Stevens provides for this opening scene suits the ordinariness of the new Hepburn character. Whether or not he was thinking of *It Happened One Night,* Stevens was doing with Hepburn what Capra had done with Stanwyck (after *Ladies of Leisure*)—deconstructing a movie star to unearth a screen personality. And he was using something like Capra's methods to do it. Versed in impromptu silent slapstick comedy, Stevens took his text, Tarkington's *Alice Adams,* only as a starting point. His real material was the actors themselves: they gave him the clues about how to rearrange the story and the dialogue as he went along. And in the next, key scene in the Adams home, Stevens shows us the family that produced an Alice like Hepburn's.

It begins with a straight-on view of the Adamses' living room, into which Hepburn bursts, screen left, with her violets. And it continues in a leisurely, fluid journey all around the house: upstairs to where Alice's father is recovering from a long illness; down to the kitchen, where Alice washes her violets; upstairs again to Alice's room, where she gets dressed for the Palmer party; down again, where Mrs. Adams nervously sends Alice off with her brother, Walter. Stevens presents these comings and goings not as mere expository information but as a portrait of the frustrations in a family where life hasn't become what the most forceful member of it, the mother, dreamed of. The timbre of their voices says it: the syrupy note of self-pity in Mrs. Adams's talk, Virgil Adams's querulous drawl, Walter's restless punk slang, Alice's mannered declarations. So does the way Stevens photographs the house. He shows wide, deep shots of a set, with characters inhabiting both the "near" and "far" parts of the screen, isolated from each other in the same frame: Walter lounging far upscreen in Alice's doorway, for instance, as she twirls downscreen before her mirror.

All through the movie, Stevens returns frequently to the different "rooms" of the house, as if sketching the family's weary paths through it: up the staircase to the narrow hall; across the dark, old-fashioned living room, where they never stop to sit and talk. These techniques point up Stevens's awareness of the story's theatrical dimension—his characters' behavior in architectural space. The melodrama of the elder Stevenses had used the physical sets as a springboard for acting. (The climax of that quintessential Belasco melodrama *The Heart of Maryland* was its star, Mrs. Leslie Carter, swinging on the bell rope to stop it ringing out her lover's dying hour.) But the young Stevens didn't simply set a scene as his parents would have done in the theater, and let the actors inhabit it. He also used a cinematic strategy of cutting rhythmically among the "rooms," so that his audience could experience the kinetic sensations of living in that house. This is Stevens's version of the newsreel dimension of *It Happened One Night*. Capra had located his realism in the look of humble public spaces—bus stations and auto courts; Stevens found his in the aural-psychological landscape of a shabby old family home.

HEPBURN, in this many-chambered house set, seems as inspired as Stevens. Her best acting before *Alice* had taken place in the family and house scenes of *Little Women*—perhaps because she herself came from a family that isolated itself, whose house was its world. But the Adamses of *Alice Adams* were not an effusive, greeting-card family like Louisa May Alcott's Marches. They were a psychologically damaged family. And with Stevens's guidance, Hepburn offers a superb rendition of the unacknowledged stresses and longings that have lodged most intensely in the family's elder child. The tone Hepburn takes with her on-screen mother (Ann Shoemaker) captures the way some middle-class daughters invariably echo their mothers' anxieties. ("I don't think *anybody* will recognize this old organdy, do you?" she asks her mother.) Her tone with her father suggests the illicit bond that a middle-class daughter and father, afflicted with such a mother and wife, would naturally form with each other. Hepburn sticks her head in at his door; she makes a mock-gruff face and says, "Poor old Daddykins"; she approaches his bed with a whispered, tender "Aw!" and a hopeless half-smile: it looks as if she's had a lifetime's experience trying to cheer up fathers. Versions of father-daughter scenes were already Hepburn's specialty in the movies. With Barrymore, her "father" in *A Bill of Divorcement,* with C. Aubrey Smith, her mentor in *Morning Glory,* and with Henry Stephenson, Laurie's father in *Little Women,* she had played her most fervently. And with Fred Stone in *Alice Adams* she achieved the most genuinely wistful manner she had yet managed in the movies.

It's the father-daughter sequences in the movie that begin to shift it away from Tarkington's *Alice* and into new psychic territory. In the novel, Alice heartlessly manipulates her father and orders her mother about. In the movie it's different: she wants to respect her father—to avoid pitying him— and she tries to enlist her mother in this effort. That makes it sadder. Here the family's misunderstandings aren't buried in habit, as in the novel; they're all on the surface, causing chronic pain.

Though Stevens's movie uses more of the novel than Jane Murfin's original script (most of the movie dialogue came verbatim from the book), it gradually alters Tarkington's fundamental emphasis. We are not observing from a distance, as readers of the novel, what poverty can do to a young girl's personality; we are watching up close while Alice struggles to be genuine in a hypocritical family. The conventions of romantic comedy weren't yet known to the movie industry as a whole. It is unlikely that Stevens intended to make an equivalent to Capra's drama, about a defiant but intimidated heroine trying to know her own mind. But by pointing up and emphasizing Hepburn's particular acting skills, he got that drama anyway. Hepburn could make Alice's self-conscious inner life, her artificiality both in and out of the family, wonderfully visible on the screen. To her parents she tries to be cheerful, but the audience hears the strain. In public she tries to be sophisticated, but the audience sees her terror. This condition of adolescent anguish is perfectly clear and familiar, even to present-day viewers, from the moment Hepburn's Alice is introduced. It is a condition that is kin to the fearfulness engendered in Colbert's Ellie by her bus trip. To Alice, the whole world seems inconsiderate and cruel, which makes her as representative a figure, to the socially thwarted Depression audience, as Capra's original heiress heroine.

ONCE HEPBURN'S ALICE has become that key type, the Depression "little man," all the events in Tarkington's story take on the extra intensity of Depression class-consciousness. The Palmer party scene, which Tarkington had written to anatomize midwestern pretentions, is transformed by Stevens into Alice's first major crisis of identity. We can tell right away that this is a swell, snobby party, because the Palmers' neo-Georgian doorway glows with prosperity on a rainy night. Alice is already on edge when she arrives: Walter has brought her in a broken-down jalopy he borrowed from a friend. (She has made him park it down the street.) Stevens exposes Alice's nervousness by cutting away from her and Walter at the Palmers' front door and planting the camera on the other side, inside, so we see the two of them entering as if through the Palmers' eyes. Instantly we cringe. Alice charges into the party like a nervous thoroughbred; she fingers Mildred Palmer's pearls too cozily in the receiving line; she compliments her brother too loudly on his dancing; she exaggerates every possible means to make an impression.

But we don't mind Alice's gaucheries, because we understand from earlier scenes why she's like this. What we mainly feel here is outrage at the ill-mannered treatment of Alice by South Renford's golden youth. Girls audibly comment on her made-over dress ("Organdy! Maybe *we're* wrong . . ."). Boys walk through her to the girl beyond. It's a detailed portrait of that primal American high-school nightmare of "unpopularity" caused by poverty—a nightmare that must have been unimaginably potent in real small towns during the Depression. Stevens underscores Alice's isolation with long shots showing a tiny, distant, white-gowned Hepburn sitting out in the hall beyond the roomful of dancing couples, which he alternates with extended close-ups of her in her chair, registering, like a seismographic instrument, every possible nuance between feigned oblivious-ness and naked hurt. These party scenes serve the same dual purpose as Capra's first bus scenes in *It Happened One Night:* they expose the worst of his heroine's affectations, then bring the sympathy back around to her. But Stevens, at Tarkington's prompting, is harsher than Capra. Instead of put-ting his heroine against a backdrop of rural loneliness, Stevens places Alice in a milieu of human indifference and watches her grow more and more agitated. When the Palmers' wealthy cousin Arthur Russell (Fred MacMur-ray) asks her to dance, she nearly goes into shock. She is so paralyzed by surprise that she dances carefully, almost gracefully, with him. But after this triumph in the waltz, Alice learns that Arthur Russell has seen her brother playing dice in the cloak room. She loses what little nerve she had mustered and makes Walter take her home.

Capra's romantic-comedy formula had dramatized a too-complacent her-oine encountering severe emotional pressure and coming undone—as if to simulate what had happened to the whole country in the worst of the Depression. Stevens, with a very different story and a different sort of heroine, creates the same effect. In *Alice Adams* the Palmer party deprives Alice of her excess nervous energy, just as the bus people had neutralized Colbert's edgy snobbery. There is a beautiful, lyric image of Hepburn sobbing against her rainy window after the party, photographed from out-side the window through the rain. It seems to mark the depths of Alice's despair and to clear the way for a new kind of life ahead. But here is where Stevens veered off from Capra. For Capra's heroines, a new life meant romance. For Stevens, the romance was not quite so important. We see all the conditions set up for a liaison: Alice, in the next scene, runs into Arthur Russell downtown, where she's gone to see about entering the local business college, and Arthur asks her to take a walk. But we never see a romance start to take shape. The two don't engage in the intimate banter that a Capra movie would have introduced at this point.

Fred MacMurray as Arthur says almost nothing—he *can't* say anything, because Alice won't let him get a word in edgewise. Hepburn does Alice "charming" Arthur superbly: the arm imperiously extended as she confesses that her career as a girl has been "one long brazen smirch" of mean things; the little embarrassed laughs between sentences, the hands creeping around her chin as she "reposes" on the porch swing the first evening Arthur comes to call. The audience watches Alice waste her formidable inventiveness on this "act" for Arthur. The movie's only attempt at a romantic exchange is a static scene in a quaint outdoor restaurant with checkered tablecloths. Hepburn and MacMurray are sitting there pensively. She, in a wistful tone, tells MacMurray that the evening "is just like that music—oh so sweet, and oh so sad." But Stevens undermines even this pseudo-love scene with a corny gag about the tired orchestra mugging as it plays Alice's favorite song one more time.

ONE COULD SAY, in fact, that *Alice Adams* is a romantic comedy without a love story. It's not because of the novel: Tarkington had provided plenty of erotic sparring between Alice and Arthur, which Stevens didn't choose to use. Something else was happening in this movie, which was related to Stevens's orientation within romantic comedy.

The next scene in which Alice talks to her mother about Arthur while they sit on the dark porch ("He's so honestly what he is; I feel like a tricky mess beside him," she says) is so much more lifelike than the little love scene in the restaurant that it reveals Stevens's essential concern: the dynamics of the family. In his mind Alice's breaking away from her parents' control counts more in the drama than her succeeding in a romance with Arthur. This porch scene shows Alice finally beginning to question Mrs. Adams's idea of correct social behavior and starting to form her own. The famous scene following it, the Adamses' dinner for Arthur on the hottest night of the year, completes Alice's awful awakening. Everything goes wrong with the dinner from the moment MacMurray appears on the porch in his summer whites. Mrs. Adams bumps into him at the door. The buttons on Virgil Adams's rented tuxedo pop continually. He has a ghastly encounter with a caviar sandwich. Hattie McDaniel, playing the hired black maid, plods through the scene with brilliant comic understatement. She serves the heavy dishes in a dubious manner, signaling that they're wrong for such a hot evening. She makes the most of the props at hand—the sliding doors she has to pry open to let the family into the dining room, a stray brussels sprout she goes after with a trowel (a recycled Laurel and Hardy gag), her lace headpiece, which keeps slipping below her eyes. As for Hepburn's Alice, she's paralyzed by her family's gaucherie: a haunted look comes into her eyes as she plies MacMurray with hollow questions, then stifles his answers with new questions.

In Capra's scheme of romantic comedy, romance forced a person to grow up. In Stevens's, that growing up needed to happen first, before a romance could occur. Capra was a director of wishes coming true; Stevens, of "realer" frustrations. Alice can't run away from this empty ceremony of a dinner, the way Ellie Andrews ran away from her wedding, because her parents, especially her mother, have spent their adult lives focusing their thwarted desires onto their daughter. She is in thrall to these. In Stevens's movies, this kind of obligation to one's parents always proved the strongest force in the shaping of a personality. Most of Stevens's Hollywood career—from the prewar *Alice* and *Vivacious Lady* through the postwar *I Remember Mama, A Place in the Sun, Shane, Giant, The Diary of Anne Frank*—would be spent examining the struggles of children or adolescents to grow up inside their families. Even when there was no visible family, in romantic comedies such as *Swing Time* or *The More the Merrier,* there were familial habits of thinking and behaving that the "children" had to overcome.

Hepburn, Stevens's first adolescent, is among his most moving, because she shows us so clearly that Alice learned her near-ruinous self-conciousness from her mother. It is evident from this movie that the collaboration between Hepburn and Stevens went on at some deep level of understanding and shared experience. Stevens's son, George Stevens, Jr., has suggested that the movie's Mrs. Adams took on some of the qualities of Stevens's own mother, a status-conscious woman whose reduced circumstances had made her socially brittle. If that is so, then Hepburn is standing in for Stevens himself, and in the drama of Alice he is telling us something about his own coming of age. The parallels between Hepburn's Alice and Stevens himself can be found all through the movie. Stevens once told his son a story about going to the school prom in Sonoma in heavy boots, the only shoes he had, and of sitting on the sidelines hiding his feet in embarrassment—obviously a source for the Palmer party episode.

Therefore, it takes a family crisis to show Alice, and us, her audience, that she actually has grown up. In the midst of the strained dinner with Arthur Russell, Walter, the absent member of the family, suddenly bursts in, demanding to talk to his father. This so panics Alice that she takes Arthur out onto the porch and asks him to leave. But then, instead of collapsing into self-pity, she strides back into the house to see what's going on. Her brother has embezzled money from his and his father's employer, J. A. Lamb's drug company, to pay for what is hinted is a girlfriend's abortion. He has also jeopardized the glue business his father has just gone out on his own to start. J. A. Lamb himself—actor Charley Grapewin in a Kentucky-colonel suit—appears at the door. The distraught Virgil Adams denounces Lamb as "a doggone mean man." But Alice stops Lamb from retaliating with an impassioned speech. "It's all my fault," she cries, to explain why her father deserted Lamb with their jointly owned glue formula. "Mother was always after Dad to make money for me." And then she volunteers to go to work and pay Lamb back what her brother owes him. "I can do things," she says, in a voice quivering with tears. "I was good at English and math. I won a prize in English once." Moved by this, Lamb goes back into the house and makes a deal with Virgil Adams.

By coming to see the truth about her family, Hepburn's Alice turns the tide for them all. This is the moment when she chooses her fate, as Colbert's Ellie chose hers by running away from her wedding. It almost doesn't matter whether she gets the romance or not—her leap into maturity carries the weight of resolution. And because the romance is downplayed here, the heroine's discovery of her intelligence—that usually secondary ingredient in a romantic-comedy climax—stands out more clearly. It's a grim discovery. All Alice can muster to support her newfound self is the fact that she was good in school. But Alice's realization that she can move from "good in school" to "good in the world" is obviously what Stevens and Hepburn wanted to celebrate.

They made up this whole scene to do it. Nothing like Alice's impassioned speech to Mr. Lamb appears in the book. But the scene rounds out the life of these characters in a way that seems more inventive than any scene in the book. The inevitable romantic-comedy father-figure-who-sets-things-right, J. A. Lamb projects a believability that Tarkington never managed to give him. He's the small-town patriarch so sure of his power that he can deign to be benign from time to time: to recognize an Alice Adams's good sense and forgive the impertinence of a Virgil Adams. Lamb also provides the ultimate occasion for Alice to show off her new maturity (and for Hepburn to play another scene with a father figure). To accentuate Alice's personal victory, Stevens caps the scene with a little coda—a silent sequence in which Hepburn goes downstairs alone and quietly turns out the lights one by one. She's not the victimized daughter anymore; she's the head of the household.

AFTER THIS SHREWDLY observed climax, the movie's actual ending comes as a letdown. Alice steps out on the porch for one last breath of night air and finds Arthur Russell still there. He has heard the whole scene, but as Hepburn starts to explain again, MacMurray finally asserts himself and tells her, affectionately, to shut up. Hepburn says one charming "Gee whiz!" and the movie fades out on their not very convincing embrace. Nowadays we might wish that Stevens had been more daring and ended the movie as Tarkington ended the novel, with Alice again starting up the steps to the business college. (In the novel, her fate seems grim at first, but in his last sentence Tarkington says that: "There was an open window overhead some-where . . . and the steps at the top were gay with sunshine.") A scene of

Hepburn starting up the steps would have made a resonant ending; likewise a scene of Hepburn leaving on a train to get work in the big city. But Pandro Berman, watching out for the studio's interests, couldn't let Arthur Russell drift out of the picture, or the romance disappear totally from a romantic comedy.

Here is where the *Alice* team divided. Stevens and Hepburn wanted Alice to go up the business-college steps. Berman wanted Alice to get engaged to Arthur. The debate inside the studio has provided us with a rare glimpse of the kind of negotiating that supported and defined the Hollywood genre system. Berman set down in a ten-page memo all the points in favor of the "happy ending" *with* romance and all the points in favor of the "story ending" *without* romance. He conceded the logic of the ending Stevens and Hepburn wanted, with Arthur Russell succumbing to the social pressures of South Renford and leaving Alice and her family to face a bleak but honest future. Such a movie, Berman admitted, would contain "art, dignity and the beauty of reality." But, Berman went on, the emotional currents that Stevens had set in motion—the attractiveness Alice has gained from leveling with herself—called for something more cathartic, for a union between Arthur and Alice. Inevitably, RKO chose the second ending. What clinched it was not anything so crass as box-office predictions, although these played a part, but rather Berman's sincere, if sentimental, feelings about the responsiveness Hollywood movies should show to the Depression audience. "The lives of most are the lives of Alice and her family," wrote Berman. "To offer these people only a philosophy that life goes on will not content the American public in its present temper after years of depression." So Alice gets her wealthy, handsome husband in the final clinch on the porch.

Despite its improbability, this ending conveys a wistful charm of its own—and anyway, it doesn't seriously alter the basic thrust of the movie. What Stevens did in *Alice* was what he was supposed to do—make Hepburn more likable to audiences. And he did it without forcing the movie into any of Hollywood's usual narrative postures of adoration toward a star. On the contrary: Stevens brought the movie's story into focus with what he had observed of Hepburn's own screen persona. This Alice was more nervous, more vulnerable, and more generous than Booth Tarkington had ever meant Alice to be; she was like Hepburn at both her best and her worst on the screen. But she was also a little like Stevens himself. He, the theater kid, the outsider, knew more about small-town mockery than Hepburn (although Hepburn says she too was mocked by Connecticut townspeople because of her mother's feminist crusading). Whatever its mix of sources, this merging of the director's and the actress's stories, in a movie which isn't literally about either of them, had become a feature of this genre. But *Alice* occupies a special place in the romantic-comedy oeuvre—a place that corresponds to Hepburn's own special position among her Hollywood peers.

If we imagine the landmark romantic comedies of the thirties as episodes in one loose story—the story of the working-girl figure and the careless-gentleman figure—then *Alice* could serve to introduce that story. It could be the prologue, the chapter that would describe the heroine's small-town origins and her decision to go off to the big city. Hepburn at this point wasn't equipped to play a sophisticated urban heroine like the ones at Paramount: she was too innocent and awkward on the screen. She was better suited, as Stevens had shown, to play a character in a small town, in a family. If Stevens and Hepburn had managed to win the dispute about the ending, the movie's potential to stand as prologue to other romantic comedies would become even clearer. We could then imagine Hepburn working in the city in a hypothetical sequel to *Alice,* the way we imagine the small-town pasts of the more typical romantic-comedy heroines in implied prologues to their movies. Most Depression romantic comedies, in fact, begin with the assumption that the heroine has come alone to the big city precisely because things are so bad out there in Main Street America. (A late romantic comedy such as Billy Wilder's *The Major and the Minor* teased the audience when it showed the heroine finally giving up on the city in disgust and buying a train ticket *back* to her small town.) At any rate, *Alice Adams* stands now as the movie that clarifies the contrast in the Depression heroine's mind between small-town "family" values and big-city independence. Alice acquires the independence at the end of the movie, even if she doesn't manage to leave the small town.

ALICE ADAMS delighted the public. It put Hepburn's career back on track, and it inaugurated George Stevens's career as a serious director. But *Alice* proved just as important to RKO as to Stevens and Hepburn. It gave the studio a style within the genre. At Paramount, Capra's original, hybrid construction was being tailored to the specifications of Colbert and Lombard. Paramount would soon become host to a whole school of romantic-comedy specialists (directors and writers)—Wesley Ruggles, Howard Hawks, Ben Hecht, William Wellman, Preston Sturges, Billy Wilder—who would work out the Paramount "flavor" of the genre. Paramount liked its love stories quick, clever, and effervescent, even if the effervescence had to be artificially induced at times: the term "screwball comedy" came out of Paramount. But at RKO, Stevens, under the protection of Pandro Berman, was working out a slower, more naturalistic, more thoughtful, more physical, and eventually more erotic approach to Depression romantic comedy. This slow style would soon become the house style at RKO. And after *Alice Adams,* as Hepburn's career slid depressingly into another slump, a different RKO actress, with an opposite sort of screen personality, would become the focus of these slower romantic comedies. Ginger Rogers, the contract player who had made her reputation as Fred Astaire's dancing partner, was beginning to emerge, in the mid-thirties, as a star on her own.

5

STEVENS AND ROGERS:

SWING TIME

Fred Astaire,
Ginger Rogers,
George Stevens,
and co. on the
set of *Swing Time*.

G INGER ROGERS came to RKO in a very different manner from Katharine Hepburn. The studio took her on in late spring of 1933, after Warner Bros.' *42nd Street* and *Gold Diggers of 1933* had suddenly brought movie musicals back into style. The twenty-two-year-old Rogers had appeared in both these landmark Warners movies, as platinum-blond chorines in the shows-within-the-movies. RKO first tried her out in a low-budget comedy called *Professional Sweetheart* (1933), a spoof of radio stardom, in which Rogers gave a delicious performance as the shallow, naughty Purity Girl who sponsored Ipsy Wipsy towels. Then RKO took out an option on a longer contract. In deciding to sign her on (or rather to take her back, since she had been briefly contracted to RKO-Pathé in 1931), the studio mentioned the "possibility of developing her."

But one gets the impression from studio memos that RKO saw Rogers as a middle-level acquisition, useful to have on the roster for the return of musicals but far from star material. That she had once starred on Broadway didn't accord her the prestige it did Hepburn, since Rogers's medium had been musical comedy (Kalmar and Ruby's 1929 *Top Speed;* the Gershwins' 1930 *Girl Crazy*), not serious drama. Moreover, Rogers had been away from Broadway since 1931, working in Hollywood at a level well below stardom. She had played bit parts in big comedies, lead parts in little comedies, and small but key roles in *42nd Street* and *Gold Diggers of 1933.* She had not appeared in the high-class weepers of the early thirties. At the time RKO hired her, the studio probably intended to use her for a B-picture line of youthful comedies. In her first RKO movie under contract, the low-budget *Chance at Heaven* (1933), she played the virtuous and colorless "best friend" of the diminutive star, Marian Nixon. She then starred with Norman Foster in an even lower-budget romantic comedy called *Rafter Romance* (1934), at a time when this genre was still considered tacky. Though Rogers (seconded by her mother, Lela Rogers) harbored serious ambitions, probably no one else at RKO then would have predicted how important she was to become to the studio—almost immediately.

FRED ASTAIRE had been hired by RKO around the same time as Rogers, in the spring of 1933. But Astaire, unlike Rogers, hadn't hung around the movie industry doing bit parts: he had arrived in Hollywood with the sheen of smart theater and high society on him. In the twenties and early thirties,

Astaire had appeared on Broadway and in London with his sister, Adele, in a series of musicals specially tailored to their bright presence. The wealthy young cabaret crowd in both cities had adopted them, and in 1932 an aristocratic English bachelor, Lord Cavendish, had married Adele. Astaire, already recognized as a dancer-auteur within musical comedy—a role that lifted him out of the debased "popular" category of most musicals—successfully ventured one more show alone in New York and London, *The Gay Divorce,* before seeking a new fortune in Hollywood.

He chose RKO instead of another studio because he was a friend of the young socialite and movie entrepreneur John Hay "Jock" Whitney, who was a friend of RKO's boss David O. Selznick. But though he came with star social status, Astaire didn't start off at RKO in a starring movie role. He had already made his Hollywood debut before his RKO contract began, playing himself, as a supporting role, in MGM's *Dancing Lady* (1933). RKO cast him in another supporting role, in its *Flying Down to Rio,* which was the studio's first large-scale bid to reenter the musical-comedy field. Astaire was supposed to have sung and have danced in *Rio* with a classy partner, an RKO starlet named Dorothy Jordan, trained in ballet. But Dorothy Jordan quit pictures just before *Rio* to marry RKO's then head of production, Merian C. Cooper. So RKO's new contractee Ginger Rogers, who happened to know how to sing and dance, was put in as Astaire's partner instead. It was the big break of Rogers's career.

THE ROLES ASTAIRE and Rogers played in *Flying Down to Rio* were not only secondary, they were corny: Astaire is a comical accordion player in a band that goes to Rio de Janeiro; Rogers is the band's wisecracking singer. Both disappear from the screen for long stretches of time while the white-blond leading man, Gene Raymond, makes love to the ebony-haired leading lady, Dolores Del Rio. But even without Astaire and Rogers in the forefront, the movie throws off a palpable excitement—about the sleek deco shape of the new Pan American airplanes, the lovely old city of Rio, and the effect of Latin rhythms on the thirties big-band sound. And when the two of them get up to perform Hollywood's version of the "local" dance called the carioca, the excitement rises to a fever pitch. "I'd like to try this thing just once," says Astaire as he gets up from their first table by a dance floor, pulling Rogers by the hand. "I guess we'll show them a thing or three," she rejoins, scrambling up to join him.

Then *she* grabs *him,* putting his forehead to hers in carioca position. For a minute they look as if they're head to head in a boxing ring, before they sweep out in unison onto the dance floor: he, thin, precise, and ennobled by his concentration on the dance; she, blond, pliant, openhearted, and willing to learn as she goes. This carioca, with its taut, mock-Spanish footwork that unclenches into dips, glides, and off-kilter circles, projects the aura of a contest. Sometimes Astaire and Rogers compete with each other; sometimes they vie with the Brazilian couples on the dance floor. Astaire's choreography displays a competitive edge, perhaps because he started out on the stage with his sister. But whatever its origins, this spectacle of the grown-up Astaire and Rogers matching wits on the dance floor, and off—a man and a woman engaging at a point of anarchic and childlike exuberance—caused audiences to respond enthusiastically in the winter of 1933–34, the worst of the Depression.

Neither Astaire nor Rogers intended this partnership. Astaire had been yoked to his sister for nearly his whole performing life; he wanted to make his reputation on his own in Hollywood. There are also hints that he didn't consider Rogers the right type of actress to co-star with him. (The more refined, and brunette, Dorothy Jordan had been Adele's understudy on Broadway and would have seemed a better choice.) Rogers, in turn, wanted to be a dramatic star in the movies instead of a song-and-dance girl. But *Flying Down to Rio* made more money in the winter of 1933–34 than any other RKO movie except Hepburn's *Little Women,* so the studio could hardly help casting Ginger Rogers as the love interest in Astaire's next movie, which was to be built around him. It was to be a remake of *The Gay Divorce,* which already had been specially tailored to his Broadway persona.

When Astaire's show was put on the screen, however, with the title lightened to *The Gay Divorcee,* Rogers's presence transformed it. The original musical (which had itself been adapted by Samuel Hoffenstein and Kenneth Webb from a play by Dwight Taylor) was a thin bedroom farce about a young woman trying to arrange a divorce at a British seaside resort who mistakes Astaire, a stranger she's attracted to, for the hired divorce co-respondent. Astaire's partner on the stage had been Claire Luce (not Clare Boothe Luce), a former Ziegfeld Follies dancer with ash-blond instead of platinum hair, pencil-thin eyebrows, a languid air, some "artistic" (not just show-business) dance training, and the artificial voice of a Noël Coward ingenue. Since the rueful, brilliantine-haired Astaire also leaned toward artificiality in his acting, the talking scenes between them must have seemed like exercises in arch double entendre. But when Rogers took over the part on the screen, her natural sincerity opened up the dynamic between Astaire and the leading lady. She enters and catches sight of her aunt, who's arrived in London on the boat from Paris. Her slightly sleepy but dazzling smile of recognition lights up the screen—and it's obvious that she brings a quality that contradicts Astaire's theatrical veneer, a lovely unguardedness.

The first Astaire-Rogers film, *Flying Down to Rio,* had proved that Rogers could match wisecracks with anybody. This second one, *The Gay Divorcee,* revealed that she had learned, somewhere in her grab-bag movie apprenticeship, a quiet unaffectedness. And such a quality turned this seamy little play, which the *Times*'s Brooks Atkinson had called "dirty but not disgusting," into a poignant story: a wronged young wife endures a painful divorce and braves a relationship with a new man, Astaire, who is cruelly flippant but who dances so beautifully.

Mark Sandrich, the movie's director, was not the source of this new dynamic between Astaire and Rogers. Sandrich was enthusiastic about musicals; it was his enthusiasm that had landed him the assignment to do this first full-scale Astaire-Rogers movie, and he, along with Astaire, can be credited with the technological innovations of RKO's new "chamber" style in musicals (as distinct from the mammoth Busby Berkeley extravaganzas being developed at Warner Bros.). But Sandrich was not very good at character development. For that aspect of the movie, he depended on the actors' making something of the stock situations of the Broadway musical. In terms of psychology, Astaire and Rogers directed themselves—or, rather, they attempted to reproduce the mischievous struggle between Maurice Chevalier and Jeanette MacDonald in Lubitsch's 1932 *Love Me Tonight.* (*Love Me Tonight* was linked to both *The Gay Divorce,* which came before it, and *The Gay Divorcee,* which came after it: the heroines of all three are called Mimi. Moreover, when RKO changed the "divorce" of *The Gay Divorce* into "divorcee" the new title became a synonym of the title of the movie Chevalier and MacDonald were just then shooting at MGM, *The Merry Widow.*)

Comparing Ginger Rogers with Jeanette MacDonald shows exactly what kind of freshness Rogers brought to those lightweight musical-comedy conventions. Where MacDonald always played for coy irony, Rogers aimed instinctively at quiet realism. In the leads' "cute meet" in *Love Me Tonight,* MacDonald's carriage breaks down as Chevalier comes by—a stock piece of stage business. She mock-fumes as he tarries and flirts. Astaire and Rogers's meeting in *The Gay Divorcee* derives from a similar piece of stage business (not transferred from the Broadway show but lifted directly from Paramount's 1932 *This Is the Night,* with Cary Grant and Thelma Todd). Rogers catches the hem of her dress in a trunk. Astaire comes sauntering along, ignores her plea to get a porter to help her, and hangs around flirting with her instead. Finally he tears the dress loose from the trunk, and Rogers, with half her skirt missing, retreats in confusion. Astaire played it predictably flip. Rogers, with no help from Sandrich—no special close-ups, no sign in the script that the director viewed Astaire's behavior as a trifle sadistic—

managed to make us feel that her character had a right to be hurt and indignant. She turned this little encounter into a Depression scene; she brought social ethics into the story.

ONE WONDERS WHERE Rogers got the instinct and then the skill to shape a heroine with a defiant emotional core. Rogers was only twenty-three in *The Gay Divorcee,* but she had a formidable mother whose presence partly explains her precocity. The Missouri-born Lela Rogers wasn't the usual stage mother; she boasted a professional past. She had married and had her daughter young, then divorced Ginger's father, Eddins McMath, left Ginger with her own mother, and gone off in the teens to be a journalist in New York for the U.S. Marines and then a scriptwriter in Hollywood for the child star Baby Marie Osborne. In the mid-twenties Lela McMath married John Rogers, an insurance broker, and "retired" to Fort Worth, Texas, to give Ginger a normal life. But when Ginger, at sixteen, won a Charleston contest in Texas and decided to go on the stage, Lela abandoned home and husband to become her daughter's coach, manager, director, and caretaker. Lela wrote and costumed Ginger's vaudeville acts, engineered her rise up the vaudeville circuits, prepared her auditions for Broadway musicals, and oversaw her transition into the movies. It must have been difficult in the early thirties, when flappers disappeared from the movies, and Ginger, who had specialized in trendy John Held, Jr., flapper costumes and baby-talk patter, was obliged to take on insignificant roles. But Rogers never stopped trying to improve herself, and Lela, a veteran of Hollywood, knew how that was done in the movies. Sometime during Rogers's early-thirties free-lancing, between playing a lumberman's girlfriend in RKO-Pathé's 1932 *Carnival Boat* and playing a newspaperwoman in Allied Pictures' 1933 *A Shriek in the Night,* she learned a crucial lesson: how to relax before the camera. In the first of these two hastily made pictures, she impersonates a cute floozie and is all over the screen. In the second, as the reporter, she focuses the movie into herself. A key scene in *Shriek*—the chaotic discovery of a murder—shows her sitting quietly, holding a lit cigarette, and projecting far more dignity than anyone else on the screen.

It was more than the rudiments of screen acting that Rogers was acquiring in the early thirties; it was a complete screen persona, which contained more poise than that of most movie ingenues. Here, Lela Rogers probably served as example as well as tutor. Because Lela had taught herself the various professions she had worked in—had all but invented her life as she went along—she possessed that grass-roots pride of the self-made. This pride was naturally passed on to Ginger. "I always carried an electric sewing machine along with our suitcases, and an electric toaster and a percolator," said Lela later about their gypsy years in vaudeville. "On tour, after a performance at night, we could have a little hot supper in our hotel room. We always stayed at the best hotel and ate the best food, because I figured if this was to be Ginger's life, she was entitled to the best." The Rogers mother-and-daughter unit undoubtedly proved claustrophobic at times— Ginger escaped it in the late twenties by briefly marrying another vaudevil-lian—but it also managed to get along very well without the usual protection from husbands or fathers. By the time of *The Gay Divorcee,* the slightly edgy self-sufficiency of this mother-and-daughter team had distilled itself into Rogers's movie persona. If what Astaire projected on the screen was the mischievous brother of Adele, what Rogers projected was the precocious daughter of Lela. When Astaire and Rogers came together in *The Gay Divorcee,* Astaire had his persona down pat: he had been playing him onstage for years. But Rogers was no green ingenue: she had survived eight years of stage and movie experience, which she had used to great advantage. She was ready to hold her own.

THE GAY DIVORCEE provided the basic outlines for the next three As-taire-Rogers movies—*Roberta* (1935), *Top Hat* (1935), and *Follow the Fleet* (1936). Astaire and Rogers would start off as antagonists; they would dance together and fall in love; then they would experience obstructive coinci-dences, mixups, and misunderstandings. Actually they spent most of their time on-screen together trading sarcastic quips. But in the *sous-entendus* underneath the quips, a dynamic was at work that concerned a trusting, needy, yet fiercely independent Rogers encountering a curiously shifty As-taire. Astaire had the mannerisms of a theatrical juvenile of the twenties— lightweight, ingratiating, a little goofy, a little nasty—except when he danced. That's when he showed his "other" nature: the passionate lover. Rogers instinctively selected the Astaire she needed. In the course of a movie, she seemed to absorb and glow from the ardor of the dancing Astaire, while she mourned and resisted the flippancies of the nondancing Astaire. What happened in an Astaire-Rogers movie was a sleight-of-hand transformation: Rogers's longing for Astaire changed him, chastened him in the audience's eyes, and elevated him, even in his juvenile moments, to his noble dancing self. The deep current of romantic tension in these movies came from Rogers's expectations about Astaire, and Astaire's callousness, off the dance floor, about those expectations.

Take the famous *Top Hat,* the first Astaire-Rogers story made up entirely at RKO. It was set in a visionary London of men's clubs and parks and an even more visionary Venice of shining bridges and piazzas that doubled as dance floors. Rogers plays a young woman who travels with a clothes designer to show off his clothes. Astaire plays an American dance star staying in the room above hers in a London hotel. They meet when she protests his tap-dancing on her ceiling. They undo their antagonism and fall in love in an exuberant number in a park gazebo, "Isn't This a Lovely Day (to Be Caught in the Rain)?" But for the rest of the movie they are mired in a misunderstanding: Rogers thinks Astaire is the husband of her best friend, Harriet, played by Helen Broderick. He assumes, fatuously, that her hesitant behavior stems from her modesty. There's a haunting moment when Harriet urges Rogers to dance with Astaire. "If it's all right with you, it's all right with me," Rogers says sorrowfully as she gives in. Then they go into the big adagio love duet, "Cheek to Cheek," in a secluded garden in the moonlight. The Astaire-Rogers unit at RKO must have seen how Rogers's sorrow and shame intensified the dance: it becomes, for her, a tragic dance about helpless acquiescence. But did Sandrich and RKO realize Rogers's importance to the whole series? Did they see how much depth they got from these fierce but needy young women she planted in their farcical plots and their beautiful dances? Did they understand that it was Rogers who performed the alchemy on Astaire and who connected the dances with the plot?

JUDGING BY RKO'S contractual dealings with Rogers, they did not. In May of 1934, midway between the release of *Flying Down to Rio* and that of *The Gay Divorcee,* the studio picked up Rogers's option again, but the bosses had to assure themselves that she could "sing and dance and play comedy or dramatic roles," that having her under contract gave them "a good trading asset, if we do not develop her and Astaire into a co-starring team." As late as July 1934, when *The Gay Divorcee* was in production, there was talk of lending Rogers to Warner Bros. for another of the *Gold Diggers* musicals or for *Sweet Adeline*—because, RKO reasoned, it could always replace her in the forthcoming Astaire-Rogers *Roberta:* Irene Dunne's was the lead role, not Rogers's. (*Roberta* repeated *Flying Down to Rio*'s formula with Astaire and Rogers as the second leads in a comic subplot; Dunne and Randolph Scott were the serious love interest.) In September of 1935, the month when *Top Hat* was released, the studio heads stalled on Rogers's request for a raise of $500 a week. (She was making $2,000, while Astaire already had won a percentage-of-profits deal.) Producer Pandro Berman stepped in and wrote a forceful memo. He pointed out that Rogers had spent all her Sundays, holidays, and nights rehearsing her dances while she was shooting nondancing *Top Hat* scenes during the day, as well as scenes from the comedy she was making without Astaire, *In Person*. He recommended that the studio give her any raise she wanted, because, he said, "I think there are so few assets in the picture business, and she being one of them and one of the three most important personalities we have, I don't think it matters very much whether we give her an extra $500 per week or not when the figures are all added up at the end of the year."

' The other "personalities" he referred to were, of course, Hepburn and Astaire. In his own mind, Berman had promoted Rogers to Hepburn's and Astaire's league. So had the movie public. Not only did *Top Hat* and *Follow the Fleet*, its sequel, each gross nearly three million dollars, but *In Person* (with George Brent), released in late 1935, also drew strong profits. Rogers had proved her power at the box office. All she needed was a director to design her a star role.

AT THIS POINT Pandro Berman gave the next Astaire-Rogers movie, *Swing Time*, the sixth in the series, to George Stevens. Rogers herself might have asked for Stevens at the end of the fifth Astaire-Rogers, *Follow the Fleet*, which, despite its profits, was not successful on all fronts: its lame narrative revealed a staleness creeping into the Astaire-Rogers formula. RKO had tried to vary the Astaire-Rogers "story" by switching from a high-class to a low-class milieu, making Astaire a dancer-turned-sailor and Rogers his former partner in vaudeville. But Sandrich had directed *Fleet* with his usual clunky humor and his habitual disregard for the Rogers character. She auditions in the movie for a singing job she needs; Astaire botches the audition by putting indigestible baking soda into her drinking water, thinking it's for another auditionee—but the movie never bothers to show us her disappointment, or her anger at Astaire's interference. If Sandrich couldn't summon the grasp of psychology to define his characters, Rogers must have thought maybe Stevens could. Stevens, as anyone on the RKO lot knew by then, always paid attention to what his heroines were feeling in their roles.

Not only had Stevens rehabilitated Hepburn in *Alice Adams*, he had rescued RKO's new recruit Barbara Stanwyck from the stigma of unstylish weepers by starring her in the sunny *Annie Oakley* (1935)—a movie one might call a romantic comedy in historical costume. Moreover, in the course of making *Annie Oakley* he had proved to Berman again that he could work with a script in disarray. The *Annie* script had come to him only partially completed; he had finished it as he went along. And that was the state of the *Swing Time* script at the start of filming in July of 1936. It was based on a story written for Astaire and Rogers by a studio writer named Erwin Gelsey, about the low-life milieu of gambling joints and small-time theaters. Broadway playwright Howard Lindsay had begun converting Gelsey's story to a screenplay, but Lindsay had gotten cold feet about working in Hollywood and disappeared abruptly, leaving a note for Stevens in his typewriter that said he was going back to New York by way of the Panama Canal.

Accordingly, Stevens prepared to begin shooting yet another movie without a proper script—this time without even a novel like *Alice Adams* to support him, or a popular legend like that of Annie Oakley. But he wasn't completely devoid of resources. He could depend on the lyrical songs written for the movie by Jerome Kern, with uncannily sensitive words by Dorothy Fields. He could be sure of four substantial dances choreographed by Astaire and Hermes Pan. The studio had hired the quick-witted rewrite man Allan Scott to help him, and the gag man Ernest Pagano. Most crucial of all, Stevens had come to trust his own instincts, which he'd honed in *Alice Adams,* about how to upset clichéd class associations that attached themselves to actors' and actresses' personae. Given Mark Sandrich's careless assumptions about the Astaire and Rogers personae, Stevens was almost fated to make a critique of the pair.

STEVENS'S REVISION of Astaire begins in the first shot of the movie. We see a stage on which Astaire is tap-dancing in front of a line of men; then we watch from the wings as he makes a whirling exit toward the camera. These images are all that were left of the intended opening number, "It's All in the Cards." To start a movie "backwards," though, at the end of a dance, provided a shorthand reminder of what Astaire did best: personified "dance." Then the pace picks up as Astaire, instead of taking a bow, rushes below stage to get dressed for his wedding, followed by his dancer buddies. In the fast dressing-room banter we learn that Astaire is John "Lucky" Garnett, a hoofer who is playing his hometown and planning, on this occasion, to marry a wealthy local girl. His backup dancers and his aging partner, "Pop," played by the small, pudgy Broadway comedian Victor Moore, don't want him to go. They stall him by convincing him to send his pants out to get cuffs put on them. There are some beautiful, mock-candid shots of Astaire in a dressing gown, gambling with the boys as he waits for his pants. We see his face in close-up as he rolls the dice like a champion bowler. We observe his physical and psychic coordination. But we also notice, as he clicks his heels in his spiffy morning costume (the pants have come back), that he's a bit too pleased with himself—too ready to slough off his aging sidekick, too cavalier about the bride who's been kept waiting while his pants were altered.

Lucky Garnett doesn't differ in temperament from the Astaire characters in earlier movies; it's *Swing Time* that displays a different attitude toward him. Mark Sandrich had pictured Astaire as a musical-comedy man of the world, with no psychological complications in his life—"No Strings and No Connections," as Irving Berlin put it in Astaire's famous number in *Top Hat*. Astaire's only "relation" in Sandrich's movies was his sidekick, Edward Everett Horton (and one of Horton's shticks was to forget Astaire was there). But Stevens wants to see what Astaire's man of the world will look like in regular, nonidealized life, so he gives Lucky some familial connections that pull on him. First there's his partner, Pop, whose affection for Lucky is shown in a close-up of the wistful Victor Moore. Then there's his prospective father-in-law, played by George Stevens's own father, Landers Stevens, who's ready to take him into the fold. Lucky's late arrival at his own wedding is milked for laughs: Astaire idles at the gleaming door; the maid opens it warily; father and daughter advance with menace; a patriarch in a portrait frowns; a dog barks; a cat hisses. But after Astaire reveals he made two hundred dollars that afternoon, the signals reverse themselves: the father pumps his hand and calls him "son"; the daughter takes his arm; the portrait smiles; the dog paws him, and the cat purrs.

A whole family changing at the mere mention of money: what a cynical version of middle America! But beneath its satiric surface, the scene presents the hitherto blithe Astaire character with a real social dilemma, embodied in the two "fathers": either he stays with sweet but small-time guys like Pop or he throws in his lot with phony go-getters like his potential father-in-law. This American dichotomy of the right side and the wrong side of the tracks was what Stevens had explored in *Alice Adams*. In fact, Lucky's hometown in *Swing Time* offers a reprise of the Adamses' South Renford—and Lucky reminds us of Alice, trying to move up the social scale via marriage. But where Alice was stuck in South Renford for a whole movie, Lucky in *Swing Time* finds an early escape hatch. He makes a bargain with his father-in-law that he won't marry Margaret until he goes to New York and earns twenty-five thousand dollars.

Stevens uses Lucky's escape to introduce the Depression into the movie. At the train station, Astaire's dancer buddies stop him from buying a train ticket by taking his money. They say it's theirs from winning a bet that he wouldn't marry. But Astaire finds a way to leave anyway. Still wearing his morning coat, striped pants, spats, and top hat, he strolls across the track and hops a freight. In an image as resonant as *It Happened One Night*'s runaway bride, we see the grinning Astaire in his wedding clothes hanging on to a moving boxcar—he's the runaway groom! It's a complex, ironic image, though. Astaire may look fancy-free, but the boxcar behind him was a reminder of the vagabond population that rode the freight trains in the thirties. It was also Stevens's sign to his audience that he recognized the unseemliness of Astaire-Rogers glamour in the Depression. This is the first time an outright picture-symbol of hard times had appeared in an Astaire-Rogers movie. And Stevens enhances his first picture-symbol by showing us several more: Pop running after the train, Pop dropping Lucky's suitcase open on the tracks, and Pop emerging over the side of the boxcar holding up the ultimate symbol of traveling light—a toothbrush.

There's a prodigious mixture of emotions in Lucky's escape—an allusion to scarcity mixed with a gleeful sensation of liberation. The gleefulness expands when Pop and Lucky arrive in New York and take a stroll on Park Avenue. Stevens's New York, though, is not the equivalent of Mark Sandrich's high-toned Rio, Paris, London, or Venice, settings of earlier Astaire-Rogerses. It's a Capraesque Depression city of cross-class encounters and fluid identities—identities that shift with the setting. Astaire on Park Avenue no longer looks like a hoofer dressed up in wedding clothes; he looks like a prosperous man-about-town—even though he only has a quarter to his name. (According to clothing historian Anne Hollander, some businessmen in thirties New York still wore formal "morning clothes," also suitable for weddings, to work.) As he stops to get Pop a smoke at a cigarette machine wedged between a newsstand and a subway stop—a Walker Evans–like graphic pile-up—we get a quick portrait of a trompe-l'oeil persona: hometown bad boy and city swell, both at once. This reminds us of Capra's portrait of Claudette Colbert smoking by the bus—both heiress and vagabond, a character adrift in a world whose rules she doesn't know. Astaire's Lucky is adrift too: his new world is the city, where the good-bad social dichotomies of the provinces disappear in a tangle of contradictions. As if to dramatize these contradictions, Ginger Rogers comes out of the subway, just as Pop is trying to fit a button into the cigarette machine. She looks chic and citified in a bold plaid cape and a fez on her platinum curls.

UP TO THIS POINT the movie has been "deconstructing" Mark Sandrich's Astaire. Now it applies itself to "reconstructing" Sandrich's Ginger Rogers. This first encounter between them involves the usual Astaire-Rogers squabble; but it's not about manners this time, it's about something more basic—money. Observing that Pop's button won't work in the cigarette machine,

Astaire asks Rogers to change his "lucky" quarter, which she does, amiably, balancing her own newly bought cigarettes on top of her packages. Then she hurries on. When a small jackpot of change comes pouring from the cigarette machine, Astaire rushes after Rogers to get his lucky quarter back. Catching up to her, he takes off his hat and tries to explain, but this only causes her to bump into someone and drop her packages. Pop finds Rogers's purse on the ground and tries to change the quarters, but Rogers swipes the purse back and finds the quarter gone. Incensed, she calls a cop. The cop looks at the situation, gives Astaire a deferential salute, and tells Rogers to move along. It's a clash like Gable's and Colbert's first dispute over a bus seat in *It Happened One Night,* in which the audience realizes that the world "out there" is rough on women who travel alone. But it's more painful than Capra's bus scene, because Rogers isn't a snobbish heiress who needs chastising; she's a working woman who's been trifled with. It's especially galling to her to be classed below Astaire, since she knows, from Pop's button in the cigarette machine, that Astaire isn't a "real" gentleman—he's a bum in disguise.

Sandrich had played earlier Astaire-Rogers meeting scenes for their comic value. Stevens set up this scene with another goal in mind—to show us what sort of mettle the Rogers character is made of. And Rogers shows us, telegraphing not just her character's reactions but the very habits of thought behind the reactions: the reluctance to change the quarter; the complying out of a sense of decency; the coolness toward Astaire when he reappears with a new demand ("You probably think I'm silly," says Astaire; "Yes, I'm afraid I do," says Rogers, striding straight ahead); the impatience when she finds the quarter gone ("Okay, give it back," she says); the unhesitating appeal to the law when he seems to feign innocence; the disbelief at the cop's bias, marked by Stevens in a long, quiet close-up; finally, the spirited attempt at a last word to the cop ("You—you Cossack!"). This is a portrait of a woman who has worked out a code of courtesy for city life, which she practices toward others and expects others to practice toward her. When they fail to do this, she doesn't hesitate to defend herself in any way she can think of. At last the "professional" dimension of Rogers, which got such short shrift in the other Astaire-Rogers movies, assumes its full importance. (In *Rio* and *Roberta* she was a singer; in *Top Hat* she was a model; in *Follow the Fleet* she was a singer and dancer; yet in none of those movies did her successes and failures seem to matter to her.) In this movie, the scene with the quarter tells us that she lives on the income from a job, even before we know what that job is. We can see that she doesn't want to be late for this work. We recognize, in fact, that she possesses the alert self-respect a woman gets from earning her own money and taking care of herself.

Ginger Rogers
and Fred Astaire
in *Swing Time*.

To utilize the full potential of the Rogers persona, a Rogers character needed to hold a serious job. The real-life Rogers was working very hard in those years, making four movies a year to Astaire's one. She was so busy, she said later, that "she would meet herself coming in and out of doors." So from her first appearance in this movie, Stevens took extra pains to explain her character's professional conscientiousness. The very nature of her work—she teaches at an Arthur Murray–style dance school—represents a joke about all the dancing Rogers was doing for Astaire on the RKO lot. And Penny, her character in the movie, displays the sort of good-natured sarcasm Rogers must have displayed in real life on the set. As she strides into the Gordon Dancing Academy after the quarter episode, she greets the other "instructresses" with a rueful "Hi, kids" and exchanges hurried wise-cracks with her friend Mabel, the receptionist (Helen Broderick). "Is that you, Mabel?" "I don't know—is it? You tell me."

But besides bringing the movie's Rogers more in line with the real Rogers, Stevens at this point was doing everything he could to explain and comment on the unexamined Astaire-Rogers dynamic from the earlier movies of the series. Mark Sandrich had relied for his drama on Astaire's man-about-town meeting up with the one character who, Sandrich vaguely knew, was bound to distrust such a figure—the quick-witted young woman who likes to earn her way as she goes. What Stevens did was give Rogers a precise reason for distrusting him. Astaire's man-about-town in *Swing Time* is not authentic: he's just good at gambling and imitating a gentleman. This makes it clear why Rogers's character, the self-respecting city woman, is wary of him. And by sharpening his focus, Stevens has brought their differences into line with the audience's own class anxieties. The fake gentleman embodies its mistrust of its old wealthy-and-suave ideal; the genuine working woman embodies its new sympathy for the struggling person at the bottom of the heap.

THESE TWO OPPOSITES meet on the street—but they engage on the dance floor. Astaire follows Rogers into the school to return her quarter. Amused to find she's a dancer, he arranges for a lesson with her. At first, in his idly sadistic way, he feigns gracelessness. Rogers gets so angry that she insults him and gets fired. But Astaire saves her job, and thrills her at the same time, by showing the boss what she's "taught" him—a fancy tap riff. And then they go into their first number, the witty, smooth, and effervescent "Pick Yourself Up" (which takes off in the pattern Ginger's been trying to get Fred to learn—"three steps to the right, three steps to the left, and turn").

What happens to Astaire and Rogers on the dance floor is what happened to Gable and Colbert on the bus ride: each opens up to the virtues of the other. Here, though, this delicate transaction occurs in concentrated form. As they dance, we can see the carefulness possessing Astaire and the care slipping from Rogers. But as Stevens has set this dance up, it actually registers more on Rogers than on Astaire. The dance begins—its opening bars come up on the soundtrack—with the close-up of Rogers's smile of wonderment at seeing Astaire's tap riff. That's also when Rogers realizes that on the dance floor, Lucky isn't a bum masquerading as a gentleman, he's a professional like her—and in the same profession! That professionalism dazzles Rogers's Penny. (It's what the real Astaire and Rogers had in common.) We see her giving in to Astaire's partnering, at first with incredulity, then with bewilderment, then with embarrassed pride, then with pure glee, then with glowing nonchalance as their syncopated one-step skims around the floor, forward, down, and center; out over the dance floor's railing in low-flying, partnered leaps; back onto the floor; and out again over the railing, to conclude in a gleeful stroll offscreen.

George Stevens didn't choreograph the dance numbers; Astaire did, with dance director Hermes Pan. But it was Stevens who noticed, as no other Astaire-Rogers director had done, Rogers's uncanny ability to show how a dance affected her even as she was executing it. Rogers's transparency allows Stevens to short-cut his plot. At the end of this number, we see that Rogers has become convinced Astaire is the man for her. She has lived a simulated lifetime of ease and harmony with him on the dance floor. Now that experience must be squared with real life. At stake is not only a love affair but her big chance as a professional dancer: Penny's boss has arranged for an audition for her and Lucky at the swankiest place in town, the Silver Sandal nightclub.

IN SANDRICH'S ASTAIRE-ROGERSES, Astaire and Rogers struggle on with ill will and misunderstanding even after they have danced together. In *Swing Time,* their first dance changes them forever—or at least it changes Rogers. Her Penny has seen a vision of romance with Astaire's Lucky which she never loses. But Astaire's Lucky proves more self-defeating. It goes without saying that Astaire, as in any Astaire-Rogers, is in love with Rogers; but he is the one who keeps wrecking things for them. First he tries to gamble for a suit of dinner clothes for the audition, with a man (Gerald Hamer) who is not just a gambler like him but a real gentleman (though a drunk one). He loses, not just his pants but his dignity in Penny's eyes (he is forced to rush after her wrapped in a tablecloth), as well as their chance to audition. Then, after he wins Penny back by picketing with Pop outside her apartment, Lucky begins to be troubled about his obligations to Margaret, the fiancée he left back home. *(Swing Time* could have been titled *The Gay Fiancé.)* There is a witty song, "A Fine Romance," which Astaire and Rogers sing to each other on the occasion of an outing to an old country hotel in the snow. In it Penny makes all the advances to Lucky, and he keeps deflecting them so as not to find himself in a compromised situation. But when Margaret herself arrives in town, unannounced, Lucky is obliged to tell Penny the truth, so he loses her again.

The trouble with Lucky is that he can't really talk to Penny—he can convey his feelings only by singing or dancing. Stevens uses inarticulateness to explain not only the Astaire persona but the whole musical-comedy medium: if Astaire can't talk, he has to sing or dance. This device comes uncomfortably close, for a musical, to evoking a real psychological disability. Lucky's weaknesses have been so fully sketched in here—his gambling, his compulsive optimism, his ambivalence about love, his confusion about choosing a "father"—that one feels at moments that he is carrying too much guilt. The potentially repentant con man doesn't quite fit with the exquisite irony of an Astaire: Lucky is actually more of a George Stevens archetype than a Fred Astaire one. Stevens was thirty-two when he filmed *Swing Time;* Astaire was thirty-seven: obviously, Stevens couldn't resist taking apart the older man's flawless gentleman image. In spite of the mismatch, the exercise taught Stevens something more about the rebel he had discovered through Hepburn in *Alice Adams*—and whom he would go on to introduce, as a male, into movie after movie in his long career. (Stevens's Jimmy Stewart in *Vivacious Lady* [1937] is an intense and inarticulate young man with a father neurosis, like Lucky; so are his postwar antiheroes, Montgomery Clift in *A Place in the Sun* [1951], the young Brandon De Wilde in *Shane* [1953], and both James Dean and Dennis Hopper in *Giant* [1956].) But even if Stevens sometimes delved too deeply into the father-son subtext of *Swing Time,* his explanation for Astaire's inarticulateness does lend an added poignancy to the singing and dancing. When Astaire sits at the piano and sings Jerome Kern's lovely ballad "The Way You Look Tonight" to Rogers, we see that though he's made mute by his feelings, he's freed by the music. And our understanding enhances the melancholy of Dorothy Fields's wistful lyrics:

> Someday
> When I'm awfully low
> And the world is cold

> I will feel a glow just thinking
> Of you
> Just the way you look tonight . . .

As a contrast to Astaire's Lucky, Rogers's Penny completely inhabits her feelings, and feels free, at almost any time, to express them in ordinary words and actions. All through this second part of the movie she keeps signaling to Lucky that she's in love with him; she keeps offering him the gift of herself. She does this even when it's a risk to her pride. She comes to stand at the piano when Astaire is singing "The Way You Look Tonight," forgetting that her head is covered in shampoo lather. She almost steps out of the bounds of propriety with her hints to Lucky about romance on their snowy outing. It's not flirting; it's trying to get him to recognize what she knows they both feel. After he rebuffs her, she sings, with irony, "A fine romance, with no kisses / A fine romance, my friend, this is." He can only repeat it after her. Even when Penny knows there's a fiancée back in Lucky's hometown, she accepts a dare from her friend Mabel to give Lucky a kiss in his dressing room at the Silver Sandal. At this point she behaves like a little kid—or like a Harry Langdon or a Stan Laurel—grinning goofily, flapping her arms and mumbling inadequate words like "Do ya like my dress?" The emotional daring that propels Rogers's character is all the more affecting because we've seen how wary and dignified she was before she met Astaire—or before she danced with him.

IN THE COURSE of the movie Rogers comes to stand for something more than the self-respecting working woman; she becomes the person who isn't afraid of the power of love. The drama then devolves back upon Lucky. Will he grow up enough to deserve that love? It's like Gable and Colbert's impasse near the end of *It Happened One Night:* they must learn to speak to each other if they're going to have each other. But *Swing Time* projects a mood even more melancholy than *It Happened One Night* because of the musical dimension of the movie.

The last part of *Swing Time* is awash with music and dancing. Kern (and his arranger Robert Russell Bennett) wrote the movie's songs—"The Way You Look Tonight," the "Waltz in Swing Time," "A Fine Romance," the lavish Astaire solo dance "Bojangles of Harlem," and the final ballroom number, "Never Gonna Dance"—so that they are interrelated melodically and harmonically. They sound like a family of songs, which play in a continuously merging undercurrent as the movie comes to its resolution.

The melodies drifting through the movie's soundtrack underscore its ideals of high style and high romance: the actual instances of singing and dancing seem to have spilled over from these melodies. But what's most impressive about this movie is not the relation between the mood music and the numbers but how the director pays attention to the meaning of the music. Stevens allows the songs and dances to communicate all the yearning of the plot. He often said that musicals made him nervous, but that didn't prevent him here from keying even the dialogue and the gags to the mood of the music and dancing. The comic delays that precede the supposed audition dance—in which Lucky and Penny find that the lugubrious band leader, Ricardo Romero (George Mextaxa) won't play their dance, since *he* loves Rogers—only heighten the effect of their finally going out on the darkened floor of RKO's grand nightclub set and dancing the "Waltz in Swing Time." This is a sometimes hushed, sometimes ecstatic waltz which dips and skims and unwinds around the space at an ever mounting pace. Astaire and Rogers lean together into the curves of the dance. And Stevens uses his cameraman's ingenuity to intensify the atmosphere: he shows Astaire and Rogers at the end of the "Waltz in Swing Time" behind venetian blinds, which seem to symbolize the privacy that so much feeling entitles them to. These stylish illuminated blinds clinch the mood of the dance.

Their last number, the great "Never Gonna Dance," which Astaire and Rogers perform in the empty nightclub after Lucky has just lost Penny for what seems the last time, is the most breathtaking dance in the picture—and perhaps the most emotionally daring dance ever devised for an Astaire-Rogers movie. It starts with what looks like a faraway portrait of Rogers standing with the band leader, whom she has agreed to marry. Then the picture melts, and we see it was a reflection in a mirrored door, which Astaire has opened to come in. The camera stays on Astaire as he looks at them. He's at his gravest. Romero leaves to let him talk to Rogers, but, as usual, he can't talk, so he starts to sing—the oddly meaningful nonsense lyrics of "Never Gonna Dance":

> Though . . .
> I'm left without my Penny
> The wolf was discreet
> He left me my feet . . .

The song merges into a dance as Rogers comes down the stairway to meet him. At first they just walk around the dance floor. Then they turn, their hands still pinned to their sides. They reach past each other—a big reach with both hands. Finally, Lucky does what he can do only on the dance floor—he grabs Penny's hand and claims her, sweeping her into an exultant reprise of their "Waltz in Swing Time." At the climax of the waltz, they separate and whirl up different sides of the double staircase to the top. There, as if in an art-deco snowstorm, he twirls her faster and faster until she whirls offstage like a white-blond torch, leaving Astaire alone and gesturing toward the illuminated place where she's disappeared.

THE DANCE WORKS as a furious outburst by both of them against the passivity in Lucky's character that would allow such a loss as this. Not a move of it is off, and Stevens has filmed almost all of it in one lyrical take, with a long, unbroken crane shot following the pair up the separate stairs, cutting to a new shot only once, unobtrusively, as he gets his camera close to them again at the top of the stairs. Both Astaire and Rogers, and Hermes Pan as well, have remembered that in the shooting of this number, the two dancers kept messing up the dance sixteen measures from the end of the music—so that everyone had to stay in the studio filming and refilming it, for forty-seven takes, till it was ten at night and Rogers's feet were bloody. Stevens had obviously caught Astaire's vision of how a dance should unwind organically before the camera, rather than being cut and pasted together from different pieces of film. But besides using his technical skill to frame this dance, Stevens has prepared all through the picture for the effect of Rogers's final exit, by associating her continually with light. Her white satin evening dresses; her white-blond hair, in blazing contrast to Romero's black; her snowy surroundings in "A Fine Romance"; even the shampoo lather on her hair during "The Way You Look Tonight"—all come back to us subliminally, to reinforce the impression that the illumination has gone from Lucky's life.

During the filming of *Swing Time,* Rogers and Stevens began an affair that would continue on and off for at least three years. Perhaps it was this personal involvement, doomed to marginality by Stevens's marriage, that lent such a melancholic tone to this "Never Gonna Dance" number. Astaire's relaxed and direct acting; Rogers's lyric gravity; the camera looking down on Astaire singing up to Rogers on the stairs; the hopeless passion of the dance—these features contribute to the tragic perception that this is what being grown-up really means: this defeat, this conviction that Lucky and Penny are never going to get together.

In the end, Stevens manages to draw a happy ending out of the material, using an old Laurel and Hardy gag to release the tight coil of regret left by the dance. It's the gag about contagious laughing. Lucky visits Margaret in her hotel room and learns that she's going to marry someone else back home. This starts a wave of laughter among the principals, which spills over into Lucky and Pop's prank to disrupt Penny's wedding to Romero. They steal Romero's pants (as Lucky's dancing buddies had stolen his when *he* was trying to get married). Marching into the wedding with the captive pants, they find Mabel at one end of a settee, doubled over in laughter, and Penny at the other end, doubled over in tears. The comedy grows a little thin here; but Rogers patches it up at the end with a good-natured burst of laughter, as Romero comes in wearing his valet's oversized pants. And Romero breaks into an obliging smile, and a snatch of song, to signal his finally giving up Penny to Lucky.

LUCKY NEVER DOES LEARN to say what he really feels; it's Penny who gives in. She agrees to substitute Lucky's message in his own language of singing, dancing, and laughing for a real declaration of love. And in this way, with the woman giving in a little more than the man, the agenda of Depression romantic comedy is fulfilled. A formal wedding ceremony has been disrupted, as it was in *It Happened One Night*—only in *Swing Time* two weddings are disrupted, one at the beginning and one at the end. The requisite informal, spontaneous union replaces all the mistaken impulses toward formal ones. It's a melodic union too: at the end of the movie Lucky is singing Penny's song, "A Fine Romance," and she is singing his, "The Way You Look Tonight." (Thanks to Kern, the two songs fit together.) Hard-nosed thirties pride, in the person of Rogers, has embraced careless twenties charm, in the person of Astaire. She has learned fun from him; he has learned persistence from her.

But there's one more element in their happy ending that must be remarked on—the picture window behind them in the final frame, offering them the big city below, glamorized by a snowstorm. This is an image that points up the importance of the city in this movie. Astaire-Lucky had escaped from the small town to confront the big city. He thought he was going to find money there, but instead he found both less and more: he found Rogers's "penny" and love and maturity and real fulfillment. It's extraordinary that Stevens, the youngest of the romantic-comedy directors, understood at this early point in his career how crucial the city had become to Depression romantic comedy. The whole genre can be seen from this point on as an inquiry into the moral composition of urban high style—the high style that had materialized for America in the twenties, around the symbol of the big city, then dematerialized with the Crash.

Swing Time is the ultimate poem to the city and the city woman. It allows the eternally provincial American male to have the lovely, city-wise woman, and it allows the audience to have that big-city glamour back, by means of a carefully crafted fable about the lovers negotiating a shared set of values. This wasn't Stevens's essential subject matter: he had already claimed small towns for himself, and literal questions of morality. But perhaps his belonging by age and experience, and ultimately by oeuvre, to the "family melodrama" which was to come after thirties romantic comedy was what allowed him to make this one light, spun-glass city romance, with its casual, unerring wisdom. Perhaps he meant *Swing Time* as a tribute to the aesthetic universe of older men, and that's why it seems so effortlessly stylized. At any rate, Stevens's "musical" directing in *Swing Time* revealed, in fact visualized, the abiding significance of the musical-comedy culture that had originated in the twenties city. This love of the city would loom large in romantic comedy in the short time that remained for it to flourish.

6

CAPRA AND ARTHUR:

MR. DEEDS GOES TO TOWN

Gary Cooper,
Jean Arthur,
and Frank Capra
on the set of
*Mr. Deeds Goes to
Town.*

I N 1936, two more actresses broke through to stardom in romantic comedies, Jean Arthur and Carole Lombard, and the circumstances of their breakthroughs marked an interesting change in the pattern. Up till then, the stars of the genre—Stanwyck, Colbert, Hepburn, Rogers—had come to the movies from the New York stage. Both Arthur and Lombard, however, started out in Hollywood, and struggled for a long time within the medium of the movies, to little avail. When romantic comedy arrived in the mid-thirties, it didn't just define them; it reclaimed them. Or, rather, individual directors reclaimed them—Capra in Jean Arthur's case, Gregory La Cava in Lombard's—by noticing qualities in their personae that almost no one had noticed before. It's eerie to see Arthur and Lombard in their earliest movies. Except for some isolated moments of eccentricity, both leading ladies seem surprisingly ordinary and dutiful. One can also see, in the early-to-mid-thirties, how sheer experience helped them to begin to open up and look freer, intermittently, on the screen. But for both of them, it took an encounter with one of the comedy-trained directors, and a role endowed with populist symbolism, to bring the intensity of stardom out of them.

JEAN ARTHUR was one of those young women drifters who gravitated to Hollywood by the thousands all through the twenties and thirties. Looking at her early career, one would have predicted anything but stardom in her future. And in terms of basic stamina, she was probably the frailest of this group of women—the one who benefited the most from romantic comedy's careful attention to leading ladies. The daughter of a New York photographer, Hubert Greene, and his Vermont-born wife, Johanna Nelson Greene, Jean Arthur was born Gladys Georgianna Greene in New York City in 1905. She left school at fifteen to become an artist's model, posing for the famous illustrator of Ziegfeld Follies girls, Howard Chandler Christy. Within three years she had reached Hollywood, having taken a stage name—a combination of Jeanne d'Arc and King Arthur—that announced a quixotic nature. She made her debut in a small role in a 1923 John Ford movie, *Cameo Kirby*, and for a few years she appeared mostly in westerns, such as the 1925 *Hurricane Horseman* and the 1926 *Lightning Bill*. By the late twenties she had graduated to some flapper supporting roles in twenties movies' compulsive explorations of loose sex, such as the Emil Jannings vehicle *The Sins of the Fathers* (1928), and a few nice-girl leads, such as Richard Dix's girlfriend in the baseball movie *Warming Up* (1928). In early 1929, Paramount ushered her into the talkies, appointing her the ingenue in the first of the Philo Vance series, *The Canary Murder Case,* starring William Powell.

The coming of sound to the movies should have helped Jean Arthur's career more than it did. She sometimes projected a note distinct to her, bewildered yet matter-of-fact. And she could act—that is, she could play characters who weren't mere variations on herself. But instead of being cast in lead roles, she got stuck at Paramount in character parts, several of them in Philo Vance–style murder mysteries. She even played the murderess in the 1929 *The Greene Murder Case.* Her problem, paradoxically, stemmed from the very conscientiousness of her acting. One of her best roles in early sound movies was a substantial one as Clara Bow's bad younger sister, Janey, in Paramount's early talkie *The Saturday Night Kid* (1929). (This was the role that Louise Brooks had played three years before in the silent version of the movie, *Love 'Em and Leave 'Em.*) Arthur didn't see Janey as Brooks had done, as an amoral little animal. She played her in a petulant style, adding a whining note when she got into trouble—as if Janey were too spoiled to focus on anything except what she wants at the moment. But one can tell why Clara Bow was the star at that time and Jean Arthur the second lead. Clara, not even in top form (she was overweight), looks straight out from the screen with that "Gee, I want to be straight with you" look, the tough little half-smile, the pleading eyes, the disheveled bob, the round face, and the wholehearted energy—and the audience adores her. By contrast, Jean Arthur's persona implies something abrasive. It's true that she's the villainess in this movie, but we can recognize the complicated temperament that would define her later heroines, the stubbornness mixed uneasily with the fragility. There's a veiled quality in her eyes that reads here as an unwillingness to play full-out on the screen. Clara Bow offered herself transparently to audiences; Jean Arthur kept a part of herself shadowed and unavailable. Moreover, Arthur didn't have the cute, round face of the prevailing Clara Bow type. She had a long face with a prominent chin, which was not flattered by the frontal curls and shaved neck-nape of twenties bobs.

It wasn't just the haircut but the whole mode of being feminine in the early-sound era that didn't favor a Jean Arthur—especially that era at Paramount. The studio was already top-heavy with female stars and starlets: there was not much room for new varieties of women. The languorous Marlene Dietrich stood for sin; the suave Kay Francis embodied style; Ruth Chatterton of the monied voice did class. Those three "serious" actresses dominated Paramount's weepers. In lighter movies, adorable flapper types still played juvenile leads. The great Clara Bow was on the way out: personal scandals and her links with the jazz age had killed her career. Her replacement on the lot, however, was a look-alike, Nancy Carroll, who had Bow's ripe, round face and curly bob, updated by a bright, refined theater voice and an on-screen nature both tougher and more wistful than Clara's. In addition, another Bow type, Claudette Colbert, was waiting in Paramount's wings. So were Miriam Hopkins, Carole Lombard, Fay Wray, Louise Brooks, and Mary Brian, starlets who didn't fit the Bow image but who dimly suggested possibilities to be developed in the future. Among these, Jean Arthur didn't particularly stand out. She wasn't elegant enough for weepers, and she wasn't cute enough for comedies. Paramount couldn't tell whether to make her a straight actress or a comedienne.

SO SHE WAS LET GO, along with Fay Wray and Louise Brooks (who had already left and returned), in the spring of 1931, during Paramount's first wave of Depression financial troubles. Brooks tried and failed to be a nightclub dancer, but the other two had better luck: Wray went to RKO; Jean Arthur, in her quixotic fashion, went to the place where no sane actress would have thought of going—New York. The Broadway theater in the early thirties was in a sorry state. Money had dried up; production had been cut back; theater people were mostly trying to get jobs in Hollywood. But Arthur was determined, she said, "to learn how to act."

Once in New York, she took any part she could get. She played first with an "uptown" (i.e., off-Broadway) company in *Lysistrata,* at a salary of fifty dollars a week. Then, in April of 1932, she made it to Broadway in a semistarring role as the serving maid in *Foreign Affairs,* a couple-switching farce set in a Tyrolean inn. Here she got her first praise from the critics: the *Herald Tribune* called her "likably simple as the pretty cook"; the *Sun* called her "dryly witty." Over the next year and a half, Jean Arthur did three more plays on Broadway—*The Man Who Reclaimed His Head* (September '32), *$25 an Hour* (May '33), and *The Curtain Rises* (October '33). The first was a political melodrama; the second and third were loose imitations of Preston Sturges's hugely influential hit comedy of 1929, *Strictly Dishonorable,* a romance in a bohemian milieu. The press continued to be kind to Arthur, if not to the plays. She got mentioned for her freshness, her "golden beauty"—she had gone blond—and her growing skill as an actress. Her last play, *The Curtain Rises,* about a theater-struck drudge who turns into an actress—stringy hair and flat shoes in the first act, radiant décolletage in the second—was essentially a vehicle for her. Brooks Atkinson of the *Times,* who had complained earlier about the monotony of her voice, praised her this time for her genuineness. "It is not profound stuff. But Miss Arthur and Mr. [Donald] Foster manage to give it a quality that enkindles the imagination and subdues a restless audience."

New York still revered comedy in the early thirties, Hollywood's weeper years, and Broadway audiences and critics still appreciated the techniques for playing it. The reviews are proof that Jean Arthur mastered those techniques—the quick sense of timing, the constant simulation of nonchalance, the line readings spiced with melody. The fact that Atkinson stopped complaining about her voice suggests that she had worked on it: in fact, the suppleness of that contralto voice would become her best feature when she finally broke through to movie stardom. She probably learned a great deal about ensemble acting, too, during her Broadway stint, from working with old hands like Dorothy Gish, Osgood Perkins, Henry Hull, Claude Rains, and Theatre Guild director Herbert J. Biberman. And by staying away from Hollywood, she avoided the worst of the weeper era. But in late 1933 Columbia's Harry Cohn, gearing up his studio for the big time, lured her back to Hollywood with a promise of "major" pictures.

He didn't exactly keep the promise: the Columbia pictures she made on her return to Hollywood in 1934 weren't major for her. In two of them, *Whirlpool* and *The Defense Rests,* she supported Columbia's aging star Jack Holt. In the third, *The Most Precious Thing in Life,* she was cast as an out-of-date weeper heroine. By 1935 Arthur must have put up a fuss, because Columbia began to do better by her. She played a smart secretary in John Ford's *The Whole Town's Talking,* a smart courtesan in Edward Sutherland and Preston Sturges's *Diamond Jim,* and a smart young lady looking for a job in William Seiter's *If You Could Only Cook.* These were roles that suited the Jean Arthur who was about to become a star. They allowed her to be tough, quizzical, pretty, businesslike, and momentarily sunlit, and quavery when in love. But except for *Diamond Jim,* they were not careful movies. Ford directed *The Whole Town's Talking* with a stilted humorlessness (though it was a success at the time); Seiter seems to have been intermittently absent from the set of *If You Could Only Cook.* Arthur is especially wasted in this movie. At moments she achieves real whimsy— when she's reading the Help Wanteds on a park bench, for instance, and convincing stranger Herbert Marshall to apply as half of a cook-butler team with her. But she doesn't look right; her face is too big; her hair is too blond; her satin maid's uniform is tacky, and, worst of all, she doesn't get any kind of a love scene. What a difference a good director would make for her, a few months later, when she was cast, supposedly at the last minute, in Frank Capra's *Mr. Deeds Goes to Town*!

BY 1936 Capra had undergone a series of painful, if imaginary, trials and tribulations. He had managed to make one more sunny movie in 1934, the underrated *Broadway Bill,* before the awesome success of *It Happened One Night* hit him. Then, like a sleepwalker who wakes up on a high wire, Capra realized that he was FRANK CAPRA, the savior of the movie industry and the voice of the little man. He panicked, and induced a debilitating attack of tuberculosis in himself, which was cured by an unassuming personage from the Christian Science Church, who called him a coward for not using his God-given gifts. Recovering from that mysterious illness, Capra began to plan another movie—one that would be sure to tap those gifts. He consulted with a friend named Myles Connolly, a scriptwriter turned producer, who encouraged him to make movies with messages. He considered Maxwell Anderson's play *Valley Forge,* about the sufferings of George Washington's revolutionary army, and he looked at Clarence Buddington Kelland's novel *Opera Hat,* about the confusion of a country boy who inherits twenty million dollars and a New York mansion. Both properties were "items" at the time: *Valley Forge* had opened on Broadway in December 1934; *Opera Hat* had run serially in 1935 (April through September) in the *American Magazine.* Eventually, Capra decided, or so he says, that *Valley Forge* was beyond his capabilities. What probably happened was that Capra and Robert Riskin recognized in *Opera Hat* a resemblance to *It Happened One Night* and decided that they were on safer territory with a light, cross-class romance than with a historical drama. So Kelland's pulp piece of Depressioniana was chosen to bear the weight of the anguished, missionary self-consciousness that had come over Frank Capra.

But *Opera Hat* was different from *It Happened One Night* in one key respect: its protagonist was an heir instead of an heiress. Capra and Riskin therefore went to work on *Opera Hat* to bring the dynamics of its love story closer to that of the earlier movies. Kelland had created a cocksure and unpleasant Longfellow Deeds; Capra and Riskin gave him something of Colbert's sheltered shyness by making him a supremely "good," even Christlike person, an overgrown boy. Deeds's opposite number in the novel was a young woman named Simionetta, of Swedish extraction, the secretary to an opera diva. Capra and Riskin transformed her, too, turning her into a near-replica of Clark Gable's Peter Warne—a smart-ass reporter named Babe Bennett. In Capra and Riskin's script, which retained little of the structure of Kelland's novel, Babe attaches herself to Longfellow Deeds for exactly the reason Warne linked up with Ellie Andrews—to get a story for her newspaper. And then she falls in love with him, just as Gable fell for Colbert.

But despite the similarities between *Mr. Deeds* and *It Happened One Night*, the fact of the male-female trade-off in the latter movie so changed its emphasis that it turned into something that partly contradicted romantic comedy's original message: it became a political fable about a rural innocent menaced by the forces of corruption in the big city. Though Capra and Riskin managed to weave a kind of love story into the fabric, the woman in question, the smart and jaded reporter, is pictured as partly responsible for the hero's downfall, even as she also brings him recognition and something like motherlove. It's a peculiarly bifurcated movie to watch. The romantic scenes display some of the qualities of Capra's earlier movies—warmth, wit, tolerance, and a real respect for the achievement of intimacy. The political scenes betray Capra's coarser side—his self-consciousness, his sentimentality, his desire to please which get funneled, for the parable's effectiveness, into a treacly patriotism with religious overtones.

For the male lead, Capra and Riskin planned from the beginning to cast Gary Cooper, Paramount's tall, silent leading man. Cooper was a clever choice. He had played the man of action enough so that his boyish manner in romantic leading roles didn't read to the audience as pathetic. For Babe Bennett, Capra wanted Carole Lombard, but Lombard turned him down in order to do *My Man Godfrey* at Universal. Capra was left once again without a leading lady. He even began to shoot the movie without casting one. Then, as Capra puts it, he "discovered" Jean Arthur, when he stuck his head into a Columbia screening room and saw the rushes of an obscure western she was making with Jack Holt. Jean Arthur, however, wasn't making westerns with Holt in those years. It's more likely that she was brought to Capra's attention by Harry Cohn, who had put her under contract in 1933. Perhaps Cohn intended her all along as a Capra leading lady. But Cohn, just about this time, made a bad mistake concerning Capra. He tried to pass off some Columbia movies in England as Capra's, and when Capra found out, he almost walked out on Cohn. One of those movies was Bill Seiter's romantic comedy *If You Could Only Cook*, starring Jean Arthur—and that could explain how Capra encountered Arthur.

However it happened, Jean Arthur proved a brilliant choice for *Mr. Deeds Goes to Town*. From her first scenes with Cooper, her veiled, shy quality lends an emotional logic to the relationship between the reporter and the terminally innocent millionaire, which Capra might not have been able to establish with a more exuberant actress like Carole Lombard. And even though Cooper provides the main focus of *Mr. Deeds,* it is Arthur's collaboration with Capra that gives the movie its occasional genuineness in the midst of its sentimental maneuverings. Capra hadn't entirely lost the habit of dramatizing the inner life of a heroine: this movie contains some scenes in which the woman's psyche registers even more strongly than in his earlier movies. And though the implications of these scenes were left out—were denied—in the movie's dramatic resolution, on their own they were still vivid and memorable enough to push Jean Arthur into stardom.

CAPRA'S NEW FOCUS on the leading man becomes clear in the first moments of *Mr. Deeds.* After a brief prologue which dramatizes, in news headlines, a New York financier's death in a car crash, we find ourselves in the train station of the comically slowpoke town of Mandrake Falls, Vermont. A New York lawyer and a publicist are visiting young Longfellow Deeds to inform him of the death of the financier—his distant uncle—and its consequences to himself. They locate Deeds's Main Street clapboard house, his housekeeper, and his dog; and finally, after they have waited a considerable time, they behold Gary Cooper, opening the screen door—all six-feet-plus of him—wearing a leather jacket and a bow tie. Cooper, with his classic profile, his dark-lashed eyes with the childlike smudges under them, his thin but self-conscious lips, rewards the gaze enough to justify this corny buildup. We see him close-up in an armchair, fitting his tuba with a new mouthpiece, then trying out a few notes. He doesn't shift his attention away from the tuba even when the lawyer informs him he has inherited twenty million dollars. Deeds in this scene isn't really oblivious of the lawyers; he's childishly flirting with them, chatting about his tuba-playing habits and his job writing greeting-card verses. There's an utterly unworldly little boy, Capra is signaling, lurking right under the surface of this slow, dear man. The movie does everything it can here to convince us that a child, artificially preserved inside a man, can be a splendid being. But the scene is missing that old Capra touch, that swift, almost impatient knowingness about everybody, which had illuminated his early-thirties movies. The folksy housekeeper, the orange layer cake, and Cooper himself, with his willed slow takes, locate us in a cartoon Americana—new to Capra and new to romantic comedy.

The next scene, however, returns us to a quintessential romantic comedy location, a New York newsroom, to introduce the leading lady. And the contrast between these two opening scenes forecasts the movie's schizophrenia. Jean Arthur as Babe Bennett is leaning against a table in her editor's office, playing with a rope, while all the male reporters project anxious looks about the assignment to get news on Longfellow Deeds, the new millionaire in town. Arthur looks natural and at ease, perhaps the most at ease she has yet looked on the screen. Her hair is not platinum anymore—it's light brown and page-boyed softly around her face. She's wearing a smartly tailored gray suit with a jaunty striped T-shirt under the jacket. Standing apart by herself, she is absorbed in this little game of trying to shake a knot into a rope. Obviously she doesn't care about this story, until the editor offers her a month's vacation if she gets it. "With pay?" she says, brightening up, and then she shoots him a command as she heads out the door—"Leave four columns open on the front page tomorrow." We can't help admiring such an offhand show of competency, even though, under the influence of the pristine Longfellow Deeds, we're supposed to see her as jaded, unhappy, and unfulfilled.

So far, though, the movie is still attempting to follow the conventions of romantic comedy which Capra himself had set up. We've met two temperamental opposites. The man is shy, naive, intense—someone who cares so little about money that he'd rather play his tuba than contemplate his new millions. The woman is smart, bored, and slightly corruptible—great at handling the world, but down on herself for it. We know from the setup that they're going to fall in love, and Capra maintains this symmetrical idea of a love affair almost to the end of the scene of their meeting.

Arthur's Babe contrives the meeting. Wearing the shapeless tweed coat and old cloche hat of a starving job-hunter, she manages to walk past Deeds's mansion just as Longfellow comes out to take a boyish walk in the rain (head uncovered, face upraised to the glories of the elements). She "faints" into his arms, thus handing him the opportunity to take her out to dinner. At the restaurant where they go, Tullio's, the hangout of "the literati," Arthur continues to play the part of Babe Bennett playing "Mary Dawson, stenographer." "Mary" eats her food with downcast eyes; she tells Cooper she's "just a nobody"; she raises her profile gratefully to the gypsy violinist who comes over to serenade her at Cooper's excited signal. But Arthur proves extremely witty at projecting Babe's skepticism through Mary's meekness. With the subtlest of deadpan looks, Arthur telegraphs what Babe might have been thinking about Longfellow. This guy is so out of it that he thinks a violin solo might be comforting to a woman who's supposed to be starving! In the next moment, however, Capra destroys his own evenhandedness, his simultaneous appreciation of Babe's cynicism and Deeds's courtliness, by shoving Deeds into an altercation with the "literati" at their customary round table.

.   .   .

THIS MOMENT IS THE HINGE of the movie, the point where Capra begins to kill a certain basic excitement about big-city life which he himself had built into romantic comedy, and which Stevens had evoked so beautifully in *Swing Time*. Tullio's literati invite the new millionaire over to sit down. Deeds is delighted at first, but when he realizes that the literati are mocking him and his greeting-card poetry, he hauls off and knocks a few of them down. The round table at Tullio's, however, an obvious reference to the famous table at the Algonquin Hotel, the geographic center of New York wit in the twenties, elicits only scorn from Capra. Moreover, Jean Arthur steps back as Longfellow resorts to his fists—she literally disappears from the frame. This is a man's fight, Capra implies. And it means that Longfellow has moved into the place of Capra's original "little man" protagonist, who was the plucky heroine. The new, male "little man" brings a set of absolutes with him, absolutes that earlier had only hovered on the edges of Capra's love stories—and one of them is this angry bias against "intellectuals." Capra might have acquired such a bias with his new position of prominence in Hollywood. Not only had *It Happened One Night* won five Academy Awards, Capra himself had accepted the presidency of the conservative Motion Picture Academy. He had become the most visible representative in Hollywood of the movie industry. And it's the cause of the whole industry versus the New York literati that he is defending in *Mr. Deeds*.

"I write my [poetry] on order," says Deeds to the falsely solicitous literati. "The people I work for just tell me what they want and I go to work." Movie directors made their art "on order" too, rather than by inspiration. And yet this too-obvious parallel between the movie's main character and its director falsifies the entire scene. Capra had always drawn on his own life and thoughts, his own view of himself and the people around him. Earlier, though, in the Stanwyck movies and *It Happened One Night,* Capra had diffused the autobiographical elements, shared them between the leading man and the leading lady and, above all, kept them metaphoric. In *Mr. Deeds* Capra not only literalized his symbols (e.g., the little man becomes a *man*), he also revealed to his audience that he might be thinking of himself as that little man. And so we are treated to the unsavory spectacle of an "auteur" musing about himself in such thinly disguised fashion that it comes out smug and overmodest at the same time.

Moreover, the fact that the man has taken center stage means that the woman, in romantic comedy's delicate balance of class and gender, must retreat to a place outside the circle of understanding between the male protagonist and the audience. Compelled by no one but himself (or maybe by himself and Riskin), Capra had come back around to the pre-Depression configuration for male and female characters in the movies: the male carries the drama; the female comments on it. Jean Arthur is obliged to effect a transformation, painful to us now, of Babe Bennett. She must show Babe changing from worldly skeptic to the maternal supporting character. When Babe and Longfellow go on a sightseeing tour of New York, Arthur listens encouragingly to Cooper's patriotic effusions over Grant's Tomb ("I see an Ohio farm boy growing up to be a great soldier . . ."). She wipes the saliva off his shoulder when he tries to spit on Times Square from the Empire State Building. On a bench in Central Park, she confesses her own—i.e., Babe's, not Mary Dawson's—origins to him, by way of reassurance. "I come from a small town too, you know," she says. Here Jean Arthur's voice sounds a kind of lyric, cracked lullaby. "Grove of poplar trees right along Main Street. Always smelled as if it just had a bath."

THE MOVIE'S AMBIVALENCE emerges most strongly here. Capra has already located "goodness" in Deeds and "jadedness" in Babe, but here he makes a detour from this grand moral purpose to give Jean Arthur the careful Stanwyck treatment. The occasion is part of Babe's maternalization; nevertheless, it's enough like the Capra signature scene of the lovers' meeting to amount to a reprise, for a time, of an earlier kind of drama. Capra quiets the movie down for this park-bench exchange, so that Jean Arthur's delicate performance can register. He shows us a smart, glamorous young woman not yet repenting of her competence but rediscovering, in a reverie, her past, which is beloved and far away and centered around her father. While in this trance of remembering, she confesses to Longfellow that he reminds her of that father. Remembering more, she offers to do "Swanee River" with drums, as her father taught her. She accepts a stick from Deeds, breaks it in two, raises the "drumsticks" in the air, gives a small "harumph," and starts beating the rhythm on a garbage can and singing "Way down upon the Swanee River" in a voice that's low, shy, and surprisingly oblivious to the microphone.

This is supposed to be the "real" Babe Bennett, before she got carried away with the excitement and corruption of the newspaper business. And the scene is so well acted that we have the impression we are seeing the "real" Jean Arthur too, before she got into this artificial business of making movies. That's not true, of course: Jean Arthur came from New York City, not a small town. Yet Capra has connected the qualities she projected best onto the screen—her shyness, her taste for privacy—with the metaphor of an old-fashioned, small-town past. This was a departure from his own convention: the personae of most of the other romantic-comedy actresses were related to the city—and to the habits of self-preservation that the city

Gary Cooper and Jean Arthur in *Mr. Deeds Goes to Town.*

required of its citizens. Barbara Stanwyck's persona, formed in collaboration with Capra, suggested the grief and vulnerability of urban survival at its most precarious. Capra's Claudette Colbert projected a certain artificial childlikeness, overlaid with irony—the essence of big-city sophistication. Stevens's Ginger Rogers showed herself alert and intensely matter-of-fact, the model of the urban working woman. Only Katharine Hepburn's persona had veered away from urbanity: as interpreted by Stevens, she was the only actress besides Jean Arthur who often expressed unease about the city, and an eager, girlish longing to return to a place where self-definition wasn't a constant struggle. Hepburn, in fact, might have been a good choice for the role of Babe Bennett. (She eventually played Babe Bennett–like characters, professional women secretly longing to regress to wifedom, in her forties and fifties romantic comedies with Spencer Tracy.)

But in the mid-thirties, Jean Arthur made a better Capraesque heroine than Hepburn, because Arthur didn't carry an upper-class aura that needed to be corrected for the Depression public. Intermittently in *Mr. Deeds*, Arthur's shy delight in herself strikes a note new to romantic comedy—a dimension of hidden sweetness not obscured (as Hepburn's sweetness was) by nerves or pretensions. We hold our breath during this scene, for fear Jean Arthur will get embarrassed and retreat—but she doesn't. Capra helps her by adding a song to the other loosening-up devices he always used in his love scenes—a cue he had probably taken from the lovers of Stevens's *Swing Time*. (His "Man on the Flying Trapeze" in *It Happened One Night* was a communal affair.) Babe dares Longfellow to make good on his boast that he can do "Humoresque" to her "Swanee River," and they render the two songs in counterpoint, with Deeds singing tubalike basso under Babe's contralto—just like Rogers and Astaire singing their final *Swing Time* duet. When Arthur and Cooper get to the lilt in the chorus—"All the world is sad and dreary"—they go at it more robustly. Arthur even turns around to look at Cooper and cracks up at the silliness of it, till they are interrupted by the sound of a siren, and Longfellow rushes off to indulge his mania for fire engines.

THIS DELICATE AND LYRICAL scene is lacking only one thing to fill it out—erotic tension. No eros could be projected at this point by Cooper's Longfellow. The sexuality of his character had been displaced from the beginning onto an adolescent fantasy of rescuing a damsel in distress. But Capra and Riskin also choose here to put the erotic mode out of reach for Arthur's Babe Bennett. They used Jean Arthur's reluctant timidity on the park bench to suggest a prudishness in Babe that matches Longfellow's own.

We have watched Babe's earlier scorn of Longfellow turn into fond mother-liness, then into empathetic girlishness. But how could such mutually chaste fondness provoke a romance? Here is where Jean Arthur rescued this movie. A more knowing actress, such as Colbert, Stanwyck, or Rogers, would have seemed silly ignoring the erotic undertones in such a scene. Arthur seems heroic.*

After the park bench, Capra switches to Babe in her friend Mabel's apartment, disturbed because she's having trouble writing her next article about "the Cinderella man," as she's dubbed Longfellow. Instead of the tremulous hopes that Capra's earlier leading ladies would have projected at this moment, Arthur displays a sad fatalism. Babe is slumped on a chintz couch in the shadows, smoking a cigarette, her face calm and serious. Cooper appears at the door, dressed in evening clothes. The two go for a walk around the block in the mist. Cooper tells Arthur that he's disillu-sioned with the city and is going home to Mandrake Falls. When they get back to her stoop, he hands her a poem he's written to her, in the greeting-card mode. She reads it aloud in the same low, private voice she had used for "Swanee River," a voice that seems to be out of the range of the microphones but is perfectly audible. The poem, notwithstanding its nur-sery rhythms, gains a certain dignity from the hopelessness of Longfellow's feelings: he wants Babe to marry him but doesn't believe she will. And reading it, Jean Arthur brings Babe's nostalgia for her own simpler past, and her maternal fondness for Longfellow, to a pitch that equals the force of eros. In the last lines ("My dreams have been answered, but my life's just as bleak / I'm handcuffed, and speechless, in your presence divine / My heart longs to cry out, if it only could speak / I love you, my angel, be mine, be mine"), Arthur modulates her voice from a low whisper to a cry of "Oh, darling!" and goes to his arms.

The hero and heroine's long-delayed embrace, full of pent-up emotion and past misunderstanding, recalls the prototype of Capra's love scenes, the cathartic embrace of Ralph Graves and Barbara Stanwyck in *Ladies of Leisure*. And there are other reminders of the early Capra here too. We see traces of Capra's particular language of eros—first codified in *Ladies*—all through this scene (actually it's two scenes, separated by a montage to show the passing of time). His telltale artist figure is present in the person of Mabel (Ruth Donnelly) with her smock and her easel—a distant echo of Ralph Graves's painter in *Ladies of Leisure*. The chintz couch recalls the chintz

---

*This is not to say that Jean Arthur always came off as sexless: George Stevens made one of the sexiest scenes in all of movies by teaming her with Joel McCrea and a suitcase in the 1943 *The More the Merrier*.

curtains in the auto-court cabin in *It Happened One Night*. The pools of light from lamps reprise Stanwyck's undressing scene in *Ladies* and the intimate auto-court scenes in *It Happened One Night:* Capra loved the look of lamplight illuminating a face in the dark. When Deeds calls on the phone, Jean Arthur moves into lamplight to talk to him. Capra's favorite aphrodisiac, rain, is also evoked in the evening mist that surrounds their walk. The scene is so full of subliminal allusions to earlier Capraesque love affairs that we could almost see it as Capra's elegy for the genre he is saying goodbye to.

Finally, however, the scene proves too squeamish about sex to serve as an elegy for anything. Capra ruins it by having Deeds rush off in embarrassment and trip loudly over a series of garbage cans. According to Capra's biographer Joseph McBride, Capra didn't think he could pull this ending off, but Jean Arthur persuaded him she could handle it. It is briefly funny (and it's widely cited as an instance of Capra's characteristic charm). But it leaves a bad taste in the memory. Deeds's pratfall recalls the awkwardness of a small boy who's just shared his private thoughts with his mother—it all but confesses the latent mother-son dynamic between Babe and Longfellow. Between *Ladies of Leisure* and *Mr. Deeds* Capra had somehow, somewhere, lost his belief in the power of romance. In that first 1930 weeper Capra had rebuilt a whole genre to give his characters the time, the space, and the opportunity to pour out their longing for each other. He had redesigned the very structure of movie romance so that we, the audience, could witness every step in his characters' experience of erotic upheaval. Graves and Stanwyck holding each other in *Ladies,* telling each other everything they had thought before they came together, takes up a substantial chunk of cinematic time. Now, in 1936, Capra not only deprives his leads of the time to live out such a moment, he even spoils his own suggestion of erotic release with the garbage-can gag.

CAPRA AND RISKIN evidently believed they had more important themes to tackle in *Mr. Deeds* than romance—themes like justice and injustice, corruption and innocence, and the power of ordinary citizens in a democracy. These themes move the movie heavily toward its conclusion. Deeds gives his money to the impoverished farmers (shown massing around Deeds's mansion in a tableau that recalls the 1932 Veterans' Bonus March on the White House); and he goes on trial for doing this. In the scenes that show his conversion and his trial, Jean Arthur makes only a few token appearances. Her absence throughout most of the movie's conclusion, plus her strikingly asexual clinch with Cooper in the fade-out after the trial, suggests a link in Capra's mind, not entirely conscious, between his new mode of political allegory and his rejection of eros. *Mr. Deeds*'s last image shows Cooper looking out toward the camera—something like Buster Keaton's projectionist in *Sherlock Junior,* who checks the movie-screen-within-the-movie to see how kissing is done—and applying tight lips momentarily to Jean Arthur's. It's a mockery of sexuality, so much so that it marks a kind of regression in Capra's work.

If we could read the script of *Mr. Deeds* without picturing Gary Cooper in the main role, Longfellow Deeds would seem more like a silent-comedy hero than a romantic-comedy lead. The Deeds on the page would make us think of Keaton or, more precisely, of Harry Langdon. Longfellow Deeds and Harry Langdon are, in fact, almost the same figure. When Capra talks in *The Name Above the Title* about formulating Harry Langdon in the twenties, he might as well be describing how he made up Longfellow Deeds in the thirties. "We gave [Langdon's] character the 'fix' that made him appealing—a grown man with the actions and reactions of a trusting, *innocent* child," writes Capra. "Chaplin *thought* his way out of tight situations; Keaton *suffered* through them stoically; Lloyd overcame them with *speed*. But Langdon *trusted* his way through adversities, surviving only with the help of God, or goodness."

To see Harry Langdon live again in Longfellow Deeds makes us forget, for a moment, that the Stanwyck movies were ever made. During Capra's Stanwyck period, Stanwyck was the one who carried Capra's favorite character trait, hopeful trust in humankind—she and the Colbert heroine who extended her. But *Mr. Deeds* brings that quality of trust right back to the persona of the baby-man Stanwyck had herself displaced. Capra disguised such an obvious regression, maybe even from himself, by having Gary Cooper, who was tall, beautiful, and pugilistic, play the baby-man, instead of the small, soft, and funny-looking Harry. And in his own time, he got away with the deception. *Mr. Deeds*'s revival of male innocence proved to be a boon for Hollywood. It gave the industry a new and virtuous prototype of a male juvenile lead, not a rowdy, unrespectable type like Gable but a nongangster, non–tough guy, noncriminal—a male lead who could be the audience's pet. But it also deprived Capra's movie universe of what had been its most sophisticated quality—the playful awareness of sex. Longfellow Deeds is the most sexless creature we could imagine, and that's a feat, given that Gary Cooper is one of the sexiest icons in movie history. The faltering manner and shy, darting looks Cooper used for Deeds, and the cute habits Capra attributed to him—sliding down banisters, chasing fire engines, listening for echoes in his mansion, talking to a woman as if she were a schoolmistress—may have seemed charming at the time, but they removed the dignity that an awareness of erotic love had conferred on earlier Capra heroes and heroines.

JEAN ARTHUR in *Mr. Deeds* gives what may be the most complete and thought-out performance of any of Capra's romantic-comedy heroines. But the absence of sex between her and her co-star ultimately distorts her persona too. Deeds's naiveté has forced Babe Bennett along with everyone else "on his side"—the Irish housekeeper, the press agent, the trial judge, the newspaper editor—to become a parent to him. In so doing, Jean Arthur is retreating backwards along the trail of the romantic-comedy heroine's emergence, forfeiting the independent spirit that gave these heroines their special status in the first place. With *Mr. Deeds,* Capra lost the ability to imagine a woman at the center of a political allegory. And that meant that he gave up the one point on which his movies had challenged the traditional assumptions of Hollywood—the female character's right to live a bolder, more independent, and more fulfilled life than whatever her origins had held in store for her. At the end of the movie, Jean Arthur's Babe Bennett, crack newspaperwoman, has tacitly agreed to become a wife in Mandrake Falls, Vermont. She is headed right back to a small town like the one she came from—smaller, even, than the town Alice Adams struggled for a whole movie to get out of. It's especially disheartening when one realizes that Babe Bennett was probably based on two of the famous female journalists of twenties New York, Dorothy Parker, the wit, and Dorothy Thompson, the sage. Capra is telling the women in the audience to forget examples like Parker and Thompson, who stood for all the new fervor of twenties feminism, to find a Longfellow Deeds and retire to a small town.

This movie marked the end of Capra's leadership in the romantic comedy he had invented in 1934. After *Mr. Deeds,* Capra would concentrate on hybrids like it, all of which contained more political allegory than romance, and all of which put the hero at the center of the drama rather than the heroine. The movies Capra made between *Mr. Deeds Goes to Town* in 1936 and World War II—*Lost Horizon* (1937), *You Can't Take It With You* (1938), *Mr. Smith Goes to Washington* (1939), and *Meet John Doe* (1941), two of these again starring Jean Arthur—emphasize a young man's search for a "good" father in a corrupt world rather than a romance between a man and a woman. Capra had returned, by his own route, to the quintessential Hollywood subject that had prevailed in the twenties and would prevail again in the forties and fifties: reconciliation between the generations, as defined mostly by the men. The women in Capra's later thirties movies, lively, helpful, thoughtful, modern though they are, still end up standing by during the hero's ordeal rather than living through an ordeal themselves. One could attribute Capra's abandonment of female protagonists to a variety of causes: the final fading of the romance with Stanwyck; his conversion to Christian Science; the audience-pleasing instincts of his scriptwriter, Riskin; the influence of the idealogue Myles Connolly; his own acceptance into the Hollywood power structure; his sentimentalization of his former outsider's status. However, Capra's skill and capaciousness as a movie-maker were such that, on his way out of romantic comedy, he helped make one more actress, Jean Arthur, into a star of the genre. She was the star who represented the softest feminine ideal within romantic comedy: a pragmatic intelligence tempered by pure sweetness.

7

LA CAVA
AND
LOMBARD:

MY
MAN
GODFREY

Gregory La
Cava, William
Powell, and
Carole Lombard
on the set of
My Man Godfrey.

JEAN ARTHUR and Carole Lombard make a near-symmetrical contrast to each other. The one's persona was shy and quizzical; the other's, gay and farcical. Jean Arthur represented the working girl of conscience; Lombard, the morally untutored debutante—almost the flapper, reborn in a Depression landscape. And yet they both embodied, each in her fashion, the stubborn persona of the romantic-comedy heroine. Moreover, Lombard's career was just as slow to peak as Jean Arthur's, and for the same reasons: Hollywood assumed that without stage experience, she couldn't be as good in the talkies as actresses who had come from Broadway. Lombard was even more obviously a Hollywood creature than Jean Arthur. She had come to Hollywood from Indiana when she was six, with her mother and her two older brothers. It had been decided in Fort Wayne, Indiana, Lombard's hometown, that Lombard's mother, Bess Peters, and her children should take a vacation from her husband, Frederick, who suffered from some kind of brain disease. The vacation lasted the rest of their lives.

Hollywood was still a small town in the early twenties. Carole Lombard, then Jane Alice Peters, was a pretty, blond little girl, who went to school with the children of movie people. It was natural that in 1921, at twelve, she should play a bit part in Allan Dwan's *A Perfect Crime,* and at sixteen, after becoming Queen of the May at Fairfax High School, she should be offered a Fox contract and given a new name. As Carol (the final "e" was added a few years later) Lombard she appeared in several Fox silents in 1925 and '26. Her progress was interrupted, though, when a car accident inflicted a small scar on her face, and Fox dropped her contract. No major studio would take her with the stigma of a scar; but Mack Sennett rescued her and made her, in 1927 and 1928, a featured Bathing Beauty in his last custard-pie silent slapsticks before the coming of sound.

The Lombard of those comedy shorts—game, pretty, breathless, demonic, jumping into swimming pools, running in goofy foot races—is the screwball heroine we know from the late thirties, except she's about twenty pounds heavier (Sennett liked his girls plump). But it would take trials and tribulations, false starts and detours for thirties Hollywood to cast her as a comedienne. During the industry's chaotic conversion to sound, Lombard managed to get Pathé, Sennett's distributing agent, to take over her contract. At Pathé she made a silent movie and three primitive talkies before she and another blond starlet were dropped from the roster because the new

Pathé star, Constance Bennett, herself a blonde, couldn't stand the competition. After some scrambling, Lombard landed at Paramount with a seven-year contract starting at $375 a week. But Paramount in 1930 had too many young starlets under contract, so it was a questionable place for Lombard to be, especially since several of the others had come from the stage.

LOMBARD'S FIRST NOTICEABLE Paramount role was in *Fast and Loose* (1930), an early two-couple cross-class romantic comedy with a script by Preston Sturges. She was brought from Hollywood to New York to do it, and it is said that Sturges modeled her part, a chorus girl courted by a rich boy, on her own rakish off-screen character. But though *Fast and Loose* strengthened Lombard's position on the lot, Miriam Hopkins and Nancy Carroll, both Broadway graduates, remained her superiors in the featured slot and always got first choice of ingenue roles. Carroll landed the role in the other "big" Paramount romantic comedy of 1930, *Laughter,* which edged out *Fast and Loose* for in-house prestige in that year. Hopkins, who had appeared with Lombard in *Fast and Loose,* went on to play roles Lombard would have liked to play in the splendid Lubitsch comedies of the early thirties *Trouble in Paradise* (1932) and *Design for Living* (1933).

Paramount made more comedies in the weeper years than the other studios, but not enough to float three young comediennes. So the studio decided in 1931 to develop Lombard for the weepers—as the "Orchid Lady." She was to have a wardrobe to rival Kay Francis's, a glamour to match Dietrich's, and a new elocution to equal Ruth Chatterton's—and she was to be photographed with orchids whenever possible. This would prepare her for hothouse weeper emotions. To kick off the "Orchid Lady" campaign, Paramount put Lombard into the 1931 *Man of the World* (actually she replaced Miriam Hopkins), about an American debutante abroad who falls in love with a gentleman blackmailer, played by the debonair William Powell. The "Orchid Lady" cause appeared to prosper when Lombard married Powell in June of '31, then made another movie with him, *Ladies' Man,* in which her debutante once again reformed his suave gigolo. But Carole Lombard never quite grew into the "Orchid Lady" image. First of all, she divorced Powell about a year after she married him, though they remained good friends. Second, her acting in these genteel roles was terrible. She was stiff and artificial—as if she thought acting were enunciating. She even walked and moved in a boxed-in fashion, despite the slinky clothes.

Meanwhile, the Paramount corporation entered formal bankruptcy in early 1932 and began to reorganize, so the studio couldn't fully realize its plans for Lombard or anyone else. There was a cutback of actresses more severe than the one that had lost Jean Arthur. This time, not just starlets but stars who weren't pulling their weight at the box office were let go or were passed on to other studios—among them Kay Francis, Ruth Chatterton, and Jeanette MacDonald. Lombard, who hadn't made any impression at the box office yet, miraculously escaped the cuts. She was loaned out, however, to cut-rate Columbia on Poverty Row, where she made a fairly successful low-life weeper with Pat O'Brien called *Virtue* (1932). Paramount's "Orchid Lady" idea fizzled definitively around this time, because Lombard began to show some moments of glee on the screen. Her second Columbia loan-out cast her in a semblance of what would later be a typical Lombard role—a bored, mischievous debutante who determines against her family's wishes to marry a poor guy instead of a rich guy. With a wink at Lombard's recent past, Cohn named the movie *No More Orchids* (1932).

Back at Paramount, she made a picture with a good director, Wesley Ruggles, and a good leading man, MGM's up-and-coming star Clark Gable, *No Man of Her Own* (1932). It was the only picture she ever made with her future husband. (The casting was, as usual in Lombard's career at that time, an afterthought: Gable replaced the originally scheduled George Raft, and Lombard replaced Miriam Hopkins.) In the first half of the movie, Lombard shone as a restless, small-town girl given to sudden whims, such as marrying Gable. But in the second half, when she was the gambler's city wife, she sank back into a dazed and glassy gentility. And the movies that followed *No Man of Her Own* in 1933 seemed designed to suppress her still-frail comic instinct. They were halfhearted melodramas such as *Supernatural* (1933), about table-tapping; *From Hell to Heaven* (1933) about horse-racing; and *White Woman* (1933), about steamy sin on a rubber plantation; and they put Lombard opposite such second-class leading men as Randolph Scott, Sidney Blackmer, and Kent Taylor, respectively.

NO ONE ELSE in Hollywood was as different from the roles she played in the movies as Carole Lombard. Off the screen she knew everybody, since she'd been around ever since she was a sixteen-year-old Fox starlet, winning Charleston contests at the Cocoanut Grove nightclub. She loved to dance. She was addicted to pranks and jokes. She was a rabid tennis player. And then there was her mouth. Hollywood gossip had it that Lombard had decided back in 1929 that her prettiness required some kind of armor in the lecherous world of the movies, so she had made her older brothers teach her all the invective they knew. By the time she came to Paramount, Lombard, the "alabaster blonde," could trade insult for insult with the crassest Hollywood producers. This kind of verbal toughness endeared her to many of the men in the movie industry, who had, after all, come to Hollywood from the uninhibited milieus of vaudeville, burlesque, and small-time salesmanship. Hollywood, in terms of power brokering and behind-the-screen authoring, was a vulgar place. And away from the eyes and ears of the public, it took pride in its vulgarity.

Lombard's language habits matched her desire, unusual in those days, to penetrate into domains within the industry that actresses didn't usually concern themselves with. Early on she knew more about how movies were put together than most actors in Hollywood. Even as she was playing prissy blond debutantes, she was hanging around with the ultra-sophisticated Ernst Lubitsch. In 1930, her instincts about dialogue were already legendary among writers on the lot: they would try a line on her, and she would tell them if it sounded natural. Later she would also be famous inside Hollywood for her knowledge of lighting, casting, and contract negotiating. But in the early thirties, her ease with invective was already working in her favor. Her good relationship with Columbia, for instance, stemmed from her unbuttoned rapport with the king of the dirty mouths, Harry Cohn. When Lombard first came to see Cohn, he told her that her platinum hair made her look like a whore, and she replied that if anyone could recognize a whore, it was he.

Lombard was a paradox. She definitely wanted to be a star, but it wasn't clear to her or anybody else what kind of a star. Her attention to her clothes and her makeup, her tireless posing for the genre photographers who "backlit" her in translucent gowns, with key lights trained on her cigarette and her halo of hair, bespoke a professional lust for glamour in the Swanson-Dietrich-Garbo tradition. The "Orchid Lady" plan hadn't been exactly a figment of Paramount's imagination. Lombard had even thought up some new ways to enhance her glamour. In 1933, for instance, she brought the cameraman Ted Tetzlaff from Columbia to Paramount because he made her look prettier. On the other hand, there was also Carole Lombard the California outdoors girl, the reckless tennis competitor, the buddy of grips, cameramen, writers, and producers, the one who swore like the boys.

These contradictions added up to a character who didn't yet exist in a movie genre. All the trappings of a major career had been put in place for Lombard by the early thirties. She employed her best friend from Mack Sennett days, Madlyn Fields, as a personal secretary. She had another old friend, Dixie Pantages, working as her stand-in. She retained Tetzlaff as cameraman. She acknowledged a few favorite directors. For contractual arrangements, she was represented by Myron Selznick, older brother of David O., who usually handled much bigger stars but kept her on because she was a friend. But she hadn't yet made a movie that clicked for her, that connected the movie-star glamour with the naughty wit.

IT WASN'T UNTIL 1934, when the frozen attitudes of the weepers began to melt, that Lombard got her first chance to discover what she could do that other actresses couldn't. That chance came from Harry Cohn. Among the high-class scripts Columbia was preparing in 1934, the year it geared up for the big time, was Ben Hecht's translation to film of his and Charles MacArthur's Broadway play of 1932, *Twentieth Century*. John Barrymore was to play the Belascoesque theater mogul; Howard Hawks was to direct. Cohn's and Hawks's first thought for the part of the leading lady—the movie star Barrymore is trying to coax back to Broadway—was to get an actual Broadway star such as Ina Claire or Tallulah Bankhead. Neither of these ladies, though, would play with the often pickled Barrymore; and for various reasons, not the least of which was Columbia's low place in the hierarchy of studios, Gloria Swanson, Ruth Chatterton, Constance Bennett, Ann Harding, and Kay Francis also turned the movie down. Howard Hawks suggested Miriam Hopkins; Cohn countered Hawks's suggestion with a candidate of his own. Why not put Lombard, his pet actress, into it? She was all but interchangeable with Hopkins, whom she had replaced in about half the movies she had made. Hawks agreed to the suggestion because he, like everyone else, knew Lombard in private. There's even a rumor that Hawks and Lombard, both born in Indiana, were distant cousins.

Twentieth Century unleashed the demon comedienne in Lombard—for a moment. As Lily Garland, the Hollywood star who had started life as plain Mildred Plotka, Lombard kicked, scratched, shrieked, and rolled her eyes with enough gusto to match Barrymore's all-time hammiest movie performance. Hawks, in his book-length interview with Peter Bogdanovich, credits himself with teaching Lombard how to act—or how not to act. Lombard cited Barrymore as her comedy mentor; and three years later, when she was a star, she thanked him by having Paramount expand his bit part in *True Confession* (1937) into a major role. But despite the relentless comic pace and inventiveness of the movie, *Twentieth Century* was not a hit, so it didn't make Lombard a star. (Nor was it a failure; but it did only lackluster business at the box office and it didn't show up in the 1934 Academy Award nominations, which were dominated by another Columbia comedy, *It Happened One Night*.) Two or three years later, it might have gone over big; but in these critical moments when movie humor was first applied to the wounds of the Depression, *Twentieth Century* not only struck the public as too raucous, it also failed to incorporate (as Carole Lombard's biographer, Larry Swindell has shrewdly pointed out) any kind of Capraesque Depression parable. There was no muted echo of warfare between rich and poor in *Twentieth Century*, no cross-class learning experiences, no last-minute renunciations of snobbery.

Lombard's next six movies, at Paramount, Columbia, MGM, and Universal, contributed nothing to her quest for stardom. In one, Paramount's *Now and Forever* (1934), she played a supporting role to Shirley Temple; in another that same year, Columbia's *Lady by Choice*, she supported the elderly May Robson. These 1934 movies failed to place her movie persona in the body of Depression myth that was accumulating in romantic comedies—though one of them, Paramount's *Hands Across the Table* (1935), came close. In preparation for this movie, her old friend Lubitsch, now Paramount's head of production, gave her a half-year's vacation—star treatment—while he oversaw the retooling of the script for her. (It had been intended for Claudette Colbert.) Another of her old friends, Mitchell Leisen, directed, and Colbert's frequent co-star Fred MacMurray came in to play the hero. *Hands Across the Table*, about a gold-digging manicurist and a gold-digging ex-playboy who fall in love and give up greed together, proved a solid item at the box office. It was Lombard's most aesthetic romantic comedy to date: Leisen and Tetzlaff got the camera up close to her face again and again, and they made lustrous use of her light eyes in moments of yearning. And it was funny: Lombard and MacMurray did comedy riffs on the idea of the flustered manicurist trying to attract the notice of the customer she thinks is rich. "Stabbed in the cuticle," says MacMurray to Lombard, through clenched teeth, across the manicure table. But *Hands Across the Table*, despite Lubitsch's efforts, didn't really fit Lombard the way *The Gilded Lily* of the same year fit Colbert. Any of the romantic comediennes could have played the gamely reasonable Regi Allen of *Hands*. No one at Paramount understood yet that Lombard needed a role created with her own qualities in mind—the hint of privilege gone awry, the eager innocence turned absurd. It would take a renegade director, hired by a troubled studio, Universal Pictures, and backed by a serendipitous comedy team, to discover that.

AMONG THE MAJOR STUDIOS, Universal Pictures had been even harder hit by the Depression than RKO or Paramount. Carl Laemmle, Jr. (known as Junior), son of Universal's founding mogul, Carl, Sr., had inherited the studio in 1929, on his twenty-first birthday. While Junior's artistic and administrative decisions generated some exemplary movies in the early thirties (Universal's distinguished series of horror pictures, for example), and also put the studio on a sound financial footing, his gambling on the big-budget musical *Show Boat* lost him his position in early 1936. Former RKO executive Charles R. Rogers took over and instituted cost-cutting procedures on the projects Laemmle had planned. One of those was the movie of a pulp novel by Eric Hatch, which had been serialized in *Liberty* magazine (May and June 1935) under the title *Irene, the Stubborn Girl,* then put into book form with a new title, *My Man Godfrey.* It concerned the reforming of a wealthy and amoral New York family, the Bullocks, by a derelict named Godfrey, whom they hire as a butler. In point of fact, Godfrey is not a real derelict but a Boston blueblood who's been hard hit by the Crash. That's why, in a profoundly conventional novel, the elder of the Bullock sisters, Irene, the "dumbest girl who ever 'came out' at the Waldorf," is allowed to fall in love with him.

Charles Rogers put together a team for *Godfrey* in his mind. For the part of Irene, he thought of Constance Bennett, who was everybody's idea of a bored debutante. For the director, he lined up the hot-tempered, difficult, but extremely talented Gregory La Cava, who had been knocking around from studio to studio since the early thirties. La Cava, however, had made two movies with the difficult Bennett (*Bed of Roses* in 1933 and *The Affairs of Cellini* in 1934) and preferred not to work with her again. Meanwhile, MGM agreed to loan out Rogers's idea of a perfect Godfrey, William Powell, but Powell consented to do the picture only if his ex-wife, Carole Lombard, got the part of Irene. Rogers was willing to replace Bennett with Lombard, since Lombard had just done a comedy for Universal called *Love Before Breakfast* which, though vapid, showed signs of being profitable. And La Cava was intrigued with the idea of Lombard. He had directed her back in 1929 at Pathé, in an early newspaper talkie called *Big News.* He knew she was lively and funny and a "good fellow" to work with. He didn't yet know how consummately her kind of humor would mesh with his own.

THE TRAGEDY OF LA CAVA'S career was that he didn't value his own talents within comedy. The high points of his achievements as a director are all comedies—two silents with W. C. Fields in 1926 and '27, the sly and raucous *The Half-Naked Truth* of 1932 (an anomaly in weeper Hollywood), and the two broadly original and self-aware romantic comedies of the later thirties, *My Man Godfrey* (1936) and *Stage Door* (1937). But La Cava was so good at the sheer mechanics of directing that he was assigned many other genres besides comedy—whatever was most prestigious at that moment—so he wasn't able to build a full comedy oeuvre. And to complicate matters still further, La Cava didn't want to be a movie director in the first place: his deepest ambition, which he cherished all his life, was to be a painter.

The conflict between the world of genteel high art on the one hand and the world of rowdy pop art, or just plain rowdiness, on the other had its roots deep in La Cava's past—in the personality of his father. Pascal La Cava was a gentleman shoemaker who had emigrated from Italy and settled in the small lumber town of Towanda, Pennsylvania. He was musical and played the violin. Pascal La Cava was raising his family in strict, old-world fashion—marching them to church every Sunday in full Edwardian dress (including corkscrew curls on his little sons)—when suddenly, in 1897, he succumbed to a wild streak in his nature and went off to search for gold in the Klondike. George Gregory, his second son, was five at the time. After several years, Pascal returned from Alaska without any gold, and died, leaving the family in dire straits. His wife, Eva, moved her family of four children to Rochester, New York, where her brother was a priest—and it was in Rochester that Gregory first found himself straddling the two worlds of his father, the rough-and-ready world of sports and humor (and gold rushes) and the more genteel world of the fine arts.

As a teenager, La Cava opted first for boxing, and took the name Kid McVay—helpful to an Italian boy in an Irish neighborhood. He was small, but built thickly on top, muscular and wide-shouldered. He had "weak hands," however: early in his boxing career, a mighty punch unhinged the small bones of his right fist, so he abandoned boxing for his other love, art. At Rochester High School his talent for drawing had been noticed. He studied for a time at the Mechanics Institute in Rochester, an arts academy. At the age of nineteen, he enrolled for one summer and fall (1911) at the Chicago Art Institute, which was one of the finest such institutions in the United States. The Art Institute employed the Ecole des Beaux-Arts' "atelier" system of small, informal workshops, and many of its instructors had been trained in Paris. "I started life with the ambition to be a master painter. I had the urge to use oils, to the exclusion of all else," La Cava later told an interviewer.

But around this time La Cava was forced to go to work in the commercial world: his older brother, Pascal, had run off and left Greg responsible for his mother and his younger brother and sister. So he turned his drawing talent to cartoons. Even before he went to Chicago, he had published cartoons in several New York papers—his hero was a luckless bum named "Unsophisticated Oscar"—and when he returned to New York, he took a job in a newspaper cartoon studio. La Cava's signed work began to appear by 1913 in the New York *Evening Globe,* the New York *World,* and the New

York *Herald*. This was the heyday of newspaper cartoons, and the young La Cava rubbed elbows with such colorful figures as Tad Dorgan, the inventor of the "Silk Hat Harry" cartoon; Damon Runyon, friend and chronicler of gangsters and street people; Jack Dempsey, the great and comradely pugilist; Gene Fowler, the wild Hearst reporter from Colorado; and Grantland Rice, the sportswriter and "virile saint" of the age—all of whom must have contributed to the comic sensibility that would flower briefly in La Cava's best movies.

Shortly after he had established himself in newspapers, La Cava realized that the brand-new art of film animation might be a more lucrative field than newspapers. In 1916 he went to work for the animated department of William Randolph Hearst's film enterprise. By 1917 he was in charge of it, commanding seven animators and twenty-five tracers and assistants, whose task was to transfer onto film all the well-known Hearst cartoon characters of the day—Silk Hat Harry, the Happy Hooligan, the Katzenjammer Kids, and a horde of others. Animation inevitably led the restless and ambitious La Cava to the movies proper. In 1921 he switched from Hearst's animated pictures to live-action comedy at a small studio in Long Island, and in 1924 he joined Paramount's East Coast studio in Astoria.

Throughout his ascent to Paramount, La Cava kept up his painting. He took art classes at the Art Students League (possibly with John Sloan) and at Robert Henri's studio school in the Lincoln Arcades, where his teacher was George Bellows. Bellows, a former student and friend of Sloan, was also connected with the influential teens and twenties painters called the New York Realists, later renamed the "ashcan school," of which Sloan was a core member. La Cava further shored up his allegiances to the world of high art by marrying Beryl Morse, the personification of New York's bohemian art world, whom he had met in his first days at the Art Students League. Beryl was a minor celebrity, an ex–child model, ex–child actress, ex–protégée of Charles Dana Gibson, former friend of Mark Twain, former sweetheart of Lewis Mumford, ardent socialist and feminist, and an artist and illustrator herself. The two would remain stormily married until the mid-thirties. Within that time, Beryl's very presence must have continually fueled La Cava's disappointment in himself for selling out for money.

At Paramount La Cava started to make feature films soon after he got there. By 1925, he had become the steady director of the studio's boyish matinee idol Richard Dix. He made five fairly sweet "sex comedies" with Dix in 1925 and '26, the usual undistinguished retellings of the boy-meets-girl-and-gets-business-break story. Subsequently, he made two silents with his buddy and drinking partner W. C. Fields—*So's Your Old Man* (1926) and *Running Wild* (1927), which are little-known gems of the era. La Cava's

Fields is not the outrageous old curmudgeon of the later talking pictures but a shy paterfamilias who occasionally runs amok. The pantomime sequences in these movies suggest a director who possessed not only a keen sense of comic timing but an interest in exploring the poignant underside of comedy—the uncertainty and embarrassment behind the jokes.

La Cava, however, didn't have a chance to stay with Fields and sharpen the persona they had created together, because he was moved by Paramount to the West Coast in 1927. (Fields didn't finally leave the New York stage for Hollywood until later, when sound was firmly established in the movies.) Once he was banished to Hollywood, La Cava's restless, prickly nature asserted itself. He left Paramount—he couldn't stand the size and the supervision. He made a picture at First National, then two at Pathé, then left Pathé in a huff and "bummed around Hollywood for a time" until he was rehired by William Le Baron, his old boss at Paramount, now at RKO. La Cava had a terrible temper. He brooded. He tended to "bend too long over the flowing bowl" and come up with fists flailing. Worst of all from Hollywood's point of view, he liked to tear up prepared scripts and shoot scenes his own way, free of supervision. Sometime in 1930 somebody persuaded La Cava to go to a psychiatrist, one Dr. Samuel Marcus. Mired in the feelings of self-betrayal that circulated in this industry which employed artists to commercial ends, he became a devoted patient, one of the first gifted analysands of the movies.

Despite his difficult nature, La Cava remained in high demand. His years as a cartoon animator had given him an internal time gauge for estimating the relation of live scenes to celluloid. "I can almost always tell just how many frames it will take to make a given gesture," he said later in an interview. And because he could shoot complicated scenes in one take, after a single rehearsal, he could complete movies quickly and under budget. In the early thirties, even without settling down at one studio, he attracted a string of prestigious assignments—and naturally, given the genre hierarchy of those years, they were weepers or gangster pictures. At RKO in 1932 he made two multigenerational melodramas, *Symphony of Six Million* and *The Age of Consent;* at Fox in 1933 he turned out an Ann Harding unwed-mother story, *Gallant Lady;* at MGM in 1934 he directed a fairly astonishing fantasy-melodrama about crime and politics, *Gabriel Over the White House.* And he did these well, though without much personal flavor. La Cava's one outright comedy in those years was the scintillating *The Half Naked Truth* (1932), in which the fast-talking Lee Tracy played a carnival barker and Lupe Velez, the "Mexican Spitfire," played a snake charmer. *The Half Naked Truth,* though, was downplayed at David O. Selznick's rather portentous RKO, despite Pandro Berman's admiration of it.

William Powell
and Carole
Lombard in *My
Man Godfrey*.

In 1935, following the genre revolution brought about by *It Happened One Night,* La Cava began to get more of the comedy assignments he was suited to by temperament: that year he directed Claudette Colbert in *She Married Her Boss* for Columbia. Colbert's melodious wit was not, however, the kind of comic quality that sparked La Cava's imagination. He needed more raucous and uninhibited characters who could go berserk on the screen like the W. C. Fields of the silent years or the Lee Tracy of *The Half Naked Truth.* In short, he needed cronies. La Cava, of all the romantic-comedy directors in this book, was the least interested in romance and the most interested in pure comedy. He was at his best when he collaborated with a team, like the teams on the old comedy lots. And for *My Man Godfrey* he got one.

Morrie Ryskind, a comedy specialist, was hired to write *Godfrey.* Ryskind was the Pulitzer Prize–winning co-author with George S. Kaufman and Ira Gershwin of the 1932 Broadway musical *Of Thee I Sing.* He was also a newsman and a political columnist, so he had little time for movie scripts. But when he did do a movie, he was willing to work in "crony" fashion—not off in a room by himself but present on the set, observing rehearsals, rewriting dialogue on the spot, and merging his ideas with those of the director and the players. Besides Ryskind, La Cava's team included that suavely witty man-about-town William Powell—as well as that wilder man-about-town Carole Lombard. One wonders how much Powell had taught, or tried to teach, Lombard, during their year of marriage, about his own subtly uninhibited mode of screen acting. When she reunited with Powell for *My Man Godfrey,* his lessons, or his example, finally "took" in her persona. Thus, it was she who permitted La Cava to make the conceptual crossover from the male-centered cartoon comedy he had worked with up till then to the female-centered, romance-flavored comedy that Capra had brought to the movies. La Cava discovered, directing Lombard on *My Man Godfrey,* that a woman in thirties Hollywood could act as a full member of the team. And the discovery registered on the movie as a wild outburst of excitement.

La Cava's finding his heroine may well have been connected to his personal life: he divorced Beryl Morse just before he shot *Godfrey.* It's as if, having disengaged from intensive combat with one woman, he could now see how to make another woman a companion in improvisation. Whatever the meaning of *Godfrey* for La Cava, it was undeniably a breakthrough. After a string of well-made movies without any special distinction or personal flavor, suddenly he made this one, a raucous tale with the mood of a communal prank. But that's not all this movie is. Paradoxically, La Cava's finding himself among a group of sympathetic cronies enabled him to tap certain parts of his experience that he hadn't yet used in his work—his lengthy psychoanalysis and his training as a painter.

The La Cava–Ryskind version of *My Man Godfrey* takes a nuclear family apart to illuminate the personality of one of the children. In the novel, Irene was the older daughter. La Cava and Ryskind reconsidered the stresses within the family, and made her the younger. So, where the novel had been a psychologically unsophisticated potboiler, the movie showed a shrewd grasp of the Bullock family dynamic: it displayed something like *Alice Adams*'s wisdom, though with an edge more farcical than weary. Moreover, the revised story didn't merely put Irene into a psychological context; it also placed her visually in the pictorial tradition La Cava had studied in his youth, that of the New York ashcan school.

Most of the ashcans had been socialists—in spirit if not in letter. They were the American painters who became aware as early as 1907 of the sensual possibilities, the qualities of light, texture, and tone, in the spectacle of social contrasts in a great city. La Cava obviously had kept their viewpoint alive in his mind since his student days; here he put it to use. Where Capra had borrowed his "visual politics" from newsreels and illustrated magazines, La Cava got his, at least in part, from the political-aesthetic slant of the ashcan school. There is a dimension of social-realist chiaroscuro in some parts of *Godfrey* that is deeply evocative at the same time it is mildly quaint. A wide-sweeping Dickensian geography of the city suggests itself from time to time—nowhere more strikingly than in the movie's opening images.

THE CREDITS OF *My Man Godfrey* are superimposed over a drawing of a city landscape by a river. This was already unusual: most thirties movies began with a photographed image. In *Godfrey* the camera pans along the river in the drawing, revealing the names of director, producer, and stars flashing on the signs of warehouse buildings, until it arrives at a great bridge over the river, and the chimneys of a shantytown in the foreground. The flare of the shantytown fires backed by the dark silhouette of a bridge recalls John Sloan's etchings, rich with social contrasts of the great city. Then the "etching" dissolves to the same scene on film. Men are moving on the dump heap amid the fires, and one of the men is William Powell in an old hat and coat and a three-day growth of beard. Powell is in the act of dryly reassuring a shantytown companion that "prosperity is just around the corner" when two shiny limousines pull up on the hill of garbage above them and let out a tall, brunette Cornelia Bullock (Gail Patrick), arrayed in shining black satin, her formally dressed escort, and a blond and silver-clothed Irene (Carole Lombard) trailing behind.

It's a beautiful first scene. The gleam of the cars, the fires in the garbage dump, the glint of light on the tin cans become the background for a clash of personalities. All the social suggestiveness of the scenery is borne out when Patrick's debutante insults Powell's down-and-outer. She offers him five dollars to be the "forgotten man" in a scavenger hunt. He refuses, backing her into a heap of trash. She retreats up the hill in a huff, but Lombard is left behind. "Who are you?" says Powell, almost bumping into her. "I'm Irene. That was my sister Cornelia you pushed in the ash pile," says Lombard. Powell orders her to sit down, and they hold a conversation, profile to profile, the light softening his face and gleaming on the shoulders of her silver evening cape. We are reassured in this opening encounter that Powell's bum isn't dangerous, only fair and reasonable in populist style: he believes that rich people should be humiliated for discourteous treatment of poor people. And soon, despite his bum's costume, Powell becomes himself again on-screen, the ironically courtly partner of leading ladies. He shifts the attention deftly to Lombard's Irene. Visually, she's a shimmering creature, with a magically pretty profile, like the "girl" in F. Scott Fitz-gerald's fiction of the twenties—the "girl" who meant money and delicacy and the good life. Temperamentally, she's an exaggeration of the spoiled heiress in *It Happened One Night:* she has only the dimmest comprehension of what "rich" and "poor" mean. She asks Powell why he lives in a place like this when there are so many nicer places to live in. (He says the altitude is good for his asthma.)

With her wide eyes, her breathless tempo extended into anxious trail-offs, Lombard evokes not just a spoiled debutante but the whole barbaric-wealthy universe that has spoiled her. She can't concentrate very long on anything, and she's never encountered the enormous fact of the Depression. Prompted by Powell's professorial irony, however, she begins to articulate a rudimentary Depression morality. "You know I've decided I'm not going to play any more games with human beings as objects," she says in her breathless way. "It's kind of sordid when you think of it—I mean, when you think it over." We marvel that such impulses have sprouted in the palpable chaos of Irene's mind. But what seems clearest in this scene is how much of a child she still is, the way the silent comics in the twenties were children, with children's dismay when they have no power. Irene, we can see, is locked in a chronically losing battle with her domineering older sister. She's already told Powell that she's been wanting to push Cornelia into "an ash pile or something" ever since she was six years old. "Let's beat Cornelia,"

Powell says suddenly, making a quick decision to go with Irene to the scavenger hunt. This way he addresses her on a child's level, and at the same time gives her the first sign she's ever received that her cause, the cause of the powerless, is a good one to fight for.

FOR THE OPENING ROUNDS of that fight, the movie plunges us into Irene's universe, the "Waldorf Ritz," where the scavenger hunt is in full cry. A horde of people in evening clothes is coming and going within the frame, carrying odd objects. Irene's father, the squat, raspy-voiced Bullock (Eugene Pallette), is standing apart at the bar. "All you need to start an asylum is four walls and the right sort of people," he comments to a fellow drinker. Irene's mother, the daffy Mrs. Bullock (Alice Brady), is hurrying toward the podium dragging a goat. Into the melee comes Irene pulling Godfrey by the hand. And Irene, we see, is the real subject of this scene, because in the wake of meeting Godfrey, she's changing. When Godfrey tells scavenger-coordinator Franklin Pangborn at the podium that he lives at City Dump 32, we get a beautiful close-up of Lombard's delight—Godfrey has come through for her. When Powell strides out of the hotel after calling the assembled throng a bunch of nitwits, Lombard, with comic dismay, runs after him. "You did something for me—now I want to do something for you, don't you see?" she explains, as if she'd invented this principle. That's how he becomes the butler—she hires him on the spot. It's curious that the two leading romantic comedies of 1936, *Mr. Deeds Goes to Town* and *My Man Godfrey,* featured outrageously innocent characters with a lot of money, Longfellow Deeds and Irene Bullock. But the atmospheres with which the directors surrounded their "innocents" provide the real measure of the two movies. Capra's neodocumentary asks us to accept the infantile Longfellow Deeds as real and believable. La Cava's farce lets us see the infantile Irene as both real and surreal—a comic idea of a character, with human emotions.

That's what the best silent comedies did in the twenties. They showed the hero in a situation that was surreally funny because of its exaggeration—the small, serious Buster Keaton, for instance, leaning against a strong wind in *Steamboat Bill, Jr.*—then they pointed out the pathos of the situation in close-ups of him. Good twenties silent comedies never made the comic hero into a joke; what was funny about him was his gravity in the midst of comically chaotic circumstances. La Cava and Lombard also kept this Irene Bullock sweetly, gravely oblivious to the maelstrom that she has partly created. Lombard's Irene is the character in romantic comedy who comes closest to a female, talking-picture version of a Keaton, Chaplin, or Langdon. She never grows leaden or sentimental the way Capra's Longfellow Deeds does, because *My Man Godfrey* keeps giving us deft glimpses of her pathos showing through the comic froth surrounding her.

But neither does *Godfrey* forget the social-realist dimension that Depression movies were obliged to provide: it finds a number of ways to show us in familial terms why Lombard's Irene is so childish. The movie's main action takes place in the Bullocks' Fifth Avenue mansion, where Powell's Godfrey has become the butler. Godfrey's dismayed face bobs above his trays of hors d'oeuvres as he makes his way through the family's daffy ensemble scenes, giving us a perspective from which to gape at their antics. And what a circus of antics it is: mother Alice Brady babbles; father Eugene Pallette blusters; sister Gail Patrick sends chilly looks into the air; protégé Mischa Auer cavorts; and little sister Lombard moons and pouts around the room trying to attract Godfrey's attention. All of them are cartoon figures, sounding their one note—except Lombard's Irene, whose portrait has more dimensions. But we can see that her behavior is logically related to what they do. She is trying, in her way, to be her mother—and in pursuit of this unconscious intention, she has picked up her mother's mannerisms. She greets Godfrey on his first morning as butler from her bed, with the news that he's her protégé—the way the "pianist" Carlo is her mother's protégé. She even echoes her mother's idiotic staccato laugh when she says this. And when she wants the family to pay attention to her, she takes another cue from her mother's self-indulgence and throws a crying fit.

But her tactics always fail, because Cornelia—who is just as much a child as Irene, but a nasty and imperious child instead of a beguiling one—mocks the innocent Irene and exposes her intentions. One might say Irene's whole character derives from reflecting her mother and resisting her sister. Nowhere in Eric Hatch's novel was the psychological knowingness of this approach suggested: Hatch didn't acknowledge in his story that he had ever heard of sibling rivalry. La Cava and Ryskind, on the other hand, are entirely comfortable with the subject. They make rivalry the focus of both sisters' lives. And there's no doubt in our minds who's been the more successful rival up till now: Gail Patrick's Cornelia is nothing less than a female bully, with Lombard's Irene as her helpless, though not unspirited, victim. It's this very persecution of her, though, that gives Irene the status of the Capraesque little man, that cornerstone of romantic comedy.

THERE'S NO DENYING that Lombard's Irene Bullock makes a very odd little man, however—as odd in her way as Hepburn's Alice Adams was in hers. Irene's basic sense of decency, the prerequisite of a romantic-comedy heroine, has been shaken up and nearly lost in the chaos of her family. That's why she falls in love with Godfrey: he provides what she needs to get it back—discipline. Irene, lying on the living-room couch after one of her bouts of moping, reaches up to Godfrey as he talks to her, and kisses him on the mouth. When he retreats in shock, she wafts into his room behind the kitchen to try it again, opening his door without knocking. He has to inform her that she can't just walk into someone's room and kiss him—a concept that's new to her. Somewhat later in the story, Godfrey administers to Irene an even stronger chastisement, which sends her hopes spiraling. While she's lying on her bed, having faked a fainting spell to get Godfrey's attention, he realizes (he sees in a mirror) that she's playing possum. He picks her up, still "unconscious," puts her on a stool in the shower, and turns on the water—at which point Lombard bounds out of the shower, dripping wet in her evening gown, jumps up and down on the bed, then rushes to the door, and announces to her mother that "Godfrey loves me, he put me in the shower!"

Lombard was the most exhilaratingly anarchic child-woman in all of romantic comedy: this scene says it all. Its humor works not because Lombard has become a child but because she plays brilliantly with a child's timing. She's jaunty. She *skips* back and forth between the shower and the doorway. Just before she gets to her mother, she careens to a stop and lowers her voice as if conveying secret information. It's like a moment out of the innocent-nasty years of slapstick Sennett comedies, when Fatty Arbuckle and Mabel Normand skipped all over the landscape. And the "romance" between Irene and Godfrey is nearly as absurd, stylized, and comically repressed as that between Mabel and Fatty.

That doesn't mean, though, that the usual romantic-comedy dynamic isn't at work here. What Godfrey and Irene exchange in their romance is something like what Peter Warne and Ellie Andrews exchanged in theirs: he gives her discipline; she gives him fun. But in *My Man Godfrey* the exchange is farcicalized. Irene doesn't know what to do with the discipline, and Godfrey doesn't know what to do with the fun. At the end of the movie, after Godfrey has revealed that he is really "one of the Parkses of Boston" and has rescued the Bullocks from financial ruin, Irene goes after him at his new address—the nightclub called the Dump, created by Godfrey on the site of the old shantytown to employ all the forgotten men. (A long shot of the illuminated nightclub on the site of the former dark and mysterious shantytown provides another pictorially beautiful moment.) Irene sashays through the club, greets the mayor of New York by name, and continues blithely through the door into Godfrey's office, marked "Private," to announce that she and he are getting married. But as the movie fades out on a spur-of-the-moment wedding tableau, accompanied by Irene's half-witted Bullock laugh, we get the unmistakable sensation that Godfrey is on the verge of a marriage as frustrating as the senior Bullocks'.

It's a deeply funny ending. Capra, in his 1936 romantic comedy, *Mr. Deeds Goes to Town,* had sentimentalized his own dramatic formula, his prescription for healing the Depression by means of a lovers' cross-class union. La Cava in *My Man Godfrey* reclaims the Capraesque romantic comedy by making fun of Capra's own prescription. The very social placement of *Godfrey*'s characters—the Fifth Avenue Bullocks, the derelict Godfrey—comically simplifies Capra's social universe. It locates Capra's idea of pre-Depression corruption not in a class of jaded politicians and literati but in an anarchic family. Then it administers the coup de grace to the mock-pious hero, by trapping him in that family through his marriage with Irene. It's true that La Cava didn't invent the idea of the berserk wealthy family standing for pre-Crash ills. Broadway had played with this idea in such plays as Gertrude Tonkonosy's *Three Cornered Moon* (1933), filmed that year with Claudette Colbert. Eric Hatch, the original author of *My Man Godfrey,* had taken his cue, in part, from vehicles like *Three Cornered Moon.* But the sustained comic frenzy of La Cava's and Ryskind's Bullocks in *My Man Godfrey* outdid anything plays, books, or Hollywood had yet seen. It was La Cava who brought the absurdly wealthy family, with its rococo plaster-of-Paris mansion and all its ludicrous affectations, into romantic-comedy symbology.

THE MOVIE'S MOST INSPIRED creation, however, remains Carole Lombard's Irene. La Cava, Ryskind, and Lombard had created this Irene from the living model of Lombard herself. She was nothing like Eric Hatch's Irene. Not one word of the novel's bovine debutante had made it into the movie; all of Irene's on-screen lines were written for Lombard. Moreover, Lombard's Irene is anything but slow-witted: she's quicksilver and breathless. Her mind seems to function like a pinball machine, where randomly circulating ideas sometimes, magically, make lights go on. At first glance, this anarchic persona offers an exception to the rule of romantic-comedy heroines. She appears generically different from the personae of Stanwyck, Colbert, Hepburn, Rogers, and Jean Arthur, projected through characters who depended on intelligence and self-reliance to make their way in the world. But Irene has her own kind of intelligence: it simply derives more from primal energy than from rationality. And her intelligence puts her, just like the others, into the classic dilemma of the romantic-comedy heroine.

She's out of step with the representatives of power in her world, notably her sister, Cornelia, and her task is to figure out how to get some respect in a Cornelia-dominated world.

In other words, Lombard's Irene reinvents the values of democracy in her head, like the rest of the romantic-comedy heroines, but she does it impulsively, in her own fashion. She's even demonstrative toward the servants. Eric Hatch had put an antiquated kitchen maid named Molly into his novel—an Edwardian tart with whom his Godfrey toys absentmindedly, like a gentleman cad. Such an Anglophiliac notion was unsuitable for thirties movies, so La Cava and Ryskind made Molly (Jean Dixon) a wisecracking Greek chorus, smarter, in thirties fashion, than her employers. Dixon's Molly is given a wonderful scene with Lombard's Irene in which the two realize they're both in love with Godfrey and embrace tearfully.

Godfrey's Irene Bullock enabled Carole Lombard to finally find her full screen potential, in a role that summed up her schizophrenic career: it contained vestiges of Mack Sennett's slapstick Bathing Beauty and traces of Paramount's rebellious "Orchid Lady." Irene represented, in short, the mischievous-child version of the romantic-comedy heroine. And if this child-woman seems incompatible now with the Lombard who was gradually acquiring a knowledge of movie-making, who was sponsoring her colleagues' careers, who once expressed the desire to be a producer like David O. Selznick, perhaps it's because Lombard in 1936 still hid her wish to be an official movie author behind her high-spirited antics. Or else she was a person of extremes, and the childlike Lombard coexisted with the potentially powerful one. It seems eerie that she was the one who died young, in a plane crash in 1942—she who represented the pure spirit and untrammeled instinct of this thirties folk figure, the romantic-comedy heroine. But before she died, she would spend six more years playing the child-woman she had brought to fruition in *My Man Godfrey*. (Her most demonic post-*Godfrey* creations can be seen in *Nothing Sacred* [1937], *True Confession* [1937], parts of *Made for Each Other* [1939], *Mr. and Mrs. Smith* [1941], and the comically flyaway *To Be or Not to Be* [1942].) Meanwhile, even as Lombard returned triumphant to Paramount after *Godfrey*, in secure possession of her special child-woman persona, La Cava, the co-creator of that persona, moved over to RKO to help realize two of the most grown-up romantic-comedy heroines the genre would ever know.

8

LA CAVA,
ROGERS,
AND
HEPBURN:

STAGE
DOOR

Lucille Ball,
Gregory La
Cava, and
Katharine
Hepburn on the
set of *Stage Door*

Gregory La Cava
and Ginger
Rogers on the
set of *Stage Door*.

N 1 9 3 7 Katharine Hepburn, whose stardom had been rescued and rede-
fined in 1935 by *Alice Adams,* found herself in trouble again. The trouble
had begun shortly after *Alice.* In the afterglow of that movie's success, the
studio had allowed Hepburn to do a pet project of George Cukor's, *Sylvia
Scarlett,* based on a 1918 potboiler by Sir Compton Mackenzie about a
Franco-English bohemian girl who travels as a boy. *Sylvia* was released in
1936 and failed miserably. Hepburn's boy disguise was unpleasantly lifelike:
she had cut her hair like a real boy, not a gamine, and she paraded around
with awkward bravado. But it wasn't just Hepburn who was "off." The
whole movie gave off a fey and oh-so-English atmosphere. This was not
what audiences wanted to see in 1936.

Nineteen thirty-six marked the ultimate arrival of romantic comedy in
mainstream Hollywood. The two biggest romantic comedies of the year,
Mr. Deeds Goes to Town and *My Man Godfrey,* showed up as nominees in
nearly all the categories of the Academy Awards, alongside the usual non-
comic blockblusters, such as *The Great Ziegfeld, The Story of Louis Pasteur,*
and *San Francisco.* And Frank Capra won Best Director for *Mr. Deeds.*
With the genre's new prestige came an industry-wide awareness of the
change in the leading ladies' roles. Romantic comedy had succeeded in
completely inverting the weepers' dramatic strategy. The new genre's heroines didn't start out in prestigious jobs or marriages, like the weeper
ladies, then abuse their authority and fall down the social ladder. They
started out in humble positions; they already possessed an innate kind of
authority unrelated to "society"; and in the end they rose socially—that is,
married someone stable or wealthy—because they'd held on to their con-
victions.

This new strategy for heroines had bred a new kind of star. Instead of the
cool, remote women of the weepers—Garbo, Dietrich, and the like—whom
the men in the audience despaired of possessing and the women despaired
of becoming, the new leading ladies—Stanwyck, Colbert, Arthur, Lombard, Rogers—projected down-to-earth, familiar qualities. They played "ordinary" people, newspaperwomen, saleswomen, manicurists, teachers of
ballroom dancing, and the occasional comradely heiress. One could almost
imagine meeting them offscreen, at the office, at a party, in a department
store: one could almost imagine *being* them. Fan magazines took note and
changed their coverage to acknowledge the new stardom: they stopped

talking about the stars' love affairs; they now talked about their kitchens and their tennis and backgammon games. This shift in style was proof that some of the humbler elements in the movies—directors, writers, some of the stars themselves—had won out temporarily over the big moguls. The moguls on the whole saw stars as remote but humiliatable women. The romantic-comedy authors saw them as regular human beings, as protagonists who voiced the emotions of the Depression audience.

And yet RKO, in the midst of this industry-wide revision, still could not get the Hepburn persona right. The trouble was indicated plainly in the box-office figures: the plebeian *Alice Adams* had made money; the preten-tious *Sylvia Scarlett* had flopped. But the studio bosses couldn't read that evidence—they were still too impressed by Hepburn's low-key "patrician" manner offscreen. A month after *Sylvia*'s release, they had her in production for Maxwell Anderson's pompous play *Mary of Scotland,* with John Ford as director. Not even messages from theater owners could stop them. HEPBURN NEEDS HUMAN STORY WITH AMERICAN BACKGROUND AND BOX OFFICE MALE LEAD STOP MISTAKE TO FOLLOW SYLVIA SCARLETT WITH MARY OF SCOTLAND, wired the head of the fifteen-hundred-seat Garden Theater in Pittsburgh. The studio paid no attention. *Mary* bombed in the spring of 1936, and RKO remained unenlightened. A week after *Mary*'s release, Pandro Berman wrote Hepburn a memo about her next movie. "Great follow-up for *Mary* would be my old favorite Josephine, and Jack Ford comes through with the suggestion of Charles Boyer for Napoleon," he wrote.

That particular Napoleon and Josephine was never made (though Charles Boyer did play Napoleon at MGM in 1937, in *Conquest,* with Greta Garbo as Marie Walewska). But other high-toned literary ideas for Hepburn were bandied about at this time, such as *Jane Eyre* (which Hep-burn was already set to do onstage with the Theatre Guild); *The Mill on the Floss;* a Sarah Bernhardt biography (this project had been around since '33); the old Maude Adams vehicle *Peter Pan* (suggested by Hepburn but nixed by the studio)—even the new blockbuster novel *Gone With the Wind,* published in June of 1936. (It was rejected because its heroine was termed "unsympathetic" and its story line resembled that of Paramount's 1935 southern epic with Margaret Sullavan, *So Red the Rose.*) Desperate, the studio returned Hepburn to the Victorian milieu of her first big hit, *Little Women.* They cast her as a bluestocking of 1870 in *A Woman Rebels* (1936), directed by Astaire and Rogers's director Mark Sandrich. Here was Hepburn once again in crinolines, demure as a girl, flashing-eyed as the girl grown into magazine editor, but out of step with the public's new sentiments about its stars. *A Woman Rebels* lost $222,000. Undaunted,

RKO plunged even further down the same blind alley. It considered Henry James's *Washington Square* for Hepburn; it thought about lending her to Paramount for *National Velvet,* or bringing Frank Capra in to direct her in a biography of George Sand. But once again the studio chose English crinolines, and Hepburn's first movie of 1937 was *Quality Street,* directed by George Stevens, based on J. M. Barrie's 1900 play about a plain schoolmistress in early Georgian England, who impersonates her own coy niece to win a suitor. Even Stevens couldn't save *Quality Street:* it lost $242,000.

It's striking how many "old maid" projects figure in this list of vehicles intended for Hepburn. To her puzzled studio, Hepburn must have seemed like an aging elder daughter, too old-fashioned for the suitors at the box office. But this time, as opposed to the last time Hepburn's career had dropped down a hole, Hepburn wasn't the only female star on the lot. RKO had a "younger daughter" who had no trouble catching the public's eye—a star who already embodied the qualities that were eluding Hepburn. Ginger Rogers on the screen was not snobbish or fey or imperious; she was thoughtful, proud, and "real" in Depression terms—perhaps the most natural female democrat working in Hollywood in the thirties. Rogers had proved her worth in the Astaire-Rogers series, and demonstrated her box-office strength in two substantial movies without Astaire—*Star of Midnight* and *In Person* (both 1935). By 1937, though, the Astaire-Rogers series was beginning to lose its phenomenal drawing power. The seventh Astaire-Rogers, *Shall We Dance,* had grossed only half the profits of the earlier movies in the series. Rogers, like Hepburn, was in need of a good contemporary drama, one that would separate her in the public's mind from Astaire once and for all. At this alarming moment for RKO—this crisis in Hepburn's career and crossroads in Rogers's—Pandro Berman did something that was unconventional but, in its own way, logical. He decided to make a movie that would star both his reigning actresses—*Stage Door.*

BEFORE IT BECAME a movie, *Stage Door* was a play, written by George S. Kaufman and Edna Ferber, about aspiring actresses in a New York theatrical boardinghouse. As early as June 1936, four months before *Stage Door* opened on Broadway, RKO's story watchdog in New York, Lillie Messenger, wrote to the studio about it. Messenger had standing orders to keep a watch out for vehicles for Hepburn. "Question every playwright and author in an attempt to find Hepburn material," RKO-Hollywood wrote her in February 1936. That was why Messenger leaped at *Stage Door,* even though she was worried about its anti-Hollywood attitude, its implications that actresses who had left the theater for the movies had no right to come back. Hepburn had already been mocked on Broadway for trying to come back. Ironically, Margaret Sullavan, a sometime movie star, was cast in the leading role—the actress who refuses Hollywood offers three times, even though she can't find a part in a play and has to take a job at Macy's.

By September 1936 Lillie Messenger had arranged for a copy of the proof sheets of the play to be sent in secrecy to RKO (Edna Ferber didn't favor that studio). Pandro Berman telegraphed his enthusiasm to Messenger. He could see it for Hepburn, Rogers, or even Margaret Sullavan. Messenger traveled to Philadelphia for the previews. She wired that the play needed work in some "dead spots" but urged RKO to buy it for Hepburn; she thought it would remind audiences of Hepburn's young-actress role in the 1933 *Morning Glory,* which had won her an Academy Award. Meanwhile, *Stage Door* opened in New York in October and became a hit. It was thought witty, wry, and poignant by almost all the critics. Several studios bid for it, and the price shot up to over $100,000 (though Messenger believed that Hepburn's agent, Leland Hayward, who had also become the play's agent, and the new husband of Margaret Sullavan, had bluffed the price up). RKO bought it in November of 1936 for $130,000.

Despite its substantial reputation, the play today reads like the outcry of puny little Broadway backed against the wall by monster Hollywood. It contains some clever, slangy lines, but it gives off an excess of spleen—the spleen of lost prestige. Kaufman and Ferber had been partial inventors of the self-referential cleverness of the twenties theater. After the Crash, their kind of rarefied wit proved impossible to finance. The Depression hadn't treated Kaufman and Ferber themselves badly: together they had turned out a Broadway hit in 1932, *Dinner at Eight;* separately they had continued other profitable activities—Ferber writing novels and Kaufman co-writing plays with other partners. Each had even had dealings with Hollywood: Ferber had sold novels to the movies, and Kaufman had worked on two movie projects, for which he earned an amazing amount (*Roman Scandals* of 1933 and, with Morrie Ryskind, *A Night at the Opera* of 1935). Nevertheless, both Kaufman and Ferber partook of Broadway's generalized grudge against Hollywood and expressed it where they could in the mode of petty snobbery. *Stage Door* was an orgy of petty snobbery. On the pretext of idealizing the "small folk" of the theater, the play took

potshots at a wide range of Hollywood types. Its cast of characters consisted of corrupt movie people who had sold out and virtuous theater
people who had kept the faith. On the "bad" side were Keith Burgess, a
Clifford Odets–like playwright; Jean Maitland, an untalented stage actress
turned movie star; and Adolph Gretzl, a gratuitously egregious version of
Paramount's founder, Adolph Zukor. On the "good" side were Terry
Randall, the street-smart and incorruptible actress heroine; David Kings-
ley, the young movie producer longing for Broadway; and assorted embit-
tered female residents of the Footlights Club who, though hard pressed,
remained true to their art.

RKO HARBORED no illusions about the new property. Even as the studio
was buying it, the bosses were discussing how to alter it to remove the
Hollywood-baiting that was such a core feature of its plot. Pandro Berman
conceived a new approach. While pondering the play, he had seen a "March
of Time" newsreel about girls in the big city looking for work. "That helped
in casting about for a treatment to supplant the phony theme of the play—
Hollywood versus the stage—and find a solid and true theme," Berman
wrote later in an August 1937 letter to the producers of "The March of
Time" (a letter that sought a marketing tie-in with the newsreels). According to studio memos, the new "solid and true" theme Berman had in mind
was a documentary-style treatment of the life of New York actresses in the
Depression. The movie of *Stage Door* would contain allusions to the newsreel mode.

But to realize his plan of co-starring Rogers and Hepburn, Berman
knew that RKO would need to change more than the look of the play.
The *Stage Door* team would have to take on the task of turning the shallow movie actress, Jean Maitland, into a substantial and likable second
lead for Ginger Rogers. And they would be obliged to give this new Jean
Maitland a meaningful relationship with the true-blue actress Terry Randall, Hepburn's character. To tackle the script, Berman chose the young
but experienced Anthony Veiller, the son of Bayard Veiller, the Broadway
melodramatist. But hiring a scriptwriter wasn't enough. Such a recon-
struction, not just of plot but of characters, required a director present in
the early stages of the work—a director with the improvisatory skills of a
Capra or a George Stevens. Capra was off-limits to RKO—he belonged at
this point exclusively to Columbia. Stevens, who was much closer at
hand, on the RKO lot, had just been assigned another directing job, Astaire's first musical without Rogers, *A Damsel in Distress.* (Moreover, Ste-

vens had failed to improve Hepburn's ratings with *Quality Street.*) But there was another prominent director in Hollywood who had mastered the Capra methodology—a man Berman knew well. Gregory La Cava had worked at RKO back in the Selznick days; now he was riding high on his success with *My Man Godfrey.* He was even advertising his mastery of impromptu directing: during the filming of *Godfrey* he had pinned a shirtcuff to a table on the set and showed it to reporters when they asked to see the script—he shot "off the cuff."

In February of 1937, Berman approached La Cava, who was happy to come back to RKO. He was signed to a one-picture contract, with built-in features that indicate his considerable bargaining power. La Cava was not required to begin shooting without at least six weeks of "story preparation"; he retained the right to engage some members of his own production staff (script girl, cutter, cameraman, assistant, as well as other writers)—a practice the studios deplored, because it meant adding extra employees whose jobs overlapped with those of studio contractees; he held the right to final okay of the first "sneak preview" of the picture and also the right to convene a press preview before the studio changed anything. It was unusual for a director to have that much control, but La Cava had earned it. Almost alone among young directors, he had chosen to free-lance throughout most of the thirties. (Only Howard Hawks was as untetherable as La Cava.) Financially this was a precarious course. He hadn't always made outstanding movies, but he had never made a flop—or so went the myth. And now that RKO had given him a contractual right to rule his own set, he could experiment as much as he wished.

AFTER LA CAVA was hired in February, he spent a week holding conferences with Tony Veiller, sketching out a story about two girls from a small town in Vermont who come to New York to be actresses: one of them, the Hepburn character, an idealist; the other, the Rogers character, an opportunist. The Hepburn character falls in love with a left-wing playwright, acts in his play, realizes she's no good on the stage, and goes back contentedly to the small town. The Rogers character meets a wealthy man-about-town, gets him to back her friend's play, then lands him as a husband. La Cava went away, and Veiller wrote the script of that story in six weeks. But when La Cava, Veiller, and Berman met again in April, they realized that they had inadvertently recreated Hepburn's Vermont-born actress from *Morning Glory.* So they made up a new story, in which Hepburn became a Long Island debutante, Rogers became a Missouri-born gold digger, the radical playwright virtually disappeared, and the man-about-town turned into a theatrical producer named Anthony Powell. Forty-seven-year-old Adolphe Menjou, Hollywood's reigning gentleman-seducer (since Ernst Lubitsch's *The Marriage Circle* in 1923), was hired to play Powell. Shooting was to begin on June 7, 1937.

Some days before shooting started, La Cava brought his imaginative and flexible writer-collaborator from *My Man Godfrey,* Morrie Ryskind, into the project—thus throwing what script there was into La Cava's favorite suspended state. ("A picture is always in solution," he once told an interviewer. "It should crystallize only at the 'high' point of any scene of action.") Veiller never spoke to Ryskind, and Ryskind never saw Veiller's scripts; Ryskind picked up the rudiments of Veiller's story from La Cava. And from the moment Ryskind signed on, all resemblance to orderly movie-making ceased.

The casting of the secondary characters was done by ear. La Cava and Ryskind hung around the studio cafeteria listening to the voices of the RKO starlets. "Try and get a voice," La Cava would say to Ryskind. He meant a distinctive voice, and they put together a symphony of them: the wistful, screwy tones of the young Lucille Ball; the ironic drawl of the even younger Eve Arden; and the Texas twang of the extremely young Ann Miller. (She was still a teenager.) Having settled on his cast, La Cava had the girls sit around for hours on the set that was the Footlights Club living room, pretending it was a real place and that they lived there. (Many of them did live or had lived in theatrical boardinghouses.) They even brought in their own clothes for costumes, which was not the custom in Hollywood. Once the supporting cast had settled into place, the next problem was to fit the principals into the picture—to give them the cinema-verité flavor of the lesser characters while not forgetting their particular box-office needs. Hepburn needed to be chastised and reformed; Ginger Rogers required equal stature with Hepburn; and Menjou, with his considerable Hollywood prestige, had to have a substantial part too.

At the time they started filming, Hepburn's character was more developed than Rogers's. La Cava had already written the snobbery into her personality, a snobbery he might have taken from Hepburn's character in *Alice Adams.* Terry Randall thinks she can act because she's been indulged, like Alice. She's not hesitant like Alice, however; she's rich, and used to being respected and deferred to. This is the attitude she brings into the Footlights Club: she thinks of the club as her Wild West, her equivalent of the territory her pioneer grandfather had subdued. But if Hepburn's Terry was clear in the authors' minds, the role of Ginger Rogers's Jean Maitland was vague.

From the beginning the project had shown a tendency to belittle Rogers, by making her "partner" Hepburn the way she had "partnered" Astaire. That's what Veiller had done in his script: he had imagined Jean Maitland as a brassy chorus girl who recognizes that her friend Terry Randall has a nobler soul than her own; he had made Rogers, in fact, Hepburn's hand-maiden. Veiller had also planned a casually crass denouement for the Rogers character: her father, a Missouri sheriff, was supposed to arrive in town and force Anthony Powell to marry her at gunpoint. Obviously Veiller had not understood the reasons Rogers was outshining Hepburn at the box office; he didn't "get" the Depression appeal of the younger star. (Veiller wasn't alone in misunderstanding: RKO at this time was still paying Rogers nearly a thousand dollars a week less than Hepburn, and both women were paid less for this movie than Menjou.)

So La Cava settled down, with Ryskind at his side, to figure out what to do with Jean Maitland—and with the whole story—on the set itself. He followed the procedure that he and Ryskind had perfected in *My Man Godfrey*. The cast "lived" the scene in the morning: they tried out the dialogue and spacing and made up new material if the old felt wrong. Over the lunch break, La Cava, Ryskind, and the script girl would write out readable versions of the morning's experiments. In the afternoon they would shoot the finished scene. It was the freest of free-form movie-making. But La Cava, with his experience in cartoon animation, could do this kind of impromptu directing faster and cleaner than almost anyone. "Now look, don't worry about the camera angles," he would tell Morrie Ryskind. "Just write it like you would a play."

The two of them had already conjured *My Man Godfrey* out of thin air. *Stage Door* presented a situation that was similar in a key respect: there were two "sisters" as there had been in *Godfrey*—or, rather, two young women who would live together at close quarters. It was already clear which part Hepburn would take in this thirties morality drama: she would be the nasty older sister. Rogers would therefore become a kind of younger sister with democratic instincts. But that's not exactly what happened. A peculiar relationship—a relationship in which the two characters seesawed back and forth in each other's estimation—began to evolve on the set.

THE CONNECTION BETWEEN *Stage Door* and *My Man Godfrey* appears in *Stage Door*'s first scene, which shows Rogers locked in combat not with Hepburn but with another "older sister," her then roommate, played by the

actress who had played Lombard's older sister in *My Man Godfrey,* Gail
Patrick. First we see the façade of a brownstone, and a plaque that says it's
the Footlights Club. Here is Berman's documentary-style approach. The
outside of the building dissolves to the inside, to reveal a group of young
women lounging about the living room and grousing to the maid, who's
singing mock arias as she sweeps up. The mature and svelte Gail Patrick,
playing "Linda," descends the staircase in the middle of the set—and then
Ginger Rogers, wearing a wholesome shirt tucked into tailored slacks,
makes a flying entrance into the scene, racing down the stairs, demanding
the return of her stockings.

The confrontation between these two unfolds in the free-for-all style La
Cava had perfected in *Godfrey:* Rogers threatens to flatten Patrick's ears to
her head; the club's proprietress flutters about, pleading "Girls! Girls!"; Eve
Arden, with a white cat draped around her neck, tries to referee; the others
offer wisecracks; and Lucille Ball, on the phone, yells at them all to shut
up. By the time the fracas has died down, Rogers's Jean Maitland has won:
Linda has agreed to move out of her room. Rogers's Jean, we see, is no
frustrated child like Lombard's Irene Bullock; she is the natural leader of
the house—she articulates the populist "philosophy" they all live by. Her
scorn is aimed not at Linda herself but at the goody-goody airs Linda has
put on because she's dating the great Anthony Powell, theatrical producer.
Her prime weapon is a quick switch back and forth between fancy talk and
slang. "Girls, girls, pheasant bordelaise!" she says, mimicking Gail Patrick's
description of her coming dinner with Powell. Then she lowers her voice
and levels a vernacular broadside—"Don't eat the bones and give yourself
away."

La Cava's Footlights Club functions as an all-women version of Capra's
Greyhound bus, a closed society that the Depression has radicalized. Into
it comes a stranger, Hepburn's Terry Randall. First glimpsed outside in
silhouette, rattling the doorknob of one of the club's French windows, she
finally locates the front door upscreen and enters, smart and imperious in
a fez and a military-type coat with double brass buttons. Her manner, at
once hesitant and authoritative, types her as rich and spoiled, like Capra's
heiress—a privileged person automatically at odds with the underprivileged
of the Footlights Club. (Veiller's original script opened with Hepburn
landing on her family's Long Island estate in an autogyro—a direct steal
from *It Happened One Night*—but La Cava and Ryskind had narrowed the
action to the club.) "How many doors are there in this place?" Hepburn
asks with awkward jocularity. "The trap door, the humidor, the cuspidor—
which one would you like?" Rogers answers crisply. Rogers's Jean has simply

replaced one symbol of snobbery in her routine with another. But Hepburn's Terry, her new victim, is not as practiced in the club's ways as Linda. For this she earns our sympathy, even as she is inciting our mistrust—just as Claudette Colbert among the bus riders inspired both sentiments at once. Terry has rallied to what she thinks is Jean's attack, but it's clear that she's never used these particular weapons—irony, puns, comic insults—and certainly not at this pace. So she retreats to condescending sarcasm, too heavy a weapon for the Footlights Club. "Evidently you're a very amusing person," she says to Jean.

This is a riff on Capra's basic romantic-comedy structure. Each of the leads has locked horns with an opposite: the heiress has met a working person; the working girl has met a wealthy person. But it's not an opposite of the opposite sex. Terry and Jean have assumed the adversary positions usually occupied by a man and a woman destined for romance. What we have here is not the usual hero and heroine but two heroines—of the two different varieties produced thus far by the genre, the heiress and the working girl. And they are pitted against each other, not against two leading men. The authors of the movie—Veiller, La Cava, Ryskind—hadn't consciously planned for the two actresses' relationship to carry such weight in the story (or at least the various scripts in the archive don't suggest that they had). They hadn't intended, in other words, to make a romantic comedy with two women in the place of the lovers. But the configuration of the co-stars flows so logically out of the class contrast—a class contrast that had accrued to Rogers and Hepburn even before they became Jean Maitland and Terry Randall—that it suffices for drama.

STAGE DOOR'S opening scenes articulate the mistrust between the classes more clearly and cleverly than any other passage in a romantic comedy. The proprietress assigns Terry to Jean's room, now that Linda has moved out. There is a tense silent exchange as Jean witnesses the arrival of Terry's three large trunks, followed by Terry herself. Rogers, taking a stance against the bureau, sidles from screen left into full-face close-up, appraising the situation. She's just gotten rid of one pretentious roommate, Linda—is she gaining a worse one? That close-up is matched by one of Hepburn looking back at Rogers from under her fez, warily and wistfully—prepared for enmity but pleading for peace. Instead, the verbal battle escalates. Rogers ribs Hepburn for flaunting her privilege and breeding, and Hepburn responds by tartly defending these. "Unfortunately I learned to speak English correctly," she says. "That won't be of much use to you here—we all speak

Katharine Hepburn and Ginger Rogers in *Stage Door*.

pig Latin," says Rogers. "And I use the right knife and fork—I hope you don't mind," says Hepburn. "All you need's the knife," says Rogers.

In their quips they're showing each other how tough they are. In their close-ups they're showing the audience how vulnerable they are. And inevitably, as in any romantic comedy, they start to reveal that vulnerability to each other. Late one night, Rogers comes limping back into the room she now shares with Hepburn, complaining about those "Seattle Romeos" whose "feet are made of wood." La Cava set this scene with the Capraesque "pool" lighting, which accentuates the Depression look of a makeshift home. The room, earlier filled with trunks, is now settled and quiet in the half-dark; Hepburn is sitting up in her twin bed, lit by a small reading lamp; and Rogers's bed is clean and welcoming. It looks like the scene in the auto court in *It Happened One Night,* and it describes, as that scene did, how the two leads start to see the worth in each other. Jean asks herself why she is telling her gripes to Terry, but her tone sounds a truce. And Terry begins to mend her manners. She begs Jean's permission to ask a question—how to get some air in the room. Here La Cava lingers on a special detail of the set. When Hepburn raises the shade and opens the window, we see a giant, flashing neon sign and hear the noise of horns and traffic. In *It Happened One Night,* the heiress's discovery of the humble America of cafés and auto courts had revealed its poetry to the movie audience. In *Stage Door,* the wealthy Terry Randall's reaction to the cramped little room dwarfed by the neon sign does the same thing. "I've always longed to live in a place like this!" she says.

This setting—the room with the sign—had been the Broadway play's scenic tour de force. Recreating it must have pleased La Cava, with his youthful dream of painting. Two women in a rented room, the physical city looming over their life: this was a subject for John Sloan, or for the great descendant of the ashcans, Edward Hopper. In this scene, though, La Cava transcended what he might have done on canvas. Besides conveying atmosphere, he also gives us psychology. The scene lets us see the inner nature of each girl, the softer self that contradicts the surface bravado. On the fade-out, Rogers's Jean has gone to sleep, clutching a blond doll: the chief needs a token of comfort. Hepburn's Terry is sitting up in bed, pushing up her sleeping mask: the haughty initiate longs to know "the other half." If Jean and Terry were a man and a woman, erotic tension would make itself felt here, as a sign of mutual attraction. But the class awareness of the Footlights Club is so strong that the drama of male and female isn't missed. It is their social differences that put Jean and Terry off each other, and attract them to each other.

. . .

AT THIS POINT in the story, with Jean and Terry's standoff turning into rapprochement, Adolphe Menjou enters. We have heard about him in the first scene—he's the Anthony Powell Linda was dating. Now we see him in his sartorial splendor. He walks into the dance studio where Rogers is running through her routine with Ann Miller; he's wearing a pin-striped suit and bowler hat. But the movie undercuts him from his first words. "Who's the little blonde over there?" he asks the dance director. A man who talks like that, about a character played by a star, puts the audience on notice: such casual patronage violates Depression decency. Rogers responds in proper prickly fashion, exiting on a "Shuffle Off to Buffalo" and leaving a giggling Ann Miller to try to talk to the big man. Powell, offscreen, arranges for Rogers and Miller to star in the floor show of the Club Grotto, which he half owns. After the show, he approaches Rogers again in her dressing room. This time she flirts back, though she's still prickly. But she agrees to go to dinner. The audience condones this because of the pragmatism of the Depression: Jean Maitland needs a job more than anything else, and in the theater Powell is the source of jobs. Moreover, dating Powell offers Jean a way to look at the kind of life she begrudges Linda and Terry but has never experienced herself.

Everyone on the set assumed that Adolphe Menjou would be the love interest, and would finish the movie as the husband of either Rogers or Hepburn. But from the minute he appears, he functions as something else: as an excuse for a new point of view on the action. His very presence points up the frailty of the Footlights Club hierarchy. In the world "out there," Jean Maitland is not a leader; she's just an unemployed song-and-dance girl, a pawn in Powell's games. Terry Randall, with no acting experience but with money, privilege, and pretensions to high drama, is the one with authority. When Terry meets Powell, she doesn't flirt with him; she reprimands him. Hepburn has bet Eve Arden and Lucille Ball she could crash Menjou's office on a designated day before noon. The club's talented but starving actress Kaye (Andrea Leeds) is there too, to audition for Powell. When Kaye faints on being told Powell can't see her, Terry marches through the forbidden door. "By what right do you barricade yourself in here and refuse to see people? Why, the greatest actress in the world might be out there!" she says to the surprised but unruffled Powell.

Powell's relations with Jean and Terry begin to change their positions in the Footlights hierarchy and in the audience's eyes, too. Terry's telling off Powell shows that she is internalizing the club's spirit of solidarity. "Are you saying you're the greatest actress in the world?" Menjou asked her, to which Hepburn replied, "Never mind about me—I don't need you. But those other girls do." The club itself realizes this. "I hate to say it, but I'm revising my opinion of that Randall," says Lucille Ball later in the Footlights living room. On the other hand, Rogers's Jean is caught by Powell in a web of patronage that threatens to erode her populist ideals. He has her to dinner in his penthouse. There are soft music, blond padded carpets, a white piano, and a big window in back, through which we see the twinkling of the whole Manhattan skyline. The chronically impoverished Jean soaks up the atmosphere. She walks around, slightly tipsy in her evening dress. "I like it like this," she says about the city below, "all rouged and manicured and dressed up like it's going out for the evening."

La Cava and Ryskind amused themselves richly in this scene. Capitalizing on the effect created by Powell's entrance, they created a seduction routine for him full of devastating clichés. It's as if they had consulted the actresses in the Footlights band on the seducing tactics of studio moguls. Powell's butler, Harcourt (Franklin Pangborn), does a silent swoop backwards into the kitchen. Powell gives Jean his standard disclaimer. "This is Mrs. Powell," he says, pointing to a picture of a woman on the piano. "Oh, we're not divorced or anything. Lots of men who are separated from their wives simply let it be understood they're not married. I believe in this day and age that a man can have his home on the one hand and still lead his own life." He dims the lights, sits down next to Jean on the couch, and offers to make her "the greatest dancer that Broadway has ever known." He sinks to the floor by the couch and takes her hand. "I know at the office I'm gruff Anthony Powell, theatrical producer," he says. "That's a pose. Here I'm just a tired little boy, with a dream."

But with all the satiric wit in this scene, it presented a problem: how was Rogers's Jean to react? Within the club, we've seen Jean demolish people less pompous than Powell. She had even started in on him, at a distance, telling the girls that he "makes me feel like I should go home and put on a tin overcoat." And yet she needs the help Powell can give her in her profession; and, more than that, she's tempted by the luxury he's holding out to her: the feel of a fur coat, the taste of good champagne, the sensation of being in a penthouse, and the allure of a powerful, if fatuous, seducer. ("I'll be the sculptor, you'll be the clay. I'll be Pygmalion, you'll be Galatea," he intones to her.) So La Cava and Ryskind opted for a compromise: they allowed Jean some passive resistance. Befuddled with champagne, she can't quite focus on what's going on, but her instinct tells her when to get mischievous. "That's big of you," she says when Powell explains he's not divorcing his wife. She hears him say "your name in lights" and asks if the lights can be as tall as the sign that flashes outside her room at night. She nods dreamily at his "tired little boy" speech, then interrupts it to ask whether Pygmalion and Galatea ever got married. Powell, mopping his brow at this reference to entrapment, hustles her out of the apartment.

AT THIS POINT Menjou's Powell is no longer fit to be a lover; he's become too much of a symbol. With his ubiquitous presence in all facets of theater (he owns half-interest in the Club Grotto, and he's producing the play *Enchanted April,* which Kaye wants to star in), he resembles one of those fat men in a Chaplin or a Keaton movie: he has all the power and money in the world. And for Rogers's Jean, he acts as a Depression devil, tempting her away from her populist code. Menjou does up the devil aspect with a comically petulant manner and a wolfish grin. But it's Rogers's response to him that gives the movie a new twist. Heroines of this genre were supposed to be indifferent to their co-stars' money. In *Alice Adams* Hepburn doesn't give a thought, at least not directly, to Fred MacMurray's wealth; in *Mr. Deeds* Gary Cooper gets rid of his money before Jean Arthur accepts him; in *Easy Living* Arthur doesn't even know that Ray Milland is rich. But in *Stage Door* Rogers's Jean Maitland embarks on a romantic liaison with Menjou *because* of his wealth and status. It's as if the movie-makers had opened an inner documentary window on this already lifelike figure of the Depression heroine, and shown us the temptations and corruptions that really came with being poor and pretty in the big city. Moreover, Rogers manages to dramatize all this without losing our allegiance. Having learned in the Astaire series to project indecision and doubt, she makes Jean's ambivalence seem inevitable.

FILMING NOW WAS half over (it lasted from June 7 to July 29). According to Ryskind, Hepburn cornered him at this point on the set with the question "Who gets Menjou, me or Ginger?" and he had to tell her he honestly didn't know. All that was known was that the various scripts were unplayable and none of the projected denouements fit with what had been filmed. The last written attempt at an ending, dated June 28, pictured Jean forcing a marriage with Powell by smashing the pictures of the fake wife and son. This was clearly impossible, the way Rogers had drawn Jean Maitland. Her Jean was too suave in public to break anything with a hammer—and too irreverent to play a straight love scene with Powell. So, sometime after June 28, La Cava and Ryskind, in an inspired burst of invention, brought in Terry to neutralize Powell's marriage.

Terry's father, we have learned, is secretly backing *Enchanted April,* provided Powell will cast his daughter in the lead. (He wants her to fail on the stage and come home.) Powell has her to dinner. We see Hepburn in the penthouse, occupying the place of Rogers in the earlier dinner scene: a satisfying piece of symmetry. But Terry is not at all impressed with Powell's habit of mixing business with pleasure. Instead of melting into Rogers's tipsy state, Hepburn paces the floor, smoking a cigarette, acting as if she's the one in charge. Her black voile evening gown, ornamented at the collar and sleeves with bands of gold, looks like an Amazon's uniform. Menjou can hardly get her to sit on the couch. When he sinks to the floor and starts his "tired little boy" routine, Hepburn pats the couch and tells him to sit back up. She demolishes Powell's "married" pose by pointing out that the pictures of the Powell "wife" and "son" are fakes: the woman, says Hepburn's Terry, "has done a lot of posing for the face powder ads," while the boy used to advertise a certain military academy—"I know because my brother went there." Powell concedes the game at this point and shakes hands with her. "My friend," he says, "you've just ended a very, very convenient marriage."

Powell, exposed as a bachelor, was now free to marry one of the heroines. But instead of resolving the movie with a marriage, the authors turned away from romance, back to the cross-class friendship between the two girls—a highly unusual occurrence in Hollywood. Rogers reenters, bursting into the dinner scene between Hepburn and Menjou. She says she's heard he's seeing another woman; she acts outraged. Hepburn's Terry gives her cause: she sinks down to the floor and assumes a languid pose. "So it's you, my own roommate," says Rogers on seeing her, and then enacts one of her vivid moments of dashed hope, familiar from the Astaire-Rogers films, taking off the ermine cape she's borrowed from Terry, and admonishing Terry, rather plaintively, not to try to borrow anything from her.

To pull off this scene, La Cava and Ryskind had to fudge the question of just how far Jean Maitland had slid in her affair with Powell. Has Jean fallen in love with Powell, or is she just using him? We never know. They simply left that question up in the air—or, rather, they let Rogers the actress absorb the ambiguity of it, as only she could do. Rogers at this point is holding complicated contradictions within her character: she is still the Footlights' most vehement democrat, yet she is also the girl who is tempted by what Powell can offer. These very contradictions, however, only deepen our respect for the character she has created, and underline the quintessential contrast between her and Hepburn's Terry. Terry is immune to temptations like these: she doesn't need to borrow status from anyone; she has a "grandfather" in her family. She's so secure in her identity that she can do what she does here—throw over her friendship with Jean so as to break Jean of a liaison that she, Terry, perceives is no good for her. Jean, however, is vulnerable from every quarter; she's a fully drawn human.

THE DECISION TO discard the romance and concentrate on the friendship left the whole rest of the movie up for grabs. No romantic comedy had yet achieved an ending without the catharsis of a romance. According to the recollections of Hepburn and Andrea Leeds, from this point on the movie was completed by sheer instinct and improvisation. The authors improvised a climax from the subplot about Kaye (a very minor character in the play, who took poison). We see Kaye at her surprise birthday party, learning that Terry has gotten her part in *Enchanted April* and collapsing over her cake in tears. We cut to Hepburn's Terry rehearsing *Enchanted April,* trying out her entrance line, "The calla lilies are in bloom again," time after time, stopping the action every few seconds to ask about her motivation. Kaye is saintly enough to coach Terry (who still doesn't know that Kaye wanted her part) on her opening night. Then, in a tour-de-force solo that won Andrea Leeds a Best Supporting Actress nomination, Kaye walks slowly up the Footlights stairs to throw herself off the roof. (Fortunately, we don't see her jump.)

This event served to bring Jean and Terry together again for the inevitable, cathartic confrontation. Jean comes to Terry's dressing room, just before the opening-night performance, and all but accuses her of killing Kaye. Terry's coach, played by Constance Collier, tries to defend her sobbing charge. "She's not responsible for Kaye's act," says Collier. "She *is* responsible," says Rogers, with that truth-telling sternness she had made part of Jean Maitland's character. "It was Kaye's part, and Kaye's life. And now it's too late. Kaye is dead." Rogers delivers this standing completely still, her umbrella in both hands. "I dare you to go on tonight" are Jean's final words to Terry as she goes out the door.

Rogers's speech is beautifully conceived and rendered, with no extra gestures, no fake hysteria—an unbroken stream of grief sharpened by anger. The stagehands reportedly stood mute at the end of it, and one of them was heard to whisper, "Throw away those dancing shoes." Best of all, it's a statement from a character who isn't afraid to say what she really thinks.

Rogers's very concentratedness shapes the mood here, and Hepburn shows herself equal to its gravity. Without missing a beat, she takes the rising emotion Rogers has handed her and brings it out in a wave of grief. "Why didn't someone tell me!" she wails. She won't go on in the play, she vows; she will go out and tell the audience why. Constance Collier convinces her she must go on "for the theatah." Hepburn allows herself to be guided onstage, grief-stricken, and gives an affecting performance in the role she had massacred in rehearsal.

Hepburn's finest moment, though, comes not in the play but in the curtain speech Terry Randall gives at the end of the play. The speech was filmed from the back of a theater, which creates the impression of a small, brave figure speaking out to a sea of audience. It is Terry's answer to Jean's earlier words in her dressing room—and Hepburn delivers it as simply as Rogers delivered hers, restraining tears to speak. She even echoes Jean's word "responsible." "I suppose I should thank you on behalf of the company—and I know that I'm grateful for your applause," says the distant Hepburn, in the spotlight. "But I must tell you I don't deserve it. I'm not responsible for what happened on this stage tonight." As she tells the audience about Kaye's death, La Cava pans the camera over the faces of the Footlights Club girls in the audience, sharing Terry's grief. "And I hope that wherever she is, she knows, and understands—and forgives," Hepburn concludes in a diminuendo.

Hepburn received the final version of her speech, she says, scribbled on an odd scrap of paper, a few hours before it was filmed. And yet it serves as the climax of the movie. It is Terry Randall's public statement that the Footlights sisterhood, with its code of courtesy and loyalty, means more to her than success—or, rather, that her success is bound up with that code. This is the movie's clearest expression of the Depression brotherly (and sisterly) love that Hollywood was trying to propagate—here movingly—as an antidote to Depression class bitterness. And Terry's declaration of it earns back Jean's friendship. Jean comes back to Terry's dressing room after the speech. We see them in a pair of close-ups that echo their first wary close-ups in their room at the club. But now, instead of mistrust, they show affection and real respect. Terry, hearing the voice of Powell outside the dressing room, takes hold of the back of Jean's coat, as if for protection and comfort. They exit arm in arm.

THE EFFECTIVENESS of this portrait of a friendship between women lies in its offhandedness. It was not meant as a polemic: it was rooted in *Stage*

Door's cinema-verité texture. Even for a romantic comedy, the movie was remarkably full of "inside" references to the circumstances of its making and the studio it was made in. The club's maid, though white, is named Hattie, after Hattie McDaniel, Hollywood's greatest black maid, who had appeared with Hepburn in *Alice Adams.* (The maid from the play was black, and her name was Mattie.) Ginger's Jean Maitland, on borrowing Terry Randall's ermine cape, does an impromptu slow strut à la Mae West, saluting the mother of romantic-comedy heroines. The two guys from Seattle are not the "Powell" and "Milhauser" of the play; they are "Dukenfield" (after La Cava's crony W. C. Fields, whose original name was Dukenfield) and "Mill-banks" (after a powerful banker who had invested in RKO). Terry Randall's portrait of her grandfather resembles the grandfather who frowned down from the fianceé's wall in *Swing Time.* (George Stevens had directed both Hepburn's *Alice Adams* and Rogers's *Swing Time;* perhaps this grandfather was a nod to him.) The aging actress in the Footlights Club who coaches Terry Randall was played by the English ex–stage star Constance Collier, who coached Hepburn in real life. The play *Enchanted April* was named after an RKO Ann Harding movie of 1935, which flopped so hard it was a studio joke. Behind the very conception of the band of girls in the Footlights Club lay the little theater company on the RKO lot, founded and directed by Rogers's mother, Lela Rogers, to give the younger actresses theatrical training. (Lucille Ball was one of Lela's star pupils.) And we assume—we hope— that the respect Terry and Jean discover for each other at the end existed between Rogers and Hepburn in real life.

They certainly play characters closer to their real selves than in any of their movies up to this time. The problems Terry Randall struggles with when she first starts to act recall some of Hepburn's own professional messes. The setting and the situation of *Enchanted April* (English manor house; decadent younger generation) come from *The Lake,* in which Hepburn bombed on Broadway in 1935. Her entrance line in *Enchanted April* ("The calla lillies are in bloom again. Such a strange flower—suitable to any occasion") was lifted from the New York text of *The Lake.* Moreover, Hepburn's own brand of movie acting furnished at least part of the plot. La Cava told interviewers that the scene in which Terry Randall nervously disrupts *Enchanted April*'s rehearsal was drawn from real experience. "[Hepburn] was a human question mark, resolving everything through her intelligence rather than through her emotions," La Cava said. "So we just turned her own guns upon her and wrote the scene true to life."

Still, Terry Randall was not a literal portrait of Hepburn in real life; she was something much more useful to RKO—a canny metaphor for Hepburn's persona, and where it fit in the cultural climate of the thirties. *Stage Door* does what *Alice Adams* did—puts the Hepburn figure through a grueling test of character. *Stage Door*'s test is even tougher than *Alice*'s, since Terry must not only grow up, she must also succeed in *Enchanted April,* in order to vindicate those girls in the club and their lives. The pressures on Terry so closely parallel the pressures on Hepburn herself, that no one, not even the RKO bosses, could miss the message this time: Hepburn was going to make it back to stardom. In other words, *Stage Door* accomplished what it had set out to do. It rehabilitated Hepburn's career, gave her a persona that really *worked* in romantic comedy—abrasive but wistful, privileged but contrite—and established a Hepburn movie ritual that would become standard. After *Stage Door* Hepburn made four straight romantic comedies full of wit and vitality: *Bringing Up Baby* (1938), *Holiday* (1938), *The Philadelphia Story* (1940), and *Woman of the Year* (1942), all of which start by stressing Hepburn's shortcomings and end by celebrating her virtues.

BUT *STAGE DOOR* didn't really change the Hepburn persona. In fact, it sealed in the original Hepburn legend of the patrician heroine, entitled to put on airs and still be rewarded, because she's basically a good egg. Hepburn's Terry gets *all* the rewards in the end—acceptance by the Footlights Club and stardom in the theater as well. TERRY RANDALL IN ENCHANTED APRIL— FOURTH MONTH, says a theater marquee in the movie. ECCENTRIC DEBUTANTE CONTINUES TO LIVE AT THE FOOTLIGHTS CLUB, reports a newspaper. This over-stretches our ideas of plausibility. It's true we want to see Hepburn's Terry make good, as long as she's been chastised, because everyone in the story has come to like her. Still, such a triumphant fate for her would seem sentimentally imprecise were it not for Rogers's Jean Maitland receiving a fate which was, in its way, just as triumphant.

The Jean Maitland character had begun like Terry Randall, as a meta-phoric portrait of her actress's persona—a proper democrat, with a reper-toire of tart remarks that Rogers had helped make up. (When filming was over, Pandro Berman sent a telegram to Rogers in Sun Valley, wanting to know if he could "engage her for *Stage Door* after the fact, as a comedy constructionist"—the industry's name for a gag man. Rogers wired back that she was considering his offer "if you can take your scripts in letter form which might be a novelty from cuffs.") But Jean didn't stay just tart. This sharp-tongued democrat became attached, at the authors' instigation, to Tony Powell, thus taking a detour into corruption. Not only she was breaking one of Hollywood's sternest unwritten rules in any genre—that a female must pay for a premarital experiment—she was also challenging the ideology of romantic comedy. Rogers's Jean isn't sure that the true-blue honest life of the little man is such an ideal one. She wants to find out what it feels like to be rich, privileged, and slightly corrupt, if only for a while. The wonder of the movie is that she doesn't have to suffer for such an impulse. *Stage Door* lets Jean quietly make her foray into kept-womanhood and then come back unscathed, to concentrate on her career. And with that trajectory, the movie takes a romantic-comedy heroine farther in the direction of work and self-realization than any heroine had yet been taken.

We expect a Hepburn character to be singular, aloof, and dedicated to her career; we don't expect it of a Rogers character. In her Astaire movies, Rogers had always forfeited her independence at the last minute, for the sake of romance. But in *Stage Door,* she comes to see that the romance offered her is not worth the price it would exact. And so she ends up back in the Footlights Club, pursuing her career, just like Hepburn. The ambivalence of that choice, the regret it brings with it, remains with Rogers's Jean to endow *Stage Door* up to the end with its extra dimension of believability. In the final scene we see the club, four months after Kaye's death and *Enchanted April*'s opening, in a general state of hilarity. The mood switches to bittersweet: Lucille Ball is leaving, reluctantly, to marry and settle in Seattle. To get her going, Rogers and Hepburn hoist her over the threshold to a waiting cab—the reverse, for them, of being carried across a threshold by a husband. As they retreat to the living room, it is clear that they share the informal chairmanship of the house, and that they're ruefully content. "I know how she feels," says Hepburn about Lucille Ball. "Leaving here would be like leaving the house I was born in." "At least she'll have a couple of kids to keep her company in her old age," says Rogers. "What'll we have? Some broken-down memories and a couple of scrapbooks which nobody'll look at." "We're probably a different race of people," Hepburn responds. "Maybe," Rogers concedes.

One could argue that by making Anthony Powell a jerk La Cava and Ryskind had trapped themselves into keeping Jean Maitland single; that they don't deserve the credit for a daring ending that they didn't intend. But one could reply that it takes more courage and skill to change a movie in midstream, to trust the players and the logic of improvisation, than it does to follow a script. When La Cava and Ryskind realized, somewhere in the filming, that Jean couldn't possibly marry Powell; when they saw that she was the only character who could balance a chastened and yet successful Terry Randall, they gave in to it. They let Jean and Terry function at the end like a romantic comedy couple, the "parents" of the Footlights Club, who have learned tolerance, loyalty, adventurousness, and all the other populist virtues, from each other.

THE MOVIE'S FINAL MOMENTS reprise the hullabaloo of the opening. A new girl arrives, carrying a suitcase and asking "whom to see about accommodations." Rogers calls up her old boyfriend Bill. "Remember, you're a ham at heart," says Hepburn, warning her against romance. Gail Patrick comes down the stairs; Rogers cries into the phone, "Hold on, gangrene just set in!" The movie fades out on business as usual at the Footlights Club—an isolated, utopian moment in the annals of Hollywood. Two women have kept their careers to the end. On this literal level, *Stage Door* articulates a truth that was present everywhere in Hollywood yet rarely, if ever, got into the movies: that some women were happy being actresses; that actresses sometimes helped each other. Most of Hollywood's "all women" pictures (*The Women* [1939], for example) were predicated on the opposite assumption: that women want to murder other women. But *Stage Door* is not only benign, it's culturally plausible. It's the movie that captures the spirit not just of Hepburn's and Rogers's personae but of Stanwyck's, Colbert's, Arthur's, Lombard's, Dunne's. Each of these actresses created her own version of the thirties Depression heroine. All of them together left a legendary kind of defiance-cum-decency in the air. In the context of Hollywood's usual lurid morality and sentimentalization of gender, these actresses did become, through their roles, a different "race" of people.

In just a few years such heroines would be mocked, punished, and subdued in the movies, and the romantic-comedy actresses would be forced to play them. Starting in the forties (while still in their thirties), they would be cast as mothers, widows, do-gooders, or, in a savage twist, criminals. Hepburn would become the token feminist, fated to be taught humility; Rogers, the silly, dizzy dame who had to be set straight; Stanwyck, the dragon lady, obsessed with power. Colbert and Arthur would turn into self-sacrificing maternal types for a time, then retire early from the screen. But in 1937 these actresses were still playing independent, successful, eccentric, and emotionally unmaimed young women in the city—characters who were related to themselves in real life. (They had all survived the Depression to earn extraordinarily high salaries.) *Stage Door* shows us the most undiluted versions of those successful "selves" ever to appear in the movies. It is the ultimate expression of a utopian Hollywood, or at least of a mythical Hollywood that offered itself as an antidote to the Depression—that world where women could once in a while be real partners with men, and sometimes even leaders; where background, money, and pretensions mattered less than energy, inventiveness, wit, common sense, and pure dedication to the communal art of making pictures.

9

MCCAREY AND DUNNE:

THE AWFUL TRUTH

Leo McCarey,
Alexander D'Arcy,
and Irene Dunne
on the set of
The Awful Truth.

RENE DUNNE was the last actress to become a major romantic-comedy star in the thirties. Strangely enough, she was also the oldest woman to star in the genre: she was a full thirteen years older than Ginger Rogers, the youngest. But it is fitting that she should be the last. Dunne came into romantic comedy just as the genre was beginning to lose its sharp edges, to merge back into the Hollywood norm. She was the Lady among the Runaway Brides. She wasn't as abrupt and earnest as the others, but she embodied modes of compromise and independence that were different from theirs—older modes, in fact, of being romantically involved. And it wasn't only her personality that gave an extra composure to her persona; it was also the long, mostly humble career she had managed to survive before she even entered the movies—a career that probably would not have materialized if her family hadn't fallen on hard times.

Irene Dunne was born in 1898 in Louisville, Kentucky. Her early childhood was apparently idyllic: her mother, Adelaide Antoinette (Henry) Dunne, was an amateur musician; her father, Joseph John Dunne, known as Captain Dunne, was a supervisor of steamship inspection for the U.S. government but also a famous raconteur in their neighborhood, and a pied piper to children. "I was pretty proud to be the owner of such a parent," she said in a 1937 interview. But when Irene was eleven, this wonderful father died, and the family moved to Madison, Indiana, to live with grandparents. The respectable aura that surrounds Dunne's career has obscured the pain of her childhood, though she gave a hint of it in some thirties interviews, remembering—amid the predictable "race horses, darkies singing, Mary Pickford-Douglas Fairbanks movies"—childhood "vacations in Memphis with rich friends of Mother's." This suggests a kind of threadbare gentility. In Madison, Irene was a paid soloist in the church choir. After high school, she became an art and music teacher at an East Chicago high school, but she soon abandoned teaching for something she loved more, singing: she began studying at the Chicago Musical College, run by Florenz Ziegfeld, the father of the Broadway Ziegfeld. In 1920 she came to New York for an audition at the Metropolitan Opera, and failed—she was too young, too inexperienced, and too slight, they said. But she had no trouble getting a job in musical comedy, a bit part in the touring company of James Montgomery's *Irene*.

That first engagement launched her into a fairly undistinguished career in musical comedy, which lasted almost a decade. She made it to Broadway in late 1922, in a small part in the first act of *The Clinging Vine,* which starred the ingenue Peggy Wood. In 1924, she got a bigger role in the musical *Lollipop,* but only in the touring company. In 1925 she achieved a few moments of prominence on Broadway in a bit part, "representing the idle rich," said one reviewer, in Jerome Kern's *The City Chap.* In 1927, she played another minor socialite in Anne Caldwell and Raymond Hubbell's musical *Yours Truly,* and in 1928 she won a second lead in the "French cabaret" show *Luckee Girl.* Finally, in 1929, she got her big break: she landed the part of Magnolia in the national touring company of the great Ziegfeld show *Show Boat.* From that pinnacle, she was easily spotted by one of the Hollywood agents scouring the country in the days of early sound, looking for performers who could not only sing and dance but look good on the screen. Dunne signed with Pathé in 1930; and later that year, when RKO bought Pathé, her contract went to that studio.

Dunne was thirty-one when she came to Hollywood. If her slow rise in the musical theater had cost her time in the movies, it had also given her the skills—patience and ingenuity—to ride out the shifts in taste that would constantly threaten her career in the volatile early talkies. RKO cast her first in a musical, *Leathernecking* (a version of Rodgers and Hart's *Present Arms*). But the movie public rejected musicals in 1930, so all the songs were taken out of *Leathernecking.* It bombed. Rather than give up on Hollywood, Dunne went for the biggest plum on the RKO lot, the role of Sabra Cravat in *Cimarron* (1931). She got it, because she showed in the screen test that she knew how to use makeup to simulate Sabra's aging from young pioneer bride to grandmother. *Cimarron,* that pious, ungainly blockbuster, won an Academy Award for Best Picture and secured Irene Dunne's entry into the pious genre of the moment, the weepers. Dunne stayed in weepers while they were popular; the high point of this part of her career was her role in John Stahl's classic 1932 weeper, *Back Street.* And when the weepers began to wane and weeper stars to founder, Dunne adroitly bailed herself out by returning to her old genre, musical comedy. In 1935 she did *Sweet Adeline* at Warner Bros. and *Roberta* (with Astaire and Rogers) at RKO; and after a detour for one more big-budget weeper, Universal's *Magnificent Obsession* (1935), she landed the plum musical role of 1936, Magnolia in Universal's big production of *Show Boat.* It was *her* role, after all: besides having played it in the stage show, she had grown up on a river herself, with a riverboat man for a father.

The key point in Dunne's career, though, came not when she landed the role in *Show Boat* but shortly before that, when she rearranged her contractual relations with RKO. Buoyed by her successful transition from weepers to musicals, Dunne decided in 1935 to abandon her exclusive contract with RKO and go out on her own to free-lance—which meant that she allied herself with three studios at once, RKO, Paramount, and Columbia (this last arrangement was for a three-picture deal, one per year). Actors such as Fredric March and Ronald Colman had already gone free-lance in this fashion, but few actresses had done it, since free-lancing didn't offer the security of a weekly paycheck. In 1935, Stanwyck was forced into free-lancing when RKO decided to split her contract with Fox. Dunne voluntarily risked it—and reaped the rewards. It was through free-lancing that she broke into a third movie genre, the one that would make her a big star: romantic comedy. While RKO was wracking its brains trying to drum up melodramas for her and Paramount was trying to fit her into musicals, Columbia offered her the lead in a frothy tale of screwball romance, *Theodora Goes Wild*. Columbia's impulse was not farfetched: even in her weeper roles, Irene Dunne had sometimes displayed a roguish gleam in her eye. In the 1936 *Show Boat* Dunne had let loose and trucked around the stage while Hattie McDaniel sang "Can't Help Lovin' Dat Man." Dunne, though, didn't think this wild part of herself was appropriate for the movies. She went on a vacation to Europe with her husband to avoid doing *Theodora*. When she came back and Columbia still pressed the role on her, she gave in. "Columbia is for untyping people," Irene Dunne said in an interview (with Regina Crewe of the New York *Journal American*) in 1937. "It changed Gable from a heavy to a comedian in *It Happened One Night*. It changed Jean Arthur from a marshmallowy ingenue to a hard-boiled wise-cracker in *The Whole Town's Talking.*" And it changed Irene Dunne herself from the gallant lady who could also sing into one of the broadest of Hollywood comediennes.

THEODORA GOES WILD, based on a magazine story, concerns a spinster authoress who writes an off-color best-seller, comes to the city, and learns, with the sometime encouragement of her illustrator, Melvyn Douglas, about big-city fun. The movie gave Dunne the chance to parade around the screen in a series of extravagant costumes—elaborate tunic-creations and cascades of feathers—that mocked the grand lady costumes by Adrian at MGM. She did not become a big star in *Theodora*: the movie didn't dazzle the critics. (It didn't have a resonant Depression parable at the heart of it.) But she did show audiences the delicious, witty, and mildly naughty appetite for life she could project onto the screen. And even more important, she associated herself in the audience's mind with that other roguish lady of comedy, Myrna Loy. It happened that *Theodora Goes Wild* was released two weeks after the MGM comedy hit *Libeled Lady* with Loy, William Powell, Spencer Tracy, and Jean Harlow. Whether by coincidence or design, both movies featured nearly identical trout-fishing scenes, in which the impeccably sporty hero and heroine get tangled up in fishing lines and running water. (Hemingway's vision of socially upscale, sportsmanlike romance had "disintegrated" to these slapstick scenes.)

And because Irene Dunne demonstrated in *Theodora* that she could be funny and still imperturbable, she joined Myrna Loy in a category that the MGM actress had occupied alone up till then, the lady-comedienne—thus making this figure available to comedy-trained directors who would never set foot in the MGM factory. As it happened, one of those directors, Leo McCarey, had just quarreled with his home studio, Paramount, and sought refuge at Columbia. In 1937 Harry Cohn allowed McCarey to make a free-form comedy based on an old play, *The Awful Truth*—which Cohn promised not to interfere with. He also gave McCarey Irene Dunne as a leading lady. The encounter between Dunne and McCarey, on the set of *The Awful Truth*, would send romantic comedy off in yet another direction.

LEO MCCAREY WAS, by temperament and upbringing, as unexpected a combination of the raucous and the genteel as Irene Dunne. McCarey's father, Tom McCarey, had come out to the dry climate of Los Angeles from Edwardsville, Illinois, following the death of his mother from tuberculosis. McCarey senior had then worked his way up from the laundry business to become "Uncle Tom" McCarey, boxing promoter and proprietor of the Vernon Fight Arena at Alameda and Main in downtown Los Angeles. But if Pop McCarey made his living in the rough world of western boxing, at home he presided over a respectable, upwardly mobile family. He had married a pretty brunette he had met in church, Leona Mistral, who was from the French Pyrenees; and they had produced three children—Leo, born in 1898 and named after his mother, followed by Ray and Gertrude. In *The Name Above the Title*, Frank Capra writes about the ragtag "Newsboys' Shoe Contests" at Pop McCarey's arena, in which newsboys raced to retrieve their shoes from a big pile. He, the urchin, took part in them, but Leo, the proprietor's son, was forbidden to attend. (Capra says McCarey assured him that he and Ray sneaked in anyway.) Pop McCarey cherished high hopes for his children. He wanted Leo to become a lawyer. He made a point of returning the children's letters to him with the incorrect grammar red-penciled. In the interests of his children, McCarey senior himself moved to a more respectable occupation in 1910. He sold his arena to Jack Doyle—it became the famous Doyle's, where young movie-rich swells like Charlie Chaplin and Fatty Arbuckle bet their salaries—and bought a liquor store in Culver City. Leo helped him out in the store after school.

None of the poverty and rootlessness of Capra's, Stevens's, or La Cava's childhood intruded on McCarey's. By high school he had grown into a tall, handsome black-haired Irishman—a good athlete and a good student—who seemed to be on the way to fulfilling all his father's expectations for him. He went to USC law school, graduated, and set up a private law practice. In 1920 he married his high-school sweetheart, the blue-eyed Stella Martin. In a photo from the time of their engagement they look as new-minted as Scott and Zelda Fitzgerald—both of them in bathing suits, squinting into the sun, the tall, dark-haired, athletic young man and the small, blond, strangely reticent-looking young woman. But Leo McCarey cherished interests that weren't part of his father's plans for him. He played the piano, and he secretly longed to be a songwriter. He wrote songs with a friend all through high school, and he always liked to tell about their aborted first sale of a song, which was called "When the Eagle Flaps His Wings and Calls on the Kaiser." It was 1918; they were celebrating the sale in a bar when suddenly they realized that the wild shouting and cheering outside was the Armistice: the song was obsolete.

McCarey also dreamed about the movies, a world contiguous to Tin Pan Alley. He knew any number of movie people who bought their liquor at his father's store—and in 1920 he finally went against his father's wishes, quit his law practice, and got a job as a third assistant to director Tod Browning on the movie *The Virgin of Stamboul*. (Browning was later to direct the cult classics *Dracula*, 1931, and *Freaks*, 1932.) When his job with Browning was over, McCarey found his way, sometime in 1923, to the Hal Roach comedy studios, also in Culver City. He worked for Roach from 1923 to 1929, starting as a director and rapidly moving up to be a production supervisor, which meant producing, writing, devising gags, and pinch-hit directing all at once. Most movie scholars credit McCarey with matching the skinny, brush-haired English comedian Stan Laurel with the hefty, dimpled American comedian Oliver Hardy, to make Roach's famous Laurel and Hardy team. McCarey, along with Stan Laurel himself, was certainly the mastermind behind the Laurel and Hardy duets between two kinds of infantile befuddlement—duets that always tipped into aggression and caused destruction of property on a scale that hadn't been seen since Mack

Sennett's early comedy shorts. For Roach, McCarey engineered what was essentially a late-twenties revival of teens-style silent comedy.

When McCarey chose to leave Roach in 1929 with the coming of sound, the range of his experience, more extensive than that of the other romantic-comedy directors', all but guaranteed a smooth transition into mainstream talkies. Between 1929 and 1932 McCarey worked at Pathé, Paramount, Fox, and United Artists. He directed, among other pictures, a musical (*Red Hot Rhythm* [1929]), a flaming youth drama (*Wild Company* [1930]), and a marital comedy (*Part Time Wife* [1930]). But in 1932 he began to slip back into a slot in pure comedy. In 1932 Sam Goldwyn got him to direct an Eddie Cantor vehicle, *The Kid from Spain*. Between 1933 and 1936 he made comedies at Paramount: a Marx Brothers picture in 1933 *(Duck Soup)*; a Mae West picture in 1934 *(Belle of the Nineties)*; and a movie co-starring George Burns, Gracie Allen, Alison Skipworth, and W. C. Fields, also in 1934 *(Six of a Kind)*. He even turned the histrionic Charles Laughton into a sympathetic clown in the wonderful and odd *Ruggles of Red Gap* (1935).

But there were signs along the way that McCarey was unhappy doing only comedy. He refused at first to direct *Duck Soup,* probably because the fevered Marx Brothers didn't take direction, but Paramount pressured him into it. While making *Belle of the Nineties,* McCarey caused a small scandal at Paramount by "wasting" whole days on the set playing the piano with the Duke Ellington orchestra, which was providing the soundtrack. (Faced with a crisis at the end of filming, the Duke made up the last song arrangement in his head and hummed the parts to the members of his band; the number was composed and filmed in an afternoon.) Paramount finally pushed McCarey too far when it insisted that he preside over one of the last appearances of the outdated silent comic Harold Lloyd, in the 1936 *The Milky Way*. McCarey made *The Milky Way,* but he suffered a freak crisis before it was finished. The cast had indulged in the habit of drinking milk during filming, for good luck. McCarey drank the milk of a contaminated cow and was taken off the set in an ambulance, a victim of the rare disease called "milk fever" or "Malta fever." Around this time, Tom McCarey, with whom Leo had been very close, died of a heart attack. Recovering from the fever and mourning his father at the same time, McCarey looked hard at his own life and work.

He had noticed the success of his former colleagues from the comedy studios. Capra, who had been a lowly gag writer at the Roach studios while McCarey was production supervisor, was now the toast of Hollywood, with his own unit at Columbia, turning out his own kind of romantic comedies. George Stevens, who had been a cameraman under McCarey, was making personalized romantic comedies at RKO. La Cava, who was McCarey's friend, got better assignments than he did at his own home lot, Paramount, even though La Cava free-lanced. And the director whom McCarey admired above all others, Ernst Lubitsch, had abandoned his own continental style of romantic comedy to embrace Capra's formula: now Paramount's head of production, he was encouraging his directors to follow in Capra's footsteps. That McCarey wanted to be a Depression comedy auteur like his colleagues is clear from the Capraesque slant of his 1935 *Ruggles of Red Gap.* It's the story, told in improvisatory soufflé style, of how the American frontier liberates an English butler from class subservience. But *Ruggles* didn't contain enough of the ingredient by which comedy directors gained mainstream status in the Depression—romance. Upon returning to Paramount after his illness and his father's death, McCarey abrogated his contract and started again with a deal to make only those pictures "in which he saw distinct possibilities." And then he shot his first Depression picture, *Make Way for Tomorrow.*

MAKE WAY FOR TOMORROW is like *Stage Door:* it's a peculiar twist on the basic romantic-comedy formula. Also like *Stage Door, Make Way for Tomorrow* acquired its romantic-comedy features in the course of its filming. In its early stages *Make Way* had nothing to do with either romance or comedy. It was based on a bleak and accusatory 1934 novel by newspaperwoman Josephine Lawrence, *The Years Are So Long,* about the trials of an impoverished old couple in pre–social security days. McCarey and his new scriptwriting team, a husband and wife named Delmar who wrote under the wife's name, Viña Delmar, began the movie exactly like the novel, with old Barkley and Lucy Cooper informing their four grown children that they've lost the mortgage on their house and have nowhere to go. None of the children is rich; they decide to separate their parents and rotate them. Life is awful for the old people, with Lucy living in the cramped city apartment of her social-climbing son, Bark in the chilly country home of their hypochondriac daughter. The movie turns a sharper ear than the novel's onto the dialogue, and a keener sense of drama onto the encounters among the characters. McCarey invented the episode of a long-distance phone call from husband to wife, which Lucy Cooper takes in the middle of a chic bridge game in her son's living room: her flat, slightly deaf voice trying to say intimate things in public communicates utter despair. In the lead roles, McCarey cast two of Hollywood's best character actors, who fleshed out these rather doctrinaire figures from the novel. The forty-five-year-old Beulah Bondi, who specialized in much older women, played Lucy Cooper as an intimidated but fair-minded old lady. Victor Moore, the comedian who had come from Broadway in 1935 to play Pop in *Swing Time,* made Bark a mischievous and contrary old man.

In the midst of this bleak story, even bleaker at the end, when the children decide to send Bark to California and keep Lucy in the East, the movie suddenly opens into a sequence of unexpected magic. The old people rendezvous in New York for the departure of Bark's train. As they wander about to pass the little time they've got, they run into a streak of good fortune. A car dealer invites them into his showroom and gives them a demonstration ride in a new car. He drops them off at the swank Fifth Avenue hotel where they spent their honeymoon. When they inform the desk clerk of this fact, the hotel adopts them: the bartender serves them Old Fashioneds; the manager offers them a free dinner; the orchestra leader interrupts his rumba to play a waltz—"Let Me Call You Sweetheart"—while the younger guests beam. The novel had set this last interlude in Newark and had made Bark and Lucy visit tenement rooming houses and eat in a greasy spoon. McCarey turned seedy Newark into high-class New York, evoking the element of Depression fantasy.

But the big-city fairy tale wasn't added to the story merely to spare the audience more pain. McCarey was interested in what happened between Lucy and Bark when they found themselves in what he saw as the kindly atmosphere of a luxury hotel. They recreate their own courtship, in a love scene that recalls the words and manners of half a century earlier. Bark tests Lucy's sobriety by having her recite a tongue-twister; they argue gently about whether they married on a Thursday or a Wednesday. But it's not what they say that sets the tone of the scene; it's their grave and tender courtesy toward each other. This hotel bar scene corresponds to the "getting to know you" scene in a Capra romantic comedy, only here the lovers are not looking forward to a marriage, they're looking back on one. The conventional romantic-comedy formula has been inverted. Instead of young adults embracing unexpected intimacy and then trying to find the psychic strength to sustain it, the two old people, their strength ebbing, are saying goodbye to intimacy. In the midst of their dinner, the Coopers telephone their ungrateful children to say that they will not attend the planned family dinner uptown; they'll stay together downtown, just the two of them. The way things have been going, the audience is ready to cheer when old Bark and Lucy decide to be lovers instead of parents. But McCarey has made it seem inevitable. As the time for Bark's train draws nearer, it's the prospect of space widening between the old married pair that seems to pull them back in time, to the beginning of their romance. Before he boards the train, Bark Cooper says a final word to this stranger he has rediscovered in his wife: "If I should never see you again, you're the nicest person I ever met, Miss Breckenridge." The movie ends as the train starts out of the station, the lighted windows slipping past Lucy Cooper's ravaged face as the reprise of "Let Me Call You Sweetheart" comes up on the sound-track.

IT SEEMS CURIOUS that a thirty-nine-year-old director would choose to imagine a romance between lovers in their seventies. But this movie not only marked McCarey's bid for seriousness as a director, it also commemorated the loss of his father. "I made the movie right after he [his father] died," he said in later interviews about *Make Way for Tomorrow*, "and we were real good friends." The lighted train passing out of the screen provides a visual metaphor for death, more stirring than a funeral or graveside scene. And the eloquent close-up of Lucy's face is a testimony to all the lone survivors of long marriages. In real life, Leo's mother, Leona McCarey, outlived her husband and moved in with her son. *Make Way for Tomorrow* can be seen as a reverie about what might have happened to the senior McCareys if they hadn't had a prosperous, movie-director son. But it was primarily a celebration of the continually spontaneous and tolerant kind of intimacy marriage can bring—viewed backwards, from the end of the story, instead of forwards, from the beginning.

Make Way for Tomorrow (1937) is one of those movies that both vindicate and condemn the Hollywood studio system, an experiment by a respected director who overrode his studio's advice and appealed to the public's broadmindedness—and who ended up disappointed. *Make Way* flopped at the box office, a fact for which McCarey blamed Paramount. The mood at that studio was edgy in late 1936, when the movie was filmed. Lubitsch had recently stepped down as head of production. Adolph Zukor, who had reassumed control of the studio, visited the set of *Make Way* constantly, trying to persuade McCarey to give it a happy ending. When McCarey refused, Paramount responded by downplaying the movie's publicity campaign, releasing it without fanfare. So after he'd finished the movie, which remained his favorite despite its halfhearted reception, McCarey sorrowfully left Paramount, where he'd been on contract for seven years, and hired himself out to Columbia for a one-picture deal.

The new picture Columbia handed him, *The Awful Truth,* seemed to belong on the other side of the emotional spectrum from *Make Way for Tomorrow.* The studio intended it to be a simple farce about divorce and remarriage—and McCarey, still smarting from the reception of *Make Way,* thought he was going to make it just that. But *Make Way* had changed him. He had learned how to draw from his own experience, and he had discovered that a major part of that experience consisted of being married. At this point his marriage with Stella, the wife of his youth, was sixteen years old; and it would last for the rest of his life. He had put his own marriage as well as that of his parents into *Make Way for Tomorrow*, and he would draw on it again for *The Awful Truth*. Whether McCarey intended this or not, *The Awful Truth* became a sequel to *Make Way for Tomorrow*.

The Warriners of *The Awful Truth* are the age of the grown-up children in *Make Way for Tomorrow*, although they belong to a much more prosperous milieu than the Coopers: the banking world of New York. This makes them as wealthy, in their way, as a successful Hollywood couple like the McCareys. If the earlier film had looked at the naive romance of humble oldsters who resembled McCarey's parents, the later film looks at a complicated romance between sophisticates who resemble McCarey and his wife. "What pleases me most [about *The Awful Truth*]," said McCarey in an interview he gave late in life to *Cahiers du Cinéma*, "is that it told, somewhat, the story of my life. (Don't repeat that; my wife will want to kill me. . . .)" And in McCarey's construction of a high-class, slapstick movie version of his own story, the presence of Irene Dunne was crucial.

According to Dunne, she and McCarey hit it off famously when they met at Columbia. They were about the same age; both were half-Irish; both had a lively sense of humor; both were Roman Catholic and Republican; both of them, in short, put a lot of emphasis on living well within traditional boundaries. Irene Dunne belonged, like McCarey, to one of Hollywood's rare long-term married couples. She had married her husband, Edward Dennis Griffin, a New York dentist, in 1927, while she was still an aspiring musical-comedy actress. When Dunne went to Hollywood in 1930, Griffin stayed in New York and commuted to see his wife; then in 1935 he joined her in California. On weekends, when Irene Dunne wasn't at the studio, the Griffins lived a conventionally prosperous life at their Beverly Hills home. They entertained friends from outside the movie business, and in 1936 they adopted a one-year-old baby girl, Mary Frances. (The McCareys also had a young daughter, Mary Virginia.) Dunne had chosen to define her private self, unlike the other romantic-comedy stars, away from her profession—as an enlightened society wife rather than as a movie star. It is true that Dunne's idea of marriage included more autonomy for the wife than most people's did—she commanded a large income of her own, and she had lived apart from her husband for almost six years—but it was still a marriage, not some kind of bohemian arrangement. This air of upper-class wifeliness was what allowed McCarey to idealize Dunne. Within their re-

spectable lives, both McCarey and Dunne cultivated a surface roguish-
ness. But at bottom, they both believed in a sleek, country-club, *married*
existence. It was their double affinity, of surface and depths, projected
onto the situation of the original *The Awful Truth,* that brought a new set
of assumptions about class, and therefore about gender, into romantic
comedy.

THE AWFUL TRUTH began as a 1921 Broadway drawing-room comedy
about marriage and divorce, written by an American dramatist, Arthur
Richman, whom *Vogue* at the time called "a fresh, polished and perhaps not
very important talent." The subject of the play was anything but fresh,
though, since plays dealing with divorce had been current in both British
and American theater since Pinero's *The Second Mrs. Tanqueray* in 1893.
And the tone of this one was more pompous than witty. "Oh, darling, I
was a brute!" says Norman Satterly to his young ex-wife, Lucy Warriner.
Then he adds wistfully, "Can a building, once destroyed, ever be put together as it originally stood? Brick by brick, room by room, the same doors
and windows?" *The Awful Truth* did well on Broadway in 1921, however,
probably because its situation was so simple and self-contained: the divorced
lady, seeking to remarry, needs to have her name cleared by her ex-husband.
She gets in touch with him, only to find herself falling in love with him
again—so she rejects the fiancé and remarries her former husband. Besides
a straightforward dramatic equation, the play benefited from the dazzling
comedy technique of its star, Ina Claire. It became so popular that Hollywood filmed it twice before the Depression, once as a silent film in 1925,
starring Agnes Ayres, and then as an early talking film of 1929, starring Ina
Claire herself. In 1935 Harry Cohn, on a shrewd impulse, bought the
property from RKO-Pathé.

When Cohn began to prepare *The Awful Truth* for filming in early 1937,
he gave Dwight Taylor, the gifted son of the actress Laurette Taylor, the
task of updating the old chestnut. This was logical: Taylor was known as
a specialist in farcical divorce, having written the play that became *The Gay
Divorcee,* as well as the script of the Astaire-Rogers *Top Hat.* First off, Taylor
did Columbia the service of changing the husband's name from Norman
Satterly to Jerry Warriner. Then, to counter the prissiness of the play, he
added some screwball humor of his own and some disillusioned "crackup"
sensibility which he seems to have borrowed from his contemporary F. Scott
Fitzgerald. He made the marriage in his *The Awful Truth* a comedy version
of the marriage that fell apart so bitterly in Fitzgerald's 1934 novel, *Tender
Is the Night.* Dwight Taylor's Jerry Warriner, like Fitzgerald's Dick Diver,

is prone to violence. He gives Lucy a black eye when they fight over their common property, which in this early Taylor script was a good-luck necklace with an elephant charm, not the little dog of the actual movie. "His address is 49 East Forty-ninth Street," Lucy tells the judge, "but he lives at the Ritz bar." Actually, in Taylor's script Jerry spends most of his time in a fantasy location—a jail that looks like an athletic club, where Wall Street divorcés live voluntarily "so their wives won't get their money." After many mishaps, in which it grows apparent that Warriner is falling apart, he accompanies Lucy to the auction of their former home. The visit calls up so many memories that they are compelled to remarry.

Dwight Taylor's sour-minded script was only the beginning of the alterations Columbia performed on *The Awful Truth*. At various times in the script's history, it was given to staff writers Mary McCall, Jr., and Sidney Buchman, as well as to free-lancers Dorothy Parker and her husband, Alan Campbell. Ralph Bellamy, who played the second lead, liked to tell anecdotes about all these writers working separately but simultaneously on the *Awful Truth* script, and he also implies in his autobiography *(When the Smoke Hit the Fan)* that when shooting began in June 1937, nothing had come together and there was virtually no script. The leads, Irene Dunne and Cary Grant, have corroborated Bellamy's impression, remembering that McCarey used to bring them speeches on bits of brown paper and that he seemed to have no system in the shooting of the movie. The very first day, according to Bellamy, McCarey filmed the famous scene of Bellamy trying to sing a duet of "Home on the Range" with Irene Dunne, which falls chronologically in the middle of the picture.

But this view of things is not quite accurate. There *was* a script, and it was written by McCarey himself, in collaboration with his favorite scriptwriter—or, rather, scriptwriters—the Delmars, who still called themselves Viña Delmar. McCarey sometimes told about how he had picked up a pretty woman at the gaming tables in Palm Springs just before he began *Make Way for Tomorrow,* and it turned out to be Viña Delmar. Whether or not this is true, McCarey did use the Delmars, who were primarily book and magazine writers, authors of many popular books, including the 1929 best-seller *Bad Girl,* as his main script collaborators on both *Make Way for Tomorrow* and *The Awful Truth*. But on both scripts the Delmars set conditions that were odd in the movie industry. They stipulated that the work had to be done in their home. They refused to visit a studio office, appear on a set, or meet the actors—a fact that explains why none of the actors knew about them. McCarey came to their house to work, first on *Make Way for Tomorrow,* then on *The Awful Truth*.

"The scene is us working for Leo in our Beverly Hills living room," recalled Viña Delmar.

We talked about the race track, politics, restaurants, and everything else. Leo did not believe in hammering persistently on any one subject. We swung back and forth to the subject at hand. Leo would suggest a scene, which drew no insistent merriment from his two listeners. He would then say something like "Okay, okay. Just don't tell anyone what I said just now." If we greeted another idea with honest laughter he was as happy as could be. When we introduced an idea that did not appeal to him, he was apologetic. Nice man, that Leo McCarey.

THE RESULTS of this collaboration emerged as a finished script on June 15, 1937, six days before actual shooting began on June 21. It contains the basic architecture of the movie: the scenes in approximate order as they would appear on the screen. The existence of such a script proves that McCarey didn't entirely improvise the movie. But many of the freshest, most surprising lines in the finished movie don't appear in the Delmar-McCarey script. (This is true of *Make Way for Tomorrow* as well.) McCarey made up these lines, and the comic business to go with them, in the course of filming *The Awful Truth,* with the help of his actors, whom he actively consulted. It was, of course, a feature of romantic comedy's methodology to collaborate with actors; but McCarey probably depended on his more than other directors—especially with a property like *The Awful Truth,* which did not provide a succession of events, merely a suggestive situation. McCarey used this situation as an excuse to put the actors onto the screen unrehearsed, almost unprepared. He liked to see them in a state of semibewilderment. In the case of Irene Dunne, McCarey's personality proved so congenial to her that she had no trouble putting herself in his hands, despite the apparent disorder of those first few days of filming. Not so *The Awful Truth*'s leading man, Cary Grant, who had just left Paramount and partially contracted himself to Columbia, and who had been gently forced into this movie by Harry Cohn. McCarey's lackadaisical methods so unnerved Grant that he offered to buy himself out of the picture by paying Cohn five thousand dollars to cover expenses—an offer he was talked out of.

It's not surprising that Grant was afraid of Leo McCarey's methods. He had spent most of his time in Hollywood in the big assembly-line studio of Paramount, playing romantic leading men with a sense of humor so subtle as to be almost invisible. Paramount had used him to throw a neutral, manly light on the stars of his pictures—Nancy Carroll, Sylvia Sidney, Charles Laughton (in the 1932 submarine melodrama *The Devil and the Deep*), and, notoriously, Mae West, who picked him herself to support her in *She Done Him Wrong* and *I'm No Angel*. But for most of the decade, Grant was not himself a star who could call his own shots; he was only a featured player who came onto the set and did what he was told.

The first glimmerings of something interesting in Grant's persona emerged when he was lent to RKO to play the cockney con man in George Cukor and Katharine Hepburn's 1936 *Sylvia Scarlett*—a role that didn't run against the grain of Cary Grant as much as one would suppose. Grant, born Archibald Leach, had come from a troubled English family. He had run away from his grocer father in Bristol with a boys' acrobatics troupe at age thirteen. Cukor had caught a glimpse of this more complicated Cary Grant under the skin of Paramount's dinner-jacketed hunk, a Grant who alternated boyish goofiness with a faintly terrifying courtly opacity. That's the character Cukor put on the screen, and therefore introduced into the industry. (It's not for nothing that both George Stevens and Alfred Hitchcock later cast him as a suspected crook.) By the time he got to McCarey, Grant had already left Paramount and done one free-lance role as the urbane George Kirby in *Topper,* Norman McLeod and Hal Roach's 1937 comedy. *Topper* had shown him his tone—the suggestion of powerful mirth sheathed in a faintly bemused manner. But *The Awful Truth* needed more from Grant than *Topper:* it put him at the center of the movie's emotions. That's where Leo McCarey helped him out—probably, for the most part, unconsciously.

If McCarey had seen in Irene Dunne his ideal of a wife, in Cary Grant he might have recognized a less-than-ideal husband to go with that wife— someone like himself, a happily married philanderer. (McCarey was known in Hollywood for his lady-killing tendencies.) Both men were tall and strikingly dark-haired. McCarey later went so far as to describe himself in interviews as a "bargain-basement edition of Cary Grant." And Cary Grant's dazzling energy on the screen, an energy that seemed to repel emotion, might have helped McCarey gloss over the movie husband's culpability in the story. At any rate, after Grant relaxed and settled down on *The Awful Truth,* McCarey and Grant together would construct the Cary Grant persona as we know it—the American husband/lover so detached as to seem slightly alarming to us today, whose only means of serious communication lay in mocking himself and others, whose good intentions had to be imagined, deciphered, and eventually coaxed out, but whose physical beauty and comic power were undeniable. Cary Grant turned out to be the wild card in *The Awful Truth*. Pairing this elegant and cruelly funny gentleman with the mischievous, impenetrable lady who was Irene Dunne, McCarey would sketch a portrait, perhaps even more revealing than he meant it to be, of the dynamic of the well-to-do American marriage.

THE MOVIE'S VERY FIRST SHOT signals "well-to-do." It's a splendid skyline of New York, but it's not the New York the audience had been used to from the gangster movies and the weepers, from romantic comedies such as *Swing Time* or *My Man Godfrey,* or even from McCarey's own *Make Way for Tomorrow*—a New York that contained the drama of great social contrasts. This is the East River panorama, the New York that doesn't suggest even a hint of Depression poverty. The first scene is set in a posh athletic club, where we see Cary Grant as Jerry Warriner getting tan under a sun lamp, explaining to a buddy that he is trying to look as if he's been in Florida for the past two weeks, to avoid "embarrassing" his wife. The movie has jumped right into its essential subject—a marriage that seems placid on the surface but has lost its emotional core. Grant's Jerry Warriner then goes home to his gleaming apartment, trailing two athletic-club buddies and their dates, to cover for him in front of his wife, only to find that the tables have been turned on him: his wife's not only out, she hasn't been home all night. What's more, she comes in while the guests are still there, wearing a feathery white evening dress and followed by her singing teacher, Armand Duval, in dinner clothes (played by Alexander D'Arcy and named after the hero of *Camille*)—his car, she says, broke down the previous evening, so they were forced to spend the night in the "nastiest little inn."

Grant's Jerry Warriner is all polite irony during this explanation; Dunne's Lucy Warriner is all mischievous innocence. No wonder they can't talk to each other. And after the guests melt away, their miscommunication escalates: Jerry objects to Lucy's "timeworn story"; Lucy tosses him one of his "Florida" oranges that is stamped "California"; Jerry sounds the chorus of the movie, "There can't be any doubts in marriage"; and Lucy picks up the phone to call their lawyer. In the movie's first ten minutes they've agreed to divorce.

We seem to have strayed far away from Capra's Depression parables, with their auto courts and forgotten men, their heroines spiritedly enduring solitude, into an Ernst Lubitsch world of marriage troubles among the smart set. In the twenties and early thirties, Lubitsch had perfected the Hollywood sex comedy, adapted from Eastern European farce, in which prosperous marriages mired in boredom were put back on track. Lubitsch was McCarey's admired friend and mentor at Paramount—and *The Awful Truth,* though it was made after McCarey left Paramount, is as close as McCarey ever came to making a Lubitsch movie. Its New York seems the equivalent of Lubitsch's chic movie Paris and Vienna, and its farcical mixups among couples display the formal choreography, the deadpan duos, trios, and quartets that Lubitsch loved to put on the screen.

And yet, for all its Lubitschean flavor, *The Awful Truth* contains more affinities with Capra's brand of romantic comedy than with Lubitsch's. The standoff between the leading players is not an elaborate Lubitschean game of flirtation; it is more of a Capraesque contest between two proud individuals who don't know how to communicate. McCarey underlines the Warriners' inadequacy by giving them a pet dog, "Mr. Smith," who is more emotionally articulate than they are. Mr. Smith, a last-minute inspiration of McCarey's (he doesn't appear in the Delmars' script), is a tribute, at least in part, to the *Thin Man* series at MGM—another clue that McCarey thought of the Warriners as more "American" than "continental." (Mr. Smith is played by the canine actor Asta, who was Myrna Loy and William Powell's fox terrier in those movies.) But this little dog has a more important function in *The Awful Truth* than to remind audiences of *The Thin Man:* he symbolizes the residue of feelings left in this marriage. When he is brought to the courtroom to help the judge decide which Warriner gets custody of him, McCarey's long close-up on his eager but bewildered fox-terrier face, looking back and forth from Grant to Dunne, shows us the longing they can't show each other. Lubitsch would never have given a dog such a role—his characters were too comically eloquent by themselves. Jerry and Lucy, however, constantly demonstrate that Capraesque failing of not being able to talk about, or possibly even feel, the love that brought them together. A dog has to remind them of it.

Irene Dunne's Lucy Warriner is also more Capraesque than Lubitschean. She's not adorable in the manner of Lubitsch's Jeanette MacDonald, nor is she intent on learning, as MacDonald always was in Lubitsch movies, how to be seductive in a well-mannered style. Her pride means much more to her than her seductiveness. And now that she's divorced, that pride is very much at stake. We see her playing distractedly in her apartment with Mr. Smith, because she doesn't want to go out without an escort: here she is the Capraesque female on her own, more knowing about emotions than her husband, and more honest. Jerry was lying about his trip to Florida—we're told so in the first scene—so we assume that Lucy was telling the truth about being caught out all night with her singing teacher.

.   .   .

Cary Grant and
Irene Dunne in
The Awful Truth.

AND YET, though she fits into the Capra tradition, Irene Dunne's Lucy Warriner also brings a new tone to the romantic-comedy heroine. She may be on her own, but she hasn't been deprived of material resources like the romantic comedy heroines before her. Lucy is not a Paramount working woman trying to get her due in the world; she's not even a Capraesque heiress temporarily demoted to waifdom. It would have been easy for McCarey, in the course of the many script revisions of *The Awful Truth,* to make her poor, or fearful, or even defiant after her separation. But instead of dwelling on Lucy's disadvantages, McCarey decided that she should be as equal as possible to her husband, in circumstance, wealth, and moral status. Both Warriners have committed "sins," which, even if one is real and the other only suspected, appear to be symmetrical. (We never find out for sure whether Lucy was lying.) After their separation, they maintain equivalent standards of living. Lucy keeps their splendid apartment, bringing in Aunt Patsy (actress Cecil Cunningham) to live with her instead of her husband. Jerry takes another splendid apartment. Lucy doesn't have to go to work. Jerry doesn't appear to go to work either. Both possess a variety of chic clothes (Dunne's hats in this movie are especially noteworthy), and both exhibit a sharp wit. It's as if McCarey had set himself the exercise of creating a female character with the same privileges, the same firm sense of self, as a man, and then engaged her in battle with her "twin."

But in raising the social level of the heroine, McCarey has also sacrificed some of the genre's expressiveness. Lucy's socialite dignity prevents her from showing vulnerability, not just to her husband but to the audience as well. Jerry's athletic-club guests in the opening scene can't embarrass her, nor does the divorce appear to hurt her much—at least not in ways that she will reveal. And since the heroine's vulnerability usually served as a barometer of emotions within romantic comedy, this movie early on acquires a kind of rigidity. Dunne and Grant both play with a glittery vitality and an infectious spontaneity, but without any of the diminuendos that would suggest the tenderness that is supposed to be part of the Warriners' past.

When Jerry comes to call on an evening soon after their separation, ostensibly to visit Mr. Smith, he finds Lucy and the elegant Aunt Patsy entertaining Ralph Bellamy's comically egregious Daniel Leeson, whom Patsy happened to meet outside at the elevator. Jerry compromises Lucy's hostessing in a duet with the dog at the piano, a loud ragtime with a stride bass, to which Mr. Smith responds with double-barks in the breaks. Our idea of good manners is swept away by this image of Cary Grant, beaming with irrepressible scornful charm in the midst of a vaudeville stunt with his dog. We feel the tremendous power of the man; it swallows up everything else in the scene, drowning out the conversation between Dunne and Bellamy, until the foppish Bellamy is forced to leave. But the scene leaves an unsettling impression. On the one hand, the Warriners display an exhilarating audacity when they go at each other; on the other, they reveal an obvious potential for cruelty. The childlike abandon of their mutual insults recalls Laurel and Hardy, who were always ready to destroy whatever they could of each other. But romantic comedy, as it was constituted up till now, couldn't quite contain a Laurel and Hardy relationship—not without altering its ideology.

The Warriners, according to the genre's conventions, are supposed to learn something about tolerance and grown-up love by the end of the movie. But no character traits have appeared in either Warriner to indicate an ability to do that. It's as if their very prosperity has allowed McCarey to gloss over the state of their souls. Just as his *Make Way for Tomorrow* showed itself naive in supposing that a luxury hotel would be proud to host shabby old Bark and Lucy Cooper, so *The Awful Truth* is too ready to assume that the Warriners' fashionableness implies some ethical worthiness in them. This social carelessness also shows in the conception of a minor character, Dixie Belle Lee (Joyce Compton), Jerry's new girlfriend, whom we encounter in a scene in a swank nightclub. We see Grant and Dixie Belle sitting at a table, talking. Then Irene Dunne, accompanied by *her* date, Ralph Bellamy, enters the club. Jerry brings Dixie Belle over to Lucy and Daniel's table, for a virtuoso quartet scene of awkward pauses, glances, and uneasy small talk. Dixie Belle reveals, in one of the pauses, that she works at the club. She soon leaves the table and reappears with the orchestra to sing her number. "I used to dream of a cottage small / A cottage small by a waterfall," she begins coyly. "But I wound up with no dreams at all / My dreams have gone with the wind!"—and a wind machine blows her skirt up, while she tries to hold it down in mock embarrassment.

This scene gives us a clever parody of a second-rate nightclub number. It had been perfected on the set: in the McCarey-Delmar script, Dixie Belle was a singer named Toots Biswanger, who sang her song in full southern regalia, as a "tribute" to the novel *Gone With the Wind* (which wasn't yet a movie). Jerry Warriner was supposed to say "It's a book!" and then her costume would blow away piece by piece—the hat, the muff, the cape—in a wind effect. But even toned down, there's something ungenerous about the scene. Underneath the parody, Dixie Belle is being blamed for the bad taste of the nightclub owner who hired her, the hack who wrote her song, and Jerry Warriner himself, who asked her out. A character who in another romantic comedy would be the heroine, a Ginger Rogers type who has come to the city to work, here serves as a too-casual foil for Irene Dunne's ladylike suavity. "I just met her," Cary Grant whispers near the end of her number, nervous that Dixie Belle's bad taste will demean him in the eyes of his wife. Irene Dunne's Lucy responds with a smart quip about how it must have been easier for Dixie Belle to change her name than for her whole family to change theirs.

The foil for Cary Grant, on the other hand, Ralph Bellamy's Oklahoman Daniel Leeson, is a worthier target for satire. He's as fine a caricature of masculine pomposity, in fact, as Adolphe Menjou's Anthony Powell in *Stage Door*. The slow drawl Bellamy and McCarey invented for Leeson; his homely homilies; the pseudoabashed grin with the hanging head; his insensitivity to Lucy and Jerry's marital history (in one scene he puts his arm around Lucy in front of Jerry)—all bespeak a swell-headed mama's boy who is blinded by the acute pleasure he takes in himself. Leeson's awfulness finds its apogee in this nightclub scene, in the dance he does with Lucy. "Care about dancing? Why, I could dance till the cows come home!" Leeson exclaims. And Bellamy, from his first elbow-pumping waltz, gives a terrific performance of a man who has no idea that he's not blending in with his surroundings and his partner's wishes. McCarey adds still more details of Leeson's fatuousness in the following scene, the "Home on the Range" duet between Dunne and Bellamy, in which Bellamy, all unaware, loses the melody when Dunne tries to sing harmony. For that failed songwriter McCarey, the primal social sin—even worse than being rude—was to be tone-deaf.

WHAT MCCAREY was doing here was turning an Astaire-Rogers–style movie musical inside out. The high points in the first part of *The Awful Truth* are all failed musical numbers, which remind us, by negative example, of Astaire and Rogers, and, by implication, of the romantic harmony that Lucy was supposed to have enjoyed earlier with Jerry. We gather, from the conversation in the nightclub, that Jerry and Lucy used to dance wonderfully together, but never realized exactly what that meant. "We never won any cups," Lucy says sadly about herself and Jerry, before going out onto the floor with Leeson. In this sense, *The Awful Truth* could be the sequel to any of the Astaire-Rogers movies, the story of the hero and heroine who got married because they danced so well together, but are about to get unmarried because they never learned that that was important. At moments in this movie it seems absurd that Lucy and Jerry can't just straighten out their situation by talking to each other—the way Lubitsch's suave ménage à trois in *Trouble in Paradise,* Gaston, Lily, and Mariette, talked, in a civilized language of erotic allusion and combative irony. But Americans, even elegant ones like Fred and Ginger or Cary and Irene, don't know that language. All they know is how to *behave* together—how to sing, dance, cry, speak halting rhymes, or, what *The Awful Truth* values above all else, make jokes with and at each other.

The jokes in this movie are the essence of the Warriners' bond: for McCarey the jokes equal love. As the movie moves into a slapstick disintegration of their efforts to retrieve the marriage, Grant and Dunne display a wonderful comic timing à deux. These are the movie's strongest scenes, in which the actors' performances show us the texture of deep familiarity and like-minded humor that is supposed to explain their attraction for each other. Grant hides behind Dunne's front door while she greets Ralph Bellamy, who wants to read her a poem he has written in his exuberance. (This is McCarey's mockery of Capra's Longfellow Deeds.) As Dunne listens to Bellamy ("To you, my little prairie flower," he recites, "I think about you every hour"), the hidden Grant keeps tickling her with a pencil so that she laughs uncontrollably on a flyaway arpeggio "woo-hoo-hoo-hoo." (This is another moment that is not present in the script and so presumably was made up on the set.) Jerry attends Lucy's supposed assignation with her singing teacher, which turns out to be a music recital. He crashes it—literally—causing a spindly chair to collapse under him, and then a table. Lucy, convinced at last that he wants her back ("He wouldn't do those funny things if he didn't care about me!"), invites Armand Duval over to ask him to persuade Jerry of her original innocence, only to have to hide Armand when Jerry drops by unexpectedly, and then helplessly watch Jerry hide himself where Armand is hiding when Daniel Leeson and his mother show up for a neighborly chat. Offscreen, from the direction of the room with the closed door, we hear some giant crashes worthy of Laurel and Hardy, and then Alexander D'Arcy emerges chased by Cary Grant.

But when McCarey gets to the emotional center of the movie, in which Grant and Dunne are supposed to abandon the slapstick and enact their longing to get back together, the movie goes limp. Lucy visits Jerry on the last day of their allotted ninety days of separation, knowing that he is about to marry a "madcap heiress" named Barbara Vance. Dunne makes an effort to stage a sentimental "remembering" of their romance, but all she manages to do is put a glum weeper look on her face. And Cary Grant never unbends his stiff irony to meet her halfway. This scene fits the dramatic requirements of the genre, but it's missing that powerful mixture of vulnerability, longing, and memory of past deprivation that equals sexual attraction in Capra's original romantic-comedy formula. It's even missing Lubitsch's shimmering, mischievous, and intermittently lewd awareness of sex.

This is not just a problem of the actors but also one of the impromptu script. The wolfish contest McCarey and the Delmars have set up for the Warriners doesn't ever allow them to acknowledge mutual attraction. It doesn't even permit the director to give a sexual aura to the leading lady in close-ups, which is what George Stevens did in *Swing Time* to compensate for the lack of sexuality between Astaire and Rogers. Irene Dunne looks handsome and roguish in this movie, but not exactly sexy. And by this time, the absence of any erotic spark between the leads has begun to throw the movie off kilter. It has put all the responsibility for the reconciliation—even more than was usual in the asymmetrical endings of romantic comedies— onto Irene Dunne's Lucy. We sense the sheer force of will beneath Lucy's fey surface, and suspect that it is this quality, rather than any physical attraction between her and Jerry, that will be called on to cement this marriage back together.

Lucy plays a trick on Jerry, to get him away from his new rich friends. She goes to a gathering at the Vances' mansion in the guise of Jerry's imaginary sister Lola, wearing a flouncy dress with fringes; talking in a flat, unbuttoned southern voice; asking for a tall sherry (really ginger ale, she whispers to the butler) and gulping it down; accosting stuffy Mrs. Vance on one couch, squeezing herself in between Jerry and Barbara Vance on the other couch—and offering a rendition of Dixie Belle Lee's song, "My Dreams Are Gone with the Wind," accompanied by her *Show Boat* shuffle and an exit on a daffy backwards cakewalk. Dunne here is at her most infectiously funny. But as an example of a romantic-comedy climax, in which the class barriers between the two leads are supposed to melt away, the scene takes on a mildly ugly cast. Jerry and Lucy don't need to be reconciled with each other across class lines. Lucy's impersonation of the lower-class Lola is gratuitous: it's designed to drag Jerry down from his high place, but it also betrays a distinct snobbery about the Lolas of this world. In the end, this scene represents only Irene Dunne doing a turn at a party, not a romantic-comedy heroine trying to introduce tolerance into the social life of America.

If Lucy's snobbery veers away from romantic comedy's principles, Jerry's attitude toward the rich people he's courting betrays these principles utterly. The movie doesn't ever admit that under the influence of Barbara Vance, Jerry has turned into that villain of the romantic-comedy universe, a social climber. (We know this from the deferential way Jerry had greeted the senior Vances at the beginning of the Lola scene, hastily reassuring them that his father was a Princeton man.) How could Jerry spend at least two months with the Vances and not realize that they were rich stiffs? He responds to Lucy/Lola's performance with his old bemused expression of glee, but he doesn't come to see the error of his ways. To get him to want her again, Dunne has to keep on maneuvering him in her direction until the end of the movie. She tricks him into giving her a ride, in her convertible, to Aunt Patsy's cabin in the country. In the car she creates as much revelry as a banshee let loose, laughing and dancing in her seat. Cops stop them because their radio gets stuck blaring jazz. "Go on, honey, truck it!" Dunne yells to Grant, as the policemen make him walk the traffic line to prove he's not drunk. Then she sends her car into a tree so the cops will ride them on their motorcycles to the cabin.

ALL THIS HYSTERIA, just to make Jerry give her a sign that he still loves her. It's true that reconciliation in romantic comedy, ever since Claudette Colbert in *It Happened One Night* broke away from her wedding to join Clark Gable, had always been the responsibility of the woman. To get back with Fred Astaire in *Swing Time,* a dreadfully hurt Ginger Rogers had resorted to a bout of laughter. To get Gary Cooper to wake up in *Mr. Deeds Goes to Town,* Jean Arthur had made an impassioned plea at his trial. To marry William Powell in *My Man Godfrey,* Carole Lombard had moved into his office. But Irene Dunne is forced to work the hardest. The plot asks her to create a veritable whirlwind of mirth around the politely vacant Cary Grant. She must become all facets of woman—a little girl in the car, an aloof, Mae Westian mama in the cabin—to coax him back to her bed before the midnight deadline of their ninety-day separation.

McCarey stages this as a gag about the door blowing open between their adjoining bedrooms, then sticking shut when a black cat lies across it. Grant's Jerry Warriner stays attentive, noncommittal, somewhat puzzled all through the gag, until Dunne finally provokes him into saying that he was a fool to be suspicious of her in the first place. But there's something not quite resolved about the ending. McCarey's clever kitsch coda, the famous routine with the cuckoo clock in which the Alpine man on the clock changes course at the last minute and skips in with the Alpine woman, betrays the movie's unacknowledged uneasiness about both marriage and marital sex. Cary Grant is wearing, in this cabin scene, a long nightshirt. His symbolic stand-in, the mechanical man on the clock,

is wearing lederhosen. Both costumes could have come out of Laurel and
Hardy's wardrobe of grown-up-sized infantile outfits. The unsuitability of
Cary Grant's clothes points up an unanswered question: is getting back
together worth this distortion of a relationship—is it worth Lucy's frenzy
and Jerry's infantilization?

The fact that this movie satisfies and delights despite these unsettling
features of its resolution indicates how deep *The Awful Truth*'s myth lies
in our experience. It is difficult enough in most romantic comedies to see
that the hero partly abdicates his will at the end of the movie and allows
the heroine to make the final gesture toward reconciliation, because this
kind of effort on the part of the woman was what the culture believed was
necessary. (Think of all the torch songs, all the country music songs, all
the weepers written or produced even in the years of romantic comedies.)
The woman was supposed to know more about emotions, and she was
supposed to teach the man. If the compromises inherent in this situation
are slightly more visible in *The Awful Truth* than in other romantic comedies, it's because this movie is missing the class drama that usually obscured the male-female bargains within the plots. Jerry and Lucy Warriner
don't have to overcome class or money prejudices to have a romance the
way other romantic-comedy leads did before them. Both the Warriners
already have their class identities. To get together, they need only redefine
their taste—their conviction that good living is an art, like singing or
dancing—and learn to ignore the gender antagonisms that come with any
marriage.

But *The Awful Truth* doesn't even let them do the final learning together:
Jerry has turned snob; Lucy, with her frenzied jazzing, has put him back
on track. Moreover, their chic, wild reconciliation takes the audience back
to pre-Depression times, when wealth and privilege allowed people to ignore their troubles and just go out and tear up the town. For this reason,
The Awful Truth marks an important moment in the short and concentrated
development of Depression romantic comedy. The genre that was born
when Capra pointed his camera up to a wild penthouse party in *Ladies of
Leisure*, with the assumption that the audience was made up of street-level
skeptics, has here shifted over, just as casually, to the assumption that the
audience looks down on people in the street (the Dixie Belle Lees) because
it enjoys an upper-middle-class existence just like the Warriners'. The heroine who came into being when *Ladies'* bedraggled Barbara Stanwyck scram-
bled up from the shore to confront the rich guy has acquired, in the Irene
Dunne of *The Awful Truth,* the worldly authority of a bourgeois wife. The
wife and the husband in this movie wield an equal authority; the class

tensions of Capra's universe have almost disappeared. *The Awful Truth*—and its huge box-office popularity—serves as proof that in 1937 the pain, panic, and social upheaval of the Depression had begun to recede from the country's memory, and a sophisticated, if negligent, "normalcy" had taken its place.

10

MCCAREY, STEVENS, AND DUNNE:

LOVE AFFAIR AND PENNY SERENADE

Irene Dunne,
Cary Grant, and
George Stevens
on the set of
Penny Serenade.

NINETEEN HUNDRED THIRTY-EIGHT, 1939, and 1940 were the peak years of Depression romantic comedy. The genre's leading directors had amassed a degree of prestige by then that allowed them the ideal working conditions they had sought for so long. Leo McCarey, for instance, had waited for years at Paramount to generate his own projects. He had made one "personal" movie, *Make Way for Tomorrow,* which had not found favor with the bosses; he had left Paramount for Columbia and made his breakthrough farce of remarriage, *The Awful Truth*—and that's when he emerged a leader. Even before *The Awful Truth* was released in 1937, its advance reputation had so awed the industry that both RKO and Columbia wooed McCarey for his next picture on terms that were unprecedented. The studios outbid each other to offer him what amounted to his own unit, practically his own corporation, inside the studio structure. He was to produce two pictures a year and direct at least one of them, own the negatives of the pictures, and employ and pay the actors in his own name. In June 1938, after a long vacation in New York and Europe, McCarey chose RKO, and began work on the picture that would become the 1939 *Love Affair.*

Meanwhile, Gregory La Cava, on the strength of *Stage Door,* had negotiated a similar deal with RKO in the spring of 1938, which gave him the right to find and develop his own stories, employ a mini-staff of writer, script girl, and assistant, and hold approval of casting and cutting. George Stevens, still contracted to RKO, continued his meteoric rise, winning the right, at age thirty-three, to produce and direct his 1938 picture, *Vivacious Lady,* starring Ginger Rogers and Jimmy Stewart. Howard Hawks, who had been studio-hopping ever since he became a director in 1926, briefly joined the impressive RKO talent bank in 1938 when he was hired to produce and direct *Bringing Up Baby.* And Capra, who had started the trend of producing and directing with *Mr. Deeds* in 1936, continued to preside over his own unit at Columbia, which turned out several blockbusters in the late thirties.

The actors were also learning to free themselves from the exclusive control of one studio, to take themselves off steady salary and negotiate their fees in accordance with their box-office power. Both Irene Dunne and Cary Grant had connected themselves to several studios around 1936 for one-picture deals. Barbara Stanwyck's contract had been split between RKO and Fox since 1935, and in 1937 she made an agreement with Paramount too. Carole Lombard finally left Paramount in 1938 to ally herself with David

O. Selznick's new company, Selznick International, and the following year
with RKO as well. Jean Arthur remained at Columbia, but she got to name
her conditions, because she was its sole star until Rita Hayworth appeared
in 1941. Fred Astaire, who had controlled his career and earned a percent-
age of his movies ever since he first came to RKO, remained cheerfully at
that studio. Ginger Rogers stayed at RKO too, having won a say about
which pictures she made and which directors she worked with. Katharine
Hepburn, however, was preparing to end her six-year-long exclusive arrangement with RKO to do *Holiday* for Columbia in 1938. (In Hepburn's words,
"Ginger was on her way up and I was on my way down.")

Actors' negotiating power was enhanced by their agents, men like Myron
Selznick, Charles Feldman, Zeppo Marx, and Leland Hayward, who became powerful in those years. Not just romantic-comedy stars but top stars
of all the genres, as well as top directors, had begun to realize that they had
a right to share in the profits of their movies. The studios, with the exception of the iron-fisted MGM, were losing the control over people they had
thought of as their creations. In the years before the war, Hollywood,
against the will of the bosses, was restructuring itself through shifting
allegiances and intricate negotiations: it was heading toward a kind of
decentralization of power. Moreover, as the workers began to assume some
control over the product, romantic comedy, with its improvisatory air,
benefited the most of any genre.

AND YET, even as the directors and actors were enjoying ideal conditions
for making romantic comedies, the social climate that had given birth to the
genre was changing. According to historians, the crisis atmosphere of the
Depression began to lift in late 1935. In "Middletown" (Muncie, Indiana),
where Robert and Helen Lynd made their classic twenties and thirties
anthropological studies, business picked up again in 1935 because General
Motors came back to the town. "The city fathers," wrote the Lynds, "celebrated the return of good times with a great public dinner." In many places
across the country, the illusion of business as usual—business as it had been
before the Crash—settled in by 1936, although there would continue to be
threats to the economy up until the war. Not coincidentally, 1936 was also
the year in which national movie attendance jumped up to a healthy 88
million a week (from an all-time low of 60 million in 1932 and '33).

Gradually, the public's complicated feelings of resentment and nostalgia
toward wealth, which Capra had articulated so brilliantly in his first romantic comedy, were giving way to a semblance of complacency, and to normal
everyday American greed. The success of *The Awful Truth* had signaled to

the industry that the audience's urgency about hating the rich and lionizing the poor was almost gone—and much of the genre followed McCarey's lead. Humor about sex replaced humor about class. Bourgeois remarriages stood in for socially healing, cross-class marriages. The couple took over some of the genre's territory from the single working woman. Class differences that had characterized earlier romantic comedy leads melted away or else appeared as momentary or abstract. *The Awful Truth* provoked a flurry of reproductions. It wasn't exactly copied, but its tone of slapstick marital frustration was caught again; its awkward moments were reproduced; its jokes were elaborated on and spun out. In 1938 George Stevens released *Vivacious Lady.* Although it was planned and begun before *The Awful Truth, Vivacious Lady* was mostly shot afterwards, and became a softer, Stevensesque replay of *The Awful Truth,* in which Jimmy Stewart, a college professor, marries Ginger Rogers, a nightclub singer, and the pair spend most of the movie maneuvering for the privacy to consummate their marriage. Howard Hawks's *Bringing Up Baby,* also made at RKO, borrowed many elements from *The Awful Truth:* its actual leading man (McCarey's "discovery," Cary Grant), its posh Connecticut country setting, and the climactic gag for its leading lady, Katharine Hepburn. Hepburn did a turn as a low-class "moll" at the end, just like Irene Dunne in *The Awful Truth,* only Hawks went further toward slapstick disreputability and actually had Hepburn arrested and put behind bars.

This shift from social justice to giddy humor was as much related to the lives of the people who created romantic comedy as it was to the new mood of the audience. Both directors and players were now removed in time and in experience from their own hungry days, when they had tried to break into the movie mainstream. The directors—Capra, Stevens, La Cava, McCarey—had all settled down, fathered children, and established households. The actors had settled down too. In 1939, Barbara Stanwyck married Robert Taylor and Carole Lombard married Clark Gable. Both couples bought estates on ranches in the San Fernando Valley. Claudette Colbert had married a well-known physician several years before and was ensconced in a Beverly Hills mansion. Ginger Rogers, between husbands, owned a celebrated Beverly Hills house with a soda fountain and a tennis court. Fred Astaire, Gary Cooper, Henry Fonda, and Cary Grant all had wives who were socialite hostesses; they played decorative roles in the soirée life of Hollywood. Most of the top romantic-comedy personnel—actors, actresses, and directors—were earning huge sums of money in those years, so huge that the stiffening of the income tax laws in 1936 caused them to cut back on work so as to earn less. All in all, we can say that the people most responsible for the texture of romantic comedy had ceased being young rebels and begun to be prosperous citizens. As the crisis mentality of the Depression drifted out of the audience's memory, so it receded from the lives of the directors and the stars.

And because of the impromptu nature of the genre—the easy parallels between the actors on the set and the characters on the screen—this prosperity, and the complacent camaraderie that went with it, were bound to make themselves felt in the movies. The population of the genre—actors, directors, writers—constituted a floating stock company within Hollywood. At the professional level, these people knew each other intimately by this time. They had worked together in all sorts of combinations. They were comfortable with the modes, tricks, and conventions of the genre and could walk through the scenes that had become habitual to it. The situation resulted in a brilliant final flowering of the genre, which today seems exhilarating but also unsatisfying.

Never was the experience of intelligent men and women trying to cope with romance caught more effortlessly on the screen than in the movies of those years. One can find countless sophisticated scenes portraying strangers turning into lovers, or married couples turning into strangers: Katharine Hepburn and Cary Grant doing tricks in a playroom in *Holiday* (1938); Hepburn and Grant shooting evil looks at each other in *The Philadelphia Story* (1940); Ginger Rogers attempting to converse with a stiff David Niven over a baby carriage in *Bachelor Mother* (1939); Rogers and Ronald Colman awkwardly sharing a dinner in a strange hotel in *Lucky Partners* (1940); Jean Arthur murmuring assurance to a broken Jimmy Stewart at the shadowy Lincoln Memorial in *Mr. Smith Goes to Washington* (1939); Carole Lombard and Stewart shouting at each other in their bedroom in *Made for Each Other* (1939); Lombard trying to put a drenched and bedraggled Gene Raymond at ease in *Mr. and Mrs. Smith* (1941); Spencer Tracy bashfully wooing Joan Crawford on his penthouse terrace in *Mannequin* (1938); Clark Gable and Myrna Loy cheering at a baseball game in *Test Pilot* (1938); Claudette Colbert and Gary Cooper encountering each other at the pyjamas counter in *Bluebeard's Eighth Wife* (1938); Colbert evading Don Ameche at a party in *Midnight* (1939) . . . The list could go on and on.

But none of these movies (with the exception of the sassy *Midnight*) holds together quite as firmly as the earlier masterpieces of the genre, *It Happened One Night, Alice Adams, My Man Godfrey,* or even *The Awful Truth.* Some late-thirties romantic comedies, such as *Made for Each Other* and *Mr. Smith Goes to Washington,* weren't even really romantic comedies: their suspense was generated not from the union of the lovers but from some extra melodramatic crisis grafted onto the story. In the former movie it concerned the illness of Stewart and Lombard's child; in the latter, Stewart's battle in

Congress to save a part of Montana with a boys' camp on it. But even such extra sob stuff looks forgivable when compared to the coy snobbery of the movies that didn't resort to melodramatic subplot. "Ordinary" 1939 romantic comedy offered brilliant ensemble scenes, ingenious improvisations on already discovered formulae, moments in which a raised eyebrow or a subtle smirk could speak volumes about human relations. But when we watch these movies now, we see that they have veered away from the collective passions that animated earlier examples of the genre. Romantic comedy's agenda, losing its political edge, had turned trivial. By 1940, the surprise meeting of a mismatched man and woman, the feistiness of their first relations, their chronic misunderstandings, and their reunion in laughter no longer retained a symbolic power. Even last-minute, *Awful Truth*–style reunions between bourgeois married partners, fresh in 1937, failed to thrill the public two years later.

The peak of romantic comedy was therefore the beginning of its decline. Most directors combated the specter of boredom within the genre by thinking up literal variations on earlier classics, almost remakes—some of which caught the public's fancy and some of which did not. Gregory La Cava's 1939 *Fifth Avenue Girl* reversed the genders of *My Man Godfrey* and brought a working girl (Ginger Rogers) into a rich man's house to fix things up in a daffy family, but the new equation of characters didn't work, and the movie failed. Howard Hawks made a box-office failure, *Bringing Up Baby* (1939), which repeated elements of *The Awful Truth,* and then a hit, *His Girl Friday* (1940), which switched the gender of the reporter in the early newspaper yarn *The Front Page.* In 1938 Billy Wilder and Charles Brackett wrote a perverse version of *Mr. Deeds Goes to Town* (or a part of it) called *Bluebeard's Eighth Wife,* for Lubitsch to direct and Gary Cooper and Claudette Colbert to star in, which flopped; the next year they created the ultimate girl-on-her-own fairy tale for Colbert, *Midnight,* which was a hit, then combined an old-maid character with a spoof of Stalinism to make a Soviet romantic-comedy heroine of Greta Garbo in another hit, *Ninotchka.*

But whether the movies pleased the public or wearied it, the principle behind most of late-thirties romantic comedy was recycling. Hollywood produced countless recyclings of older romantic comedies in those years: besides the above-named, well-known examples, there is also a host of little-known movies such as RKO's *You Can't Fool Your Wife* (1940), in which the married Lucille Ball and James Ellison part and reunite; or Paramount's *Thanks for the Memory* (1938), in which Bob Hope and Shirley Ross do the same; or Paramount's *Invitation to Happiness* (1939), in which Irene Dunne and Fred MacMurray (as a lady and a prizefighter) barely manage to get together at all. It was in the midst of all this routine reshuffling of old inventions that Leo McCarey made his next romantic comedy, which veered away from recycling toward real synthesis. McCarey had come into the genre late, so perhaps he was not yet tired of it, like some of the other directors. But he was also too shrewd a judge of the zeitgeist to pretend, even to himself, that the slapstick story of remarriage, which he had all but invented, could still hold a real tension for the public. Moreover, McCarey had taken a long trip to Europe with his wife at the end of *The Awful Truth*. He had witnessed the approaching war on that continent, and that sight had cast the romantic-comedy couple in a different light for him. To McCarey the future of romance held tragedy.

LOVE AFFAIR contains even less of a plot than *The Awful Truth*. It is based on the merest sketch of a situation that McCarey had thought up on his voyage home from Europe. Two people meet on a ship in the middle of the Atlantic and fall in love. The woman is an American ex-singer, now the fiancée of a wealthy man. She is sailing back from Europe to join him and be married. The man is a French playboy painter, also engaged to someone wealthier—an American heiress in New York. Before they dock, the two decide that their love for each other is the real thing. They give each other six months to get their affairs straightened out, and arrange to meet at the end of that time on top of the Empire State Building—"because it's the nearest thing to heaven we have in New York." This is what McCarey, aided by writer Mildred Cram, had come up with for a story, and a host of other writers had turned it into a facsimile of a screenplay. But this screenplay was not finished when shooting began. At the start of filming, no one had any idea how the story would resolve itself.

The woman was a recognizable romantic-comedy heroine—smart, independent, and vaguely restless—waiting for something new in her life. McCarey cast Irene Dunne in the part: this was predictable; she had become his quintessential leading lady. But the man was a brand-new figure for romantic comedy, because he was not an American. To play him, McCarey chose Frenchman Charles Boyer, who was known in Hollywood not as a comedy star (although he had played comedy) but as a "great lover." Boyer's very presence opened the genre's love affair to the world beyond America—to Europe. Europe's troubles were not exactly unknown in Hollywood. The European revenue from American movies, which had accounted for one fourth to one third of the studios' income throughout most of the thirties, was drying up in 1939. There was hardly a Europe left where normal conditions for going to the movies existed. Up to this time, though, romantic comedy had been too focused on class tensions in America to concern itself with the tensions in Europe. But McCarey started a trend with his international couple in *Love Affair*. Following that movie, a rash of early-forties mixed-genre movies would mingle the themes of Capraesque romance with the ominous news from abroad—movies that ranged from Hitchcock's *Foreign Correspondent* (1941), to Mitchell Leisen's *Arise My Love* (1940) and *Hold Back the Dawn* (1941), both written by Brackett and Wilder, to McCarey's own *Once Upon a Honeymoon* (1942).

War was not a literal presence in *Love Affair*. It made itself felt more as a kind of melancholy, a vague threat of danger, and, in the end, an explosion of accident and tragedy—all, however, dramatized on the personal, rather than the political, level. The end of the movie, where this ominous atmosphere surfaced most sharply, was the result of pure improvisatory instinct. When, in the course of filming the story, McCarey and the actors arrived at the moment when the boat docked in New York, there was still no ending. McCarey was obliged to shut down the set for two weeks until he could figure one out. He finally settled for a melodramatic event: he arranged for the woman to get hit by a car on her way to the Empire State Building rendezvous. Irene Dunne's Terry had stopped to buy a new dress, McCarey imagined, which made her late, so she didn't pay attention when crossing the street in front of the Empire State Building. We see her in the hospital after her accident; we learn that she probably won't walk again but we understand that, in keeping with such a heroine's pride, she doesn't want to burden the man with that knowledge. So she doesn't tell him anything; she just disappears, and he thinks she stopped caring about him and forgot about the appointment. He finds out what happened much later, when he discovers her address and pays her a cynical goodbye visit on Christmas Day—and in the end they are finally reunited.

IT SOUNDS LIKE a typical 1939 hodgepodge—a man and a woman embroiled in romantic delays, the whole brought to a conclusion by means of an artificial injection of melodrama. And yet McCarey, from the opening scenes, managed to introduce a coherent mood into the story, a mood that had not yet appeared in romantic comedy. In the long first sequence, which describes the man and woman meeting and falling in love, we experience a real-life sense of a deepening acquaintance, respect, and ardor, achieved without recourse to music or dancing or slapstick gags. It's a mature kind of love affair, keyed to the persona of Irene Dunne, who was forty-one years old when *Love Affair* was made. But she isn't shown as past her prime; we see her, rather, as a splendid, radiant, American female. The unfamiliarity of that kind of splendor points up the degree of Hollywood's habitual addiction, even in romantic comedy, to the figure of "the girl." Dunne seems here like a new addition to romantic comedy's pool of stock characters, the definitively grown-up woman. Her hair in this opening scene is pinned up in a classical filet, as befits the gowns for formal shipboard wear. It's a hairdo like the one Ginger Rogers often wore when she danced with Astaire, but on Dunne it looks right and natural, not precocious as it did on Rogers. Dunne wears her clothes, her severe hairdo, her age, with superb ease—as if they belong to her and give her pleasure. It's true that her character, Terry, is being "kept" by an offscreen businessman, whom we encounter briefly later on. But as she emerges from her stateroom door in a floor-length satin gown, and strides down the corridor for dinner with that wonderful female thoroughbred stride of the thirties, we see the embodiment of someone on her own. She looks handsome, content, experienced, and mischievous all at once, a woman who's neither intrigued nor intimidated by the renowned playboy (Boyer) on the same boat.

This playboy, Michel, displays an equivalent personal distinction because of Boyer's habitual aura of quiet melancholy and his grave attentiveness to leading ladies. The beginning of their affair, as arranged by the movie, not only dispenses with the slapstick interruptions McCarey had depended on so heavily in *The Awful Truth;* it requires an extra smoothness from the sophistication of both characters. Boyer and Dunne first meet outside their staterooms. He offers a slickly flattering remark; she rebuffs him. But in the course of trying to avoid her, Boyer visits the ship's bar alone, orders a pink champagne cocktail, and absents himself for a moment, during which Dunne enters, sits down, and orders the same. He reenters in back of her; they become aware of each other, and without a word they raise their glasses, as if saluting the chance that brought them together. Then they begin to talk, in the unhurried, poised, and self-aware manner that suits them both.

The most unusual part of their courting, however, is not how they talk but how they share silences. There is a long night scene in the fog by the railing of the ship, the night before the ship is due to dock in New York, in which they finally realize that loving each other means they will need to change everything. Up till now in a romantic comedy, this climactic acknowledgment of love had been accompanied by pratfalls, freak accidents, and uncontrollable laughing or crying. Here the scene is played out on a gently rising and falling dynamic line, which matches the simulated motion of the ship itself. It's practically a whole scene of murmurs. Dunne and Boyer are both swathed in greatcoats. She wears a veil over her head; he wears a soft checked scarf and a beautiful, low-brimmed hat. The camera just stays on them, making minute adjustments to keep them in the frame, changing angles only once to look at them from the other diagonal.

Perhaps Boyer's quintessentially French persona was what precluded the usual slapstick hysteria. Europeans were always more at home with romance than Americans were, and *Love Affair* contains more quiet, if oblique, conversation about love than any other romantic comedy of the era. The movie implies that the genre has finally learned how to be peaceful, or at least poised, about strong emotion. Boyer and Dunne's talk proceeds in that illogical manner of long, long sympathetic conversations, conversations that are put down and taken up again, not in sequence. The two talk about not being able to sleep. Dunne quotes her father, who liked to say that "wishes are the dreams we dream when we're awake." She teases Boyer when he gets too ardent. They refer fatalistically to welcoming telegrams from their respective lovers. They're testing each other, thinking out loud, completing each others' thoughts. "You know, I've never worked in all my life," says Boyer, very dreamy and yet surprised at what he's saying. "In all my life I've never worked." Then there is a silence, and she says, "What did you say?" He turns his face with the dark, comprehending eyes toward her and says, gently, "I didn't say anything." "Yes you did," she responds. "You said I was very fond of expensive things—furs and jewels . . ." "I wonder what your father would think of me, never working, not once," muses Boyer in another apparent illogical leap. Here again, muted and distant, is sounded the leitmotif of romantic comedy: the idea that the aristocratic partner must learn the values of hard work and independence from the democratic partner. But despite the breaks in the sequence, nothing in this scene seems emotionally forced, the way scenes did in other romantic comedies of 1939. Even Irene Dunne's irritating habit of smiling reflexively at the end of her lines doesn't manage to trivialize their exchanges. This mannerism of hers becomes absorbed in the luster, the melody of Boyer's acting. Together Dunne and Boyer combine like a great gourmet pairing: she with the piquancy, the sudden tartness of an American wisecrack; he with a full-bodied Gallic charm.

LOVE AFFAIR relies for its drama on Capra's original device of putting the hero and heroine together in a place that's far away from both their daily lives, a place that represents socially neutral ground. But McCarey has taken the device to its farthest extreme. Where Boyer and Dunne meet is the middle of nowhere—even more nowhere than Colbert and Gable on *It Happened One Night*'s night bus. Their boat is on the high seas, not in any

Irene Dunne and
Charles Boyer in
Love Affair.

country. One would think, therefore, that Dunne and Boyer would seem even more "alone together" than other romantic-comedy couples. But because they're an international couple, they encounter the weight of history that Europe symbolized at this moment in time. The ship makes a call in Madeira. In a scene of remembering, the kind of scene that had become habitual in McCarey's movies, Boyer's Michel brings Dunne's Terry to visit his old grandmother (Maria Ouspenskaya), the retired widow of a diplomat. Dunne and Boyer kneel together in the grandmother's backlit chapel; she sings "Plaisir d'Amour" to Ouspenskaya's piano accompaniment. In the middle of the song, the haunting sound of the ship's horn causes Ouspenskaya to break off her playing. All this would strike us as shamelessly sentimental if we forget what year the movie was made. It was 1939. The movie is not just about romance but also about the fate of Europe, this "perfect" world of the past, with its pianos and flowers and tea, its lace shawls and private chapels, which was about to disappear.

The possibility of this kind of disaster, never named as such but hovering on the edges of the story, is the source of the potent aura of melancholy that permeates the movie. It explains why a hokey image such as Irene Dunne's face superimposed over the raging waves of the Atlantic, introduced for no apparent reason, seems right for the drama. McCarey, we have to remember, was French on his mother's side. His usual mode for devising movie plots was autobiographical, and never more so than in *Love Affair*, which completes the autobiographical triptych that is his special achievement within thirties romantic comedy. The first movie of the triptych, *Make Way for Tomorrow*, treats the marriage of McCarey's parents at the end of their lives. The second, *The Awful Truth*, describes a situation that resembled his own marriage. And the third movie, *Love Affair*, presents the circumstances of an imaginary ideal marriage—the kind of marriage a middle-aged man might dream of making if he were given a chance to start over.

Plans for this ideal marriage, however, do not proceed smoothly: they threaten early on to founder in melancholy and tragedy. Nor does the threat originate in the lovers' psyches, the way it did in earlier romantic comedies. It comes from outside, from the world around them. *Love Affair*'s lovers are emotionally wiser than any other romantic-comedy lovers before them— they do each other the honor of trusting their newfound love to a six-month separation. But they live in an emotional climate where separations, such as their own, or Michel's from his grandmother, seem chronic and inevitable, and where sudden accidents, such as Terry's in the street, seem all but foreordained. This is a world heading toward war. McCarey undoubtedly sensed, when he put his couple into such a dangerous climate, that war was threatening the raison d'être of the whole genre—that war's priorities, acting on the collective sensibility of Hollywood, would soon push the independent and urbanized American romantic-comedy couple back to a conception of marriage that had prevailed before the Depression began.

LOVE AFFAIR'S unusual mixture of hopefulness and despair was achieved by means of an aesthetic McCarey had developed over the course of his other two romantic comedies, consisting of a stripped-down visual code combined with a loosened-up temporal quality. In most images of his main characters, McCarey eliminated everything else from the space around them—in contrast, for instance, to George Stevens, who always paid great attention to the furnishings, objects, and minor characters that surrounded his leads. McCarey frequently showed nothing but two heads, or two figures from the waist up. In the comic atmosphere of *The Awful Truth,* this stripped-down approach had produced prolonged and close-in views of human awkwardness. In the serious aura of *Love Affair,* it conveys a clear and passionate idea of what's most important emotionally within the movie. And the sense of time in *Love Affair* underscores the images. This movie alternates between swift, sketched-in "time passing" scenes done almost in montage technique, and long, seemingly desultory duets between Boyer and Dunne. Those duets form the core of the movie. It's as if McCarey barely concerned himself with how the story was progressing: instead, he gave all his attention to the couple's hesitant rhythm of exchange, orchestrated as it would be in real life, with the pauses, uncertainties, and digressions left in. There's a purity in this approach, as if McCarey were letting the element of character determine the look and the timing of the whole movie. By the end, these lengthy seances between the two leads have so mesmerized us that the movie seems to have flipped over into the abstract and become a chart of the rhythms of a romantic interaction. Despite the melodrama that McCarey was obliged to throw in to resolve the movie, in *Love Affair* he came as close as he ever would to writing music—music realized by actors in front of a camera.

One could say that McCarey applied the means of a folk artist to the ends of a sophisticate. He deployed objects or buildings nakedly too, as if they were characters. We see the Empire State Building again and again in *Love Affair*: appearing as a reflection on the outside of the glass door on Irene Dunne's Park Avenue balcony; presiding visionarily over the giant Schlitz beer billboard that Boyer is painting to prove he can do honest labor; looming up out of the snow on the climactic Christmas Day of their reconciliation. Gradually we get the idea that the Empire State Building is standing in for the idea of a great city and its civilization—and not merely one great city. When Boyer paces the top of the Empire State Building on the stormy day they had set for their rendezvous, the close-ups of its exposed iron girders look so much like the Eiffel Tower that they evoke a faraway, darkening Paris along with a menaced New York. McCarey's stationary images always force up a sequence of associations. When he shows us Dunne rediscovering her independence during her six months, working at her old profession of singer, in Philadelphia, he lets his camera rest on her face while she renders an entire song, "Come On and Sing, My Heart!" He gives us time to be charmed by her singing, to grow impatient at the sight of her, to wonder why we don't see something or somebody else, then to find our own way to the idea that this dumb song was all she had, that it was significant because she's buying her independence with it.

Love Affair's simplified landscape of object-symbols also includes children. One doesn't understand at first what they're doing in this movie. At the end of Boyer and Dunne's first long duet by the railing of the ship, just before they part for that evening, she asks him out of the blue if he likes children. "Yes, I do," he says simply. A little later they have a seemingly gratuitous encounter with a matter-of-fact little boy on one of the ship's stairways. They're going up the stairs; he's sliding down the railing. And still later, when Dunne is recuperating from her accident next door to an orphanage, she begins teaching the orphans to sing a cappella in close harmony. McCarey could have given her any number of occupations during the time she was recuperating: she could have done needlepoint. But instead she interacts with children, because suddenly, around 1939, the movies were being invaded by a motley assortment of grubby kids.

Kids became a national compulsion in the years leading up to the war, and this marked an abrupt turnaround from the ethos of romantic comedy. How many carefree movie couples during the Depression had negotiated the problems of love, money, class, and jobs without the awkward presence of babies! A baby in *The Awful Truth* would have been a sacrilege. It wasn't that thirties Hollywood had banished children: on the contrary, child stars made huge profits. But Shirley Temple didn't embody a child in her movies, nor did Mickey Rooney, Deanna Durbin, or Judy Garland; they were miniature stars, children invested with the wit and skill of adults. Their precocity defined them. One of the most unsentimental, if minor, stock figures of thirties Hollywood was the precocious little girl with a nasty tongue, who was able to make the unpleasant observations that polite adults were not permitted. (The most horrid one can be seen in La Cava's *She Married Her Boss* [1935], a high-strung, spoiled rich child played by Edith Fellows.)

But in the late thirties, with war overtaking Europe, Hollywood and the movie public suddenly lost their tart humor and clasped to their hearts a new type of movie kid—the plain, homely, pathetic, even outright dumb child with absolutely no frills or glamour attached. As early as 1937, the Dead End Kids, a group of belligerently unattractive real juvenile delinquents from New York, who had been a Broadway phenomenon in the play *Dead End,* hit Hollywood in Samuel Goldwyn's movie version of the play. In 1939 Frank Capra made *Mr. Smith Goes to Washington,* that awesome machine of a movie in which the freckle-faced, snaggle-toothed boys of America were so humorlessly idealized that in the end his hero, Jimmy Stewart, became completely identified with them. "I feel like I've just sent my kid off to school in his first long pants," says Stewart's soon-to-be-lover, Jean Arthur, as she watches him leave his office to do battle with the corrupt United States Senate. Also in 1939, Mickey Rooney, playing a boy-next-door named Andy Hardy, took over the top of the star charts from Shirley Temple—and thus the claustrophobic American equation of children and mischievous, small-town virtues was put back into place, eclipsing Hollywood's decade-long encounter, via romantic comedy, with risky, grown-up urban wit. Even McCarey, author of the finest marital farce in the movies, *The Awful Truth,* in which the place of a child was unapologetically occupied by an intelligent dog, gave in, at least in part, in his next movie, *Love Affair.* He forced its heroine, once she was injured, to ride in a wheelchair and display maternal impulses. And he sneaked little freckled Patsy Jane and a whole slew of caricatured orphans into this most romantic of romantic comedies, so they could provide proof of Irene Dunne's selflessness while she was waiting for Charles Boyer to come back.

TO US NOW, Boyer entering Dunne's apartment as the orphans are leaving constitutes an abrupt, though welcome, leap back from the forties to the thirties, back from the "new" world of families to the "old" romantic milieu of couples. In the final moments of the movie, the two enact one of the most subtle scenes in romantic comedy, in which Boyer tries to find out why Dunne didn't show up on the top of the Empire State Building. And here again, although it's now on record that no less than seven writers, including McCarey, worked on the *Love Affair* script (Anthony Veiller for five days; Mildred Cram for forty-two days; Barry Benefield for thirty-six days; Delmer Daves for sixty-six days; S. N. Behrman for nine days; and Donald Ogden Stewart for forty-one days), the dialogue that was actually shot in this scene flows like a spontaneous example of two complicated, civilized people trying to make up a way to talk about something that is emotionally dangerous to them both. Irene Dunne is lounging on the couch where the landlady has helped her settle, a blanket covering the telltale crippled legs. She assumes a cool, self-sufficient air in Boyer's presence. Boyer lingers on and on, hat in hand. He tries a ruse, portraying himself, falsely, as the faithless one, the one who didn't turn up at the rendezvous. He turns bitter, describing himself as "the mad painter," who asks every woman he meets, "Where will you be in six months?" But in the company of this woman he fell in love with, he can't keep up the self-lacerating anger for long. He softens; he presents her with the shawl that his now dead grandmother had promised her in Madeira; and he tells her about the painting he made of her, in which he imagined she was wearing the shawl. The painting, his dealer told him, was bought by a crippled woman—suddenly Boyer breaks off. He walks quickly into the bedroom. There he finds the painting, which she has managed to buy, hanging on the wall. In a flash he knows the whole story. The tenderness, the broken assurances that Boyer and Dunne now offer each other are irresistibly moving.

But it's a curiously contradictory ending. McCarey's stripped-down story and pictures allow us to recognize how romantic comedy has grown up prodigiously and yet faltered on the brink of full flowering. The hero is a painter, like the hero in Capra's very first sketch of the genre in 1930, *Ladies of Leisure.* He has painted a picture of the woman he's in love with, just as Capra's hero did in *Ladies of Leisure.* But it's not the movie's hero, foreign though he is, who registers the differences between 1930 and 1939; it's the heroine. Barbara Stanwyck's Kay Arnold in *Ladies of Leisure,* the "party girl" longing for a better life, would never have thought to own the painting her lover Jerry has made of her. She wouldn't have dared to advertise her personality like that. It's natural, though, for Irene Dunne's self-made socialite Terry to hang a portrait of herself on her wall, even though she's now poor: she's that kind of a vivid, self-assured woman. With the evolution of romantic comedy over the decade, and especially with McCarey's own contribution to that evolution, the woman had grown up to the man's level in sophistication, in intelligence, and in the self-knowing flexibility that can be called entitlement. In *Love Affair* she is fully realized, complete in herself, and she also represents a larger ideal. Irene Dunne is the American of the two lovers; she stands for America's readiness to participate in, if not to coopt, the kind of sophisticated romance that once had been reserved in the popular mind for Europeans such as Charles Boyer's Michel.

And yet, having allowed Dunne's Terry this stunning maturity, McCarey can't bring her out of the movie unscathed. She ends up in a state worse than Barbara Stanwyck's Kay Arnold at the end of *Ladies of Leisure,* after Kay had tried to jump off the cruise ship to Havana and drown herself. She's a cripple at the end: she's been brought down from her high flight of independence and made physically dependent on her lover. Moreover, the effects of Terry's accident cannot be overcome by love, as Kay's self-doubts were overcome at the end of *Ladies of Leisure:* Terry and Michel must now live in this world where the threat of accident and separation have put the whole enterprise of falling in love into jeopardy. Irene Dunne's dignity is such that we don't register her crippled state as mere helplessness. The movie doesn't dwell on her handicap—we don't see her trying to walk, for instance. But it was McCarey's own decision, when he was casting anxiously about for what to do with his characters after their boat docked, to cause this harm to fall on her. His intuitively brilliant perception that war was sapping the strength of the romance in romantic comedy has come down to the idea that the woman must be maimed and brought back to earth, to hearth, home, and family. The "family" theme of their reunion is deliberately accentuated in the final fade-out. Boyer's and Dunne's heads are together; they are laughing and crying with the emotion of the reconciliation—and yet between them is the shawl, the memento of another generation.

Though the couple can look forward to a rich and wise adult life together, it is to be a life that embraces the memory of grandparents and the presence of children (if only orphans). The intrusion of the shawl between Boyer and Dunne marks a kind of end of the thirties couple, those two beings who brought nothing to each other that was more important than wit and responsiveness. Soon there would be war: the men would go off to fight; marriage would grow to mean something more urgent and reassuring than the union of two individuals arrived at through misunderstanding, surprise, and then delight. And when the war was over, all the marriages in the movies would be overtaken by the agenda of children and new housing. The magical but ordinary romance of romantic comedy would all but disappear, squeezed out between those antithetical postwar worlds in the movies, the "heaven" of families with children and the "hell" of sin, crime, and antisocial wandering. Even before the end of the war, McCarey had crossed over to the "heaven" side, to make two subversions of romantic comedy, *Going My Way* (1944) and *The Bells of St. Mary's* (1945), in which the hero, a priest, joined in the second movie by a heroine, a nun, were cut off from the very possibility of romantic love, and made to serve as selfless conduits among the generations.

THE IMPULSE to weigh down heroines with pain and disability, the impulse that Capra had rejected when he first coaxed his Depression romantic comedy out of the early-thirties weeper, had returned to the movies. Romantic comedy had emerged from one kind of melodrama. Now it was heading into another—a melodrama with a different atmosphere, but one that threatened the characters, especially the women, with just as much misery. The ultimate epitaph of the romantic-comedy couple is written in the strange, fitfully brilliant hybrid of a movie made by George Stevens at Columbia in 1941, *Penny Serenade.* Stevens came to Columbia in much the same emotional state as McCarey four years earlier: he had broken with his longtime home studio, RKO, over a dispute about his movie *Gunga Din* (1939). He had gone over budget, had been reprimanded, and sought refuge at Columbia, in a deal with features just like McCarey's: autonomy over his own set, a writer and stars of his own choosing. For the writer he chose La Cava's two-time collaborator Morrie Ryskind, and for stars he cast McCarey's "discoveries" Irene Dunne and Cary Grant. But Stevens didn't make a La Cava or a McCarey movie. In his usual fashion, he made something that was unmistakably Stevensesque—that is to say, a movie that challenged whatever was predictable within the genre.

Penny Serenade concerns a marriage and a near-divorce, described by means of flashbacks. But what a solemn, precarious marriage it is, authored by those former masters of abrasive wit Stevens and Ryskind! The movie races in five short scenes through Dunne and Grant's meeting and getting acquainted. This opening sequence presents a shorthand version of a romantic comedy, predicated on the assumption that the experienced audience could grasp the conventions as fast as the movie-making team could think them up. We barely even have time to register the facts—that Grant works as a newspaper reporter and Dunne as a phonograph-record saleswoman—before the leads are off and married. The movie settles into its drama only after the two have moved to Japan, sent by Grant's newspaper. An earthquake hits Japan while they're living there, and Dunne loses the baby she is carrying. Back in the States, Grant decides to fulfill a dream and start a newspaper of his own. He and Dunne install themselves in the country, in an apartment over a printing press. But foremost in their minds, even more urgent than the newspaper, is their desire to adopt a baby to replace the one they've lost. Beulah Bondi, the head of an orphanage, plays a fairy godmother to the couple. She persuades them to accept a tiny baby girl instead of the two-year-old boy they had thought they wanted. But they encounter continual trouble making enough money to justify their adoption of their child. The bulk of the movie portrays their efforts to keep the child, their utter despair when the child accidentally dies at age ten, and the inevitable decay of their marriage in the face of so much loss.

In his usual fashion, Stevens plays McCarey's former sophisticates against the grain of their personae: in Stevens's movie they bear no resemblance to the bourgeois clowns of *The Awful Truth*. Stevens's very humor here seems to have a different intent than McCarey's. The movie's longest scene is an elaborate semislapstick sequence in which Dunne tries helplessly to give the tiny baby a bath, while Grant looks on. Like everything Stevens directed in those days, this scene is flawlessly timed, with doubts and fears registered as long, blank, comic pauses. Despite the occasional slapstick, however, the mood of this movie proves the opposite of farcical. Dunne and Grant look more relaxed on the screen than ever before, and both seem more comfortable with emotion. The effect on Dunne is very beautiful. For long scenes, her face is absolutely unanimated, quiet. There are no cheesy smiles. In fact, the strongest image in the movie is of Dunne's tear-stained face when she says goodbye through the banisters to the one-year-old baby she thinks she and Grant are going to lose in the custody court. It's a deeply concerned, deeply serious face. We can see all the vulnerable planes on it—it looks like a tired, "real" face that's not acting, just letting itself be seen. And Grant, usually the skittish charmer, plays his court scene with an unaccustomed earnestness. He pleads movingly to the judge to keep his baby—his voice even breaks. It's a powerful scene, one of the least evasive Grant ever played.

BUT WITH ALL THIS melodramatic emotion spilling out of the scenes, the movie as a whole fails to project any romantic sensation between the husband and the wife. They don't even share the sarcasm that had stood in for erotic complicity between McCarey's Grant and Dunne. Here they share no feelings at all, except about the child. And when the child dies of an illness, something unexpected happens cinematically. The movie becomes a film noir, graced by shadows, psychological menace, and suspense, heavily underscored with Roy Webb's gloomy, passionate background music. We see Dunne at a darkened desk, writing a letter to Beulah Bondi about her husband. "Since that night when the child died," she writes, "we have been like strangers. . . . He does not realize that by punishing himself he's punishing me." We see the doomed couple through the rain-drenched window of their upstairs living room, each sitting alone, staring fixedly into the fire. Suddenly there comes a knock at the door downstairs. When Grant joins Dunne to see who it is, we're afraid there's going to be a murder. It turns out to be a mother with her little boy. Their car has broken down, and they're simply asking for the telephone; yet the movie's mood darkens even more. Stevens's "happy" ending, in which Dunne and Grant receive a telephone call from Beulah Bondi about another adoptable child and decide to take it, hardly compensates for the gloom, since the movie shows them receiving the news on the shadowy stairwell and, in the last image, disappearing arm in arm into the absolutely dark nursery where their first child died and their new child will live. The disparate but hopeful elements that once had combined to create the nature of romantic comedy—the sentiment, the slapstick, the warm, close-in duo-ensemble playing—have been overpowered in *Penny Serenade* by these shadows and this emptiness. It's an eerily knowing movie. What it knows is that the love between men and women, presented all through the thirties as a force that could heal the ills of America, can become, upon the death of a child who was supposed to crown it, something bogus and empty.

A number of late-thirties, early-forties movies unintentionally prefigure the end of Depression romantic comedy—among them (all from 1940) La Cava's *Primrose Path* with its small-town naturalism; Hawks's *His Girl Friday* with its cynically frenetic pace; George Cukor's (and Hepburn's) *The Philadelphia Story,* with its barely concealed cult of the upper crust. But *Love Affair* and *Penny Serenade* are probably the most prescient elegies for the genre. Their actual subject is the leaking away of vitality from the thirties vision of romance, even though they use opposite means to convey the same message. McCarey plays out the failure of romance in an international setting, using probably the most sophisticated characters the genre ever produced. Stevens sets it at the other end of the scale, in an isolated, rural spot, where characters who are the inverse of McCarey's sophisticates gradually slip into despair. In fact, *Penny Serenade* is a social-determinist drama of the kind Depression Hollywood might have produced if it had concentrated more on the politics of the Depression. *Penny Serenade* matches many of the socialist-realist novels of the era: it recounts how the endless struggle of the lower middle class to make ends meet ultimately wears away its capacity to enjoy the "finer things" in life—not just fancy dinners, nightclubs, dancing, and smart hats but romance itself.

Placed as it was at the end of the Depression, *Penny Serenade* could have become romantic comedy's most incisive comment on its own demise. Its very flashback structure implies a commentary on the genre. At the start of the movie, Irene Dunne has decided to leave her husband. She plays phonograph records of the songs of their youth, and we see the scenes that match the songs. The "youth," as reproduced by the movie, is a reprise of the conventions of romantic comedy; the "middle age" concerns the realization of the falsity of the genre's promises. This is one of the bleakest, most tragic and downright weary movies of its day, and yet it fails to stand up as the great and self-aware artifact it might have been, or should have been, because Stevens himself got caught in the sentimental currents he had set loose in it. *Penny Serenade* is really two movies, trying uneasily to blend on the screen. The scenes concerning the child—this freckled, impish, but curiously listless little creature surprising her mother with a birthday present or appearing as an angel in the school Christmas play—are nothing but heart-wringing soap scenes, while the glimpses of the empty romance between husband and wife, transmitted through the subtlety of Grant's and Dunne's acting, belong to another, sharper movie.

Penny Serenade fails in the end to distinguish between its own keen social insights and its easy melancholy. McCarey had gotten similarly confused in *Love Affair:* he had intermittently let go the tension of the ensemble playing in favor of the wet-handkerchief stuff with the orphans. At the end of this era, even the boldest and most imaginative directors of romantic comedy couldn't follow through on the bleak revelations the genre had led them to. That's when the whole enterprise had to die.

THE FOLLOWING YEAR, 1941, George Stevens recovered his sense of humor, or so it seemed. At Katharine Hepburn's urging, he made a movie with her at MGM, *Woman of the Year,* which would inaugurate a whole new cycle of romantic comedies starring Hepburn and Spencer Tracy. And yet, for all its surface obeisance to the independence of the Hepburn character, *Woman of the Year* brings Hepburn down from her heights more cruelly than Irene Dunne was ever struck down by fate in *Love Affair* or wearied by poverty in *Penny Serenade.* In a tour-de-force kitchen scene that forecasts television situation comedy, Hepburn, the world-famous journalist, at-tempts to cook breakfast for Spencer Tracy, the sportswriter. But it's not funny like the scene of Irene Dunne washing the adopted baby in front of a concerned Cary Grant—it's mean. Tracy watches Hepburn's helplessness with a complacent smirk on his face. *He's* not supposed to know how to cook a breakfast. This guy has never been subject to the impulse of a Clark Gable in *It Happened One Night,* to turn domestic in front of a spoiled but good-natured heiress like Claudette Colbert. *Woman of the Year* sees noth-ing wrong with Tracy's arch detachment from Hepburn: its intention is to reprimand Hepburn for her highfalutin tendencies, her failure to know how to make a breakfast, her all-consuming nervousness. *Woman of the Year,* and the eight Tracy-Hepburn movies that followed it over the years, all con-tained the implication that the stuck-up Hepburn would have to submit to a series of humiliations in order to be worthy of the boyishly rueful yet quietly manly Spencer Tracy. For that reason the Hepburn-Tracy "come-dies" of the forties and fifties belong in another category from Depression romantic comedy. They are actually inversions of the genre; they seem to pay lip service to the spunk of the thirties heroine, only to humiliate her and put her back, in the end, into an inferior, and properly adoring, position in a man's world.

But Depression romantic comedy hadn't compromised itself everywhere in Hollywood in the early forties. At Paramount, the genre was enjoying a late fling, an Indian summer. The man responsible for this event was not one of the directors who had pioneered the genre in the thirties, but a scriptwriter who had tried all through the thirties to become a director and had finally made it in 1940 through sheer persistence combined with uncanny talent. Preston Sturges, this aristocrat-turned-populist-turned-consummate-satirist, was one of the strangest characters who ever flourished in the strange town of Hollywood. Among other odd traits, he showed himself immune to the sentimentality about the approaching war that had overtaken the other romantic-comedy auteurs in the late thirties and early forties. Sturges alone kept his manic wit intact in those years. He also brought a new, personal, at times farcical but in fact intensely serious set of thoughts about wealth and gender to the once socially conscious romantic comedy of the Depression. He made it live again for a moment, in all its childlike excitement and its grown-up humility.

11

STURGES, STANWYCK, AND COLBERT:

THE LADY EVE AND THE PALM BEACH STORY

Joel McCrea, Mary Astor, Preston Sturges, Claudette Colbert, and
Rudy Vallee on the set of *The Palm Beach Story.*

THE WORK OF PRESTON STURGES closes the circle of the romantic comedy that came out of the Depression, using the heroine to dramatize the plight of the country's nonwealthy. The two romantic comedies Sturges wrote and directed between 1940 and 1942, *The Lady Eve* (1941) and *The Palm Beach Story* (1942), are both complex tributes to Capra's genre as it had evolved till then. They even make use of Capra's original leading ladies: *Eve* stars Barbara Stanwyck, and *Palm Beach* stars Claudette Colbert. Both of these movies belong as well to the late, decadent phase of Depression romantic comedy. They knit together recycled bits of earlier romantic comedies, and they make intentional use of previous directors' strategies, fantasies, and slapstick business. And yet, for all their self-conscious commentary, each of them contains the extra urgency that belongs to the best romantic comedies, that has to do with the metaphoric truth-telling of director and leading lady. They base their very plot structures on the personae these two actresses had created, not just with Capra but with other romantic-comedy directors. And they do that in part by borrowing the outlines of certain episodes taken from Preston Sturges's own life. One could say that these two movies, in the tradition of Capra and his confreres, are portraits, projected through the persona of a favored leading lady, of their director's psyche.

Edmund Preston Biden was born in 1898 in Chicago. In 1901, at the age of two, he was wrenched from whatever tranquil environment he might have enjoyed during his mother's brief marriage to his father, a small-time entrepreneur, by her sudden ambition to sing on the stage. Mary Dempsey, later Mary Desti, a colorful character who had studied homeopathic medicine but aspired to something more worldly, took Preston off to Paris, where, because of a chance meeting between her and the then largely unknown Isadora Duncan, Mary and her child were swept up into the Duncan clan's bohemian life. That life consisted in giving in to a whole series of half-gay, half-self-righteous impulses to *épater les bourgeois* by means of impromptu dancing, practical jokes, and makeshift *grandes fêtes*. Mary Desti became Isadora Duncan's most devoted follower, sister, and look-alike for many years, taking time out from this probably dominant relationship only to shore up her shaky finances by means of several shrewd marriages, the most important of which was her second (in January 1902), to Chicago stockbroker Solomon Sturges III, who adopted her son.

Back and forth between Europe and Chicago Preston was sent, between

two poles of experience. In Europe, he shared the theatrical Duncan life-
style, distinguished by costumes of tunics and Grecian sandals, with miniature versions for children; hired autos, express trains, arrivals at all hours
of the night; dancing through the streets of major capitals; swooping down
suddenly on the Lido, Helgoland, Bayreuth, Paris, Florence. The children
of the party (Preston and Isadora's young niece Temple) were cared for
intermittently: picked up and squeezed fervently, prayed for when ill, fed
spoonfuls of champagne—or else forgotten during revelries, parked somewhere with some convenient older person. This was small Preston's experience between the ages of two and three, and then again between five and
six. In Chicago, on the other hand, at ages three to five and seven to eight,
he lived the opposite sort of life, consisting of regular school, regular
bedtimes, sedate childrens' birthday parties, nurses—all the spacious, muted
routine of a wealthy household in a mighty midwestern city. When Preston
was eight, Mary Desti formally divorced Solomon Sturges and took her son
back to Europe to live with her, though Preston didn't stop visiting his
stepfather in Chicago. As Preston grew older, the financial disparity between his two lives diminished: Isadora, by taking up with the sewing-
machine heir Paris Singer, moved out of the demimonde, and Mary Desti
became an entrepreneur to match Isadora's affluence. She sold perfumes and
cosmetics to wealthy friends and clients, bluffing her way into prosperity,
with her son as her occasional assistant. But the philosophical underpin-
nings of Preston's two lives remained violently opposed. Art versus business;
spontaneity versus routine; adventure versus domesticity; bohemia versus
Main Street; Europe versus America—these polarities continued to war in
his young mind even as he grew to maturity.

When Preston emerged from the patchwork of French and Swiss schools
his mother had haphazardly sent him to, capped off by officers' training in
America at the end of the First World War, he was educated, but he had
no clue about who he was or what he should do. Instead of deciding those
matters, he arranged, in between stints of managing the Maison Desti
cosmetics business, to slip into the lives of other people equipped to provide
for him. In 1923 he married Estelle Mudge, an heiress on a moderate scale,
who supported him for four years on her small country estate, until she got
tired of his refusal to make a career in the world. When this marriage ended
in 1927, Preston struggled to live on nothing in Manhattan but periodically
returned to his stepfather in Chicago, who fed and clothed him and offered
him comradely and unjudgmental affection. During these years of seclusion,
Preston wasn't entirely idle; he fancied himself an inventor. He took out
patents: on grooved leaf springs for cars; a plate-glass carrier for trucks; a
new photoengraving process; a flying machine that went straight up. To-

ward the end of the twenties, he turned his inventiveness to an old hobby, writing popular songs; and in 1928, while recovering from a burst appendix in a Chicago hospital, he tried his hand at a play, *The Guinea Pig*. He managed to get the play, a wacky romance between two playwrights (male and female) produced in a small theater near Broadway. Buoyed by the public's appreciation of *The Guinea Pig*, he wrote a second play, *Strictly Dishonorable*, and persuaded the great Brock Pemberton to produce it, this time on Broadway, at the Avon Theater. *Strictly Dishonorable*, which opened on September 17, 1929, became the runaway comedy hit of the 1929–30 season.

OVERNIGHT, the thirty-one-year-old Sturges, hitherto something of a genteel bum, had turned into the author of a celebrated Broadway play. Ironically, it was a play about a genteel bum—except that Sturges had changed the bum's gender to make the story more palatable to the public. The protagonist of *Strictly Dishonorable* is Isabel Parry, a pretty girl from an impoverished old southern family, who, to get out of the South, has come north to marry the straitlaced and petulant Henry, from New Jersey. In the play, Henry and Isabel find themselves in Manhattan, in a cozy Italian speakeasy. Henry has a fit of ill humor which so offends Isabel that she breaks with him, throwing herself upon the mercy of the speakeasy's all-male population. "Poor" and "unworldly" are written all over her, but Isabel also displays a cheerful pragmatism. Magically, the men of the speakeasy—the Italian owner, the kindly old judge, the Irish cop on the street, and the young Italian opera singer who lives upstairs (who is also a count)—rise up in a body and become fairy godfathers to her, offering food and shelter. The young tenor-count even offers love. Isabel returns his love and decides to become his mistress, but is a little scared to take the plunge. Finally, after a chaste night in the tenor's apartment over the speakeasy, through a series of happy accidents and timid suggestions from the godfathers, Isabel finds both respectability and happiness as the noble tenor's bride-to-be.

Sturges was no ordinary playwright. He didn't teach himself to write plays step by step. Instead, he fell into a fully formed dramatic universe, a place already equipped with a unique set of rules. Of course Sturges had to learn to make all this comprehensible in a play—and he proved superbly good at writing dialogue and devising structure. But from the beginning of *Strictly Dishonorable*, we can recognize the special qualities of a Sturgean situation. The protagonist is a waif, who appears to be heading toward danger, poverty, and abandonment. Rescue comes to her, however, before she endures even a moment's discomfort. And what a rescue! She doesn't just get the necessities—she gets a whole kingdom. She is showered with luck and generosity, in a way that is so transparently wishful it's funny. Moreover, it's through no effort of her own. All that Isabel possesses to make her worthy of good fortune, besides looks, is a vague willingness to be adventurous. It's a charming quality, but in terms of the drama she stands as a peculiarly passive character. She doesn't have to change to get what she gets. The only suspense in the play concerns the terms of her transformation. Will she be looked down on because she's an object of charity for the others? Naturally not: in Sturges's universe the heroine receives everything and gives up nothing.

Undoubtedly this scenario came from Sturges's own life, from watching first his stepfather and then his wife rescue him from penury, and hoping they didn't think any the less of him. And the irony of Sturges's story is how closely the work paralleled the life—or vice versa. In the afterglow of *Strictly Dishonorable*'s success, on the train to Palm Beach, where he was heading to write a new play, Sturges met a woman who had the means to take care of him for life, the twenty-year-old Eleanor Post Hutton, granddaughter of C. W. Post, the cereal king, and one of the fabled heiresses of America. He eloped with her in 1930 in a splash of publicity. The marriage was strained from the first by Sturges's violently contradictory impulses toward his new wife. First he tried to dominate her: he made her move into his tiny apartment and put her on a strict budget. After all, he had written a hit play; he was now a successful man of the world. But he still needed, in some part of himself, to be supported by her kind of money, so he eventually moved into a twenty-room townhouse she bought, and allowed her to back an unwieldy operetta *(The Silver Swan)* he had written. Not surprisingly, the marriage failed after two years. But as messy as it must have been, it gave the writer Sturges a glimpse into the lives and psyches of the fabulously wealthy, which he would shortly put to use—in Hollywood.

Sturges went to Hollywood in 1932, for the reasons all the New York writers did: he didn't have any more money. He had written two plays after *Strictly Dishonorable,* and the operetta, all of which had bombed. Universal, the studio that had made the 1931 movie of *Strictly Dishonorable,* brought Sturges to California, but Universal was in even worse economic shape than the other studios in the early thirties, and Sturges was soon dropped. Finding himself at large, he did something unusual. He wrote an original script, not under contract to any studio, and he set about marketing it to the highest bidder. Even more unusual, he managed to sell it to the prestigious Jesse Lasky, one of the founders of Paramount, now a producer at Fox, who staked a lot of money on it and brought it to the screen in 1933. The movie is called *The Power and the Glory.* Surprisingly, in the light of Sturges's earlier work, it is not a comedy but a drama, almost a melodrama, about a self-made tycoon modeled on Sturges's erstwhile grandfather-in-law, C. W. Post. Fox's young tough Spencer Tracy played the tycoon, whose story is told in flashback, through the perspective of his former boyhood friend. The film has a brooding, literary style. The narrator's measured voice is heard almost constantly, giving his doom-laden commentary. And shadows accumulate in the tycoon's life as the movie progresses.

The Power and the Glory did not become a hit, though it proved to be strangely prophetic. It has been called a forerunner of the ultimate Hollywood tycoon biography, *Citizen Kane,* and anybody who has seen both films will find the resemblance marked, and beyond coincidence. What concerns us here, though, is that in this movie Sturges enlarged his own dramatic territory to include the life of America's very rich. The concept of unlimited wealth was implicit in his work before *The Power and the Glory:* his "core story" of the waif's rescue depended on the rescuer's possessing some kind of surfeit wealth or privilege. But in *The Power and the Glory* Sturges approached the equation from the other side. He made a serious examination of what it might be like to be the possessor of unlimited money and power. So, though *The Power and the Glory* wasn't a comedy, it was important to the gestation period of one of the most brilliant comedy writers the movies have ever known. The next year, 1934, Capra's *It Happened One Night,* with its part-time waifs and benevolent tycoons, would burst upon the scene. But even before Capra brought his romantic-comedy formula to the movie industry, Sturges the writer had found his own versions of Capra's stock characters. He was ahead of the game.

DURING THE YEARS when romantic comedy was taking hold, 1933 to 1936, Sturges was doing piecework, scripts by the job, mostly for Universal. Among these were an orphan story, *The Good Fairy* (1935), starring Margaret Sullavan as a naive cinema usherette, and a tycoon story, *Diamond Jim* (also 1935), starring Edward Arnold as Diamond Jim Brady. Neither was a romantic comedy in the Capraesque sense. But there is no doubt that Capra's ascendancy in Hollywood came as a revelation to Sturges. We can imagine his shock of recognition when he saw *It Happened One Night:* Peter Warne and Ellie Andrews meeting on the Florida–New York bus all but dramatized his own meeting on the New York–Florida train with the heiress Eleanor Hutton. (And Capra and Riskin might well have remembered the Sturges-Hutton marriage while preparing their script.) It wasn't until years later, after he began to direct his own scripts, that Sturges paid recognizable tribute to Capra, by writing a sort of pro-Capra polemic into his semiautobiographical *Sullivan's Travels* (1941) (the sequence in which the movie's director hero, in an audience of chain-gang prisoners, realizes the force of comedy) and by building his two romantic comedies around Capra's original leading ladies, Barbara Stanwyck and Claudette Colbert. But Sturges's first outright romantic comedy script, *Easy Living,* written when he went to Paramount in 1937 and starring the third of Capra's "discoveries," Jean Arthur, reveals how much he had borrowed in spirit not just from Capra but from the other romantic-comedy directors who had followed Capra's lead.

Plot-wise, *Easy Living* is one of the cleverest romantic comedies released in that peak year of the genre, 1937—the year of *Stage Door* and *The Awful Truth.* It's about a junior editor at the *Boys' Constant Companion,* Mary Smith, who is riding on the top of a double-decker bus when a sable coat falls on her head. Trying to return the coat, she meets J. B. Ball, "the Bull of Broad Street," who threw it from his mansion roof during an argument with his wife. Ball impulsively gives her the coat. Suddenly, people think she's his mistress. Everybody in town starts to offer her things for free—a luxury apartment, new clothes, tips on the stock market. Coincidentally, she encounters J. B. Ball's son, Johnny, in an automat, where he is working to prove to his father that he can earn his own living. At the movie's climax, the stock market plunges because of something Mary casually told a stockbroker. J.B. faces ruin. And all the lead characters get tangled up—literally—in the ticker tape that is spewing out of a machine in Ball's office, before they untangle themselves, and the market, enough to allow Mary and Johnny to get engaged.

One can see how seamlessly Sturges had merged his personal comic agenda with Paramount's romantic-comedy conventions. The story spins out from a typical Sturgean barbed act of charity—J. B. Ball's giving the coat to Mary Smith. But with the entrance of J.B.'s son, it turns into a Capra-esque cross-class romance. Mary herself is a version of Sturges's original orphan heroine, Isabel Parry—she has Isabel's crazy good luck—but she's also a smart working girl in the tradition of Paramount's Colbert and Lombard heroines. Sturges carefully constructs the opening scenes—Mary on the bus, Mary at her job, Mary in her apartment—to convey the familiar documentary approach to the working woman's life. By contrast, he writes scenes for the Ball family that are full of the surreally daffy aura that rich people had acquired in other romantic comedies. J. B. Ball is a descendant of Sturges's earlier movie tycoons (he's even played by Edward Arnold, who starred in the Sturges-scripted *Diamond Jim*), but he and his family also resemble Gregory La Cava's spoiled and unbalanced Bullocks from *My Man Godfrey.* (Sturges might well have observed La Cava on the *Godfrey* set; at the time *Godfrey* was filmed, Sturges was still working at Universal.) The crowd of colorful supporting characters in *Easy Living*—speculators and bums—can already be recognized as Sturgean, but they are also descendants of Capra's down-and-out types. And the movie's habit of frequently overflowing into slapstick owes a lot to Leo McCarey's movie-making strategies. In his first nearly original romantic comedy (he had based it on a story by Vera Caspary), Sturges had made a compendium of the genre's styles that fit together neatly in one movie.

He had also added a radical new dimension to romantic comedy—a grand vision of social chaos. In earlier romantic comedies, there had been two more or less stationary social layers, "rich" and "ordinary." No characters but the two leads crossed between the layers. Capra's Ellie Andrews may have ventured onto a Greyhound, but old Mr. Andrews, her father, never would have done that. Nor would Gregory La Cava's Bullocks have changed places with the forgotten men on the dump. In Sturges's world, though, society is not fixed but in constant motion. Orphans and tycoons are part of the same unbalanced urban system; people bounce back and forth crazily and temporarily between the layers. Mary Smith bounces into a higher cadre because of the windfall of the sable coat, but she doesn't have the cash to buy a meal at the automat. Johnny Ball bounces into a lower cadre by working at the automat, but then he meets Mary, who has a swank apartment and a sable coat. In this respect, *Easy Living* carries a social critique that is more radical than the instinctive populist fervor of the earlier romantic comedies. Everybody in this movie is an impersonator; everybody is interconnected financially; and everybody except the two leads is greedy enough to throw away the common good for the sake of profit. The merest rumor about Mary and J.B. leads all kinds of people to try to cash in on it. An idle comment about the price of steel almost causes a new Crash. And *Easy Living*'s tycoon, J. B. Ball, emerges as the least substantial figure in the movie. His empire almost disappears in a day, in a swirl of ticker tape. The movie, in fact, gets as close as romantic comedy ever did to positing a world where it's permanently October 29, 1929.

But for all its zaniness, *Easy Living,* in terms of characterization, never advances beyond a brilliant synthesizing exercise. The personalities of the leads are essentially blank. Despite Jean Arthur's sweet-tempered perplexity, Mary remains as passive and unreadable as Sturges's earliest heroine, Isabel Parry. Ray Milland's Johnny Ball proves even vaguer. He's simply a likable, well-behaved young man with no distinguishing characteristics. And their romance holds no tension. They meet, fall in love, then wait like people in a cyclone for the lull that will let them get engaged. If anything, Mary's relations with J.B. show more dramatic kick than her relations with his son,

Johnny. Mary and J.B. have a lively argument in a taxi about the proper way to do a multiplication problem. Mary and Johnny never manage to hold even an intimate conversation. It's clear that Sturges hadn't yet become interested in the "romance" part of romantic comedy. He had shrewdly seen how his fascination with the rich giving things away to the poorer fit in with Capra's Depression genre. But in 1937, the complications of giving and receiving were still more important to him than whatever lovers went through when they fell in love.

IN 1938, all that began to change. Sturges married for the third time, an Iowa-born woman named Louise Tevis, whom he had known casually for some years. She and her husband, an older stockbroker, had been regulars at the restaurant Sturges owned at this time, the Players. When Sturges fell in love with her, Louise divorced her first husband to marry him. And the effect was immediately apparent in Sturges's work. In early 1939 he wrote an original romantic comedy for Paramount which he called *Beyond Those Tears,* after an anonymous Scottish love song, but which the studio re-named *Remember the Night.* It is conceived in a completely different style from *Easy Living,* and, as directed by Mitchell Leisen, it reproduces the script word for word. The heroine isn't a passive young working girl who stumbles onto wealth and good fortune. She's a nightmare exaggeration of that figure—a shoplifter, who breaks the law to acquire those things. The first image we see in the movie is a glittering jewel in a case, a typical Paramount opening, telegraphing glamour and high life. Then we see the leading lady, played by Barbara Stanwyck, reach into the case and steal the jewel. She is arrested. Enter the hero, played by Fred MacMurray, who is not only someone from the opposite social class but her formal adversary, the prosecuting attorney who tries her case. MacMurray, on an impulse, pays Stanwyck's bail so she can be out of prison over Christmas, and, finding she's from Indiana, decides on another impulse to drive her to her family on his way to his.

As usual, a Sturgean impulsive act of charity—MacMurray's footing Stan-wyck's bail—precipitates the drama. But "drama" doesn't mean the comic complications of earlier movies; it means a tragicomic love affair. MacMur-ray's lawyer falls in love with Stanwyck's criminal, and she with him, in the car trip to Indiana. (Starting with *Remember the Night,* Sturges would wholeheartedly embrace Capra's original device of a journey as the proper setting for a love affair.) This is the movie in which Sturges discovered romance. He discovered, in fact, what the other romantic-comedy directors had found out each in turn: that romance makes people feel weak because of what they can't offer the loved one, and strong because of what they dream of getting from the loved one. In *Remember the Night* Sturges's script dramatized these strengthening and debilitating powers of romance more starkly than any romantic comedy had yet done, by widening the gulf between the two lovers. His heroine is a criminal—the ultimate have-not—while his hero is the ultimate "have," one of society's guardians of property. Sturges even attempts to explain how each of them got this way by showing us their contrasting homes. Stanwyck's is a broken-down, unpainted house, inhabited by a mean, uncaring mother. MacMurray's home, where he decides to take her after he sees hers, represents the other Indiana—bright and warm with a Christmas tree, fresh-baked bread, and Beulah Bondi's mother love. It is romance that allows the Stanwyck and MacMurray figures to bridge their seemingly impassable social gulf: romance teaches Stanwyck to believe in MacMurray's generosity and lets MacMurray believe in Stanwyck's retrievability. Stanwyck and MacMurray's characters are not just passive juveniles like *Easy Living*'s Mary and Johnny, waiting for comic accidents to bring them together; they're complex adults, using their intelligence to reverse old habits. In the end, not just the dictates of love but the demands of justice are met too. Stanwyck goes back to prison to finish out her term, and MacMurray promises that he will wait for her.

Though Sturges would write many movies that were cleverer and more balanced than *Remember the Night,* he never again wrote one as emotionally revealing. The fact that most of the movie takes place in the Midwest, where his new wife grew up, tips us off to the personal content. Louise Tevis was the first "ordinary" American Sturges had fallen in love with; she was not an heiress like his two former wives. But she was richer, in one sense, than they were: she boasted a settled and secure small-town upbringing, which Sturges obviously admired and envied. These complicated feelings of envy were played out in the movie, in Sturges's usual reverse-gender fashion. The character who had often stood in for Sturges's own wish for wealth—the adventuress—here stands for his shame about having the wish. She's what an adventuress is called in legal language—a thief—and she comes from a cruel, bloodless America that doesn't want her. The lawyer is the Louise figure, the one with the normal ethics and the American-dream background, where people bake and clean and go to square dances and care about their children. There are no actual wealthy people in this drama. For this once, Sturges omitted the tycoon and his milieu, in order to turn the focus from real wealth to the wealth and poverty of the psyche. What counts here is not money but food, shelter, warmth, and the sensation of abundance that the heroine has never known. The movie almost froths over in its eagerness to portray these sappy customs of Louise's mythical past. (Sturges seems transfixed by Carrie Jacobs Bond's treacly song "When You Come to the End of a Perfect Day.") But the melancholy Stanwyck figure, placed in relief against the American cornucopia, carries the real message of the movie: that poverty can warp a personality, and a warped personality can only be reclaimed through love.

It is not known, given the absence of a Paramount archive, whether Sturges wrote *Remember the Night* specifically for Stanwyck. He could have: Stanwyck had a new contract with Paramount, and Sturges was a new Paramount writer. But whether it was by design or coincidence, *Remember the Night* proved to be one of Stanwyck's finest movies of the thirties. It drew out the grief and loneliness she could reveal so movingly beneath her tough and efficient façade. Canny directors, who had helped create parts explicitly for her, had seen this side of Stanwyck and made use of it. Capra had been the first, but John Cromwell in *Banjo on My Knee* (1936) also dramatized Stanwyck's wild loneliness, and so, in another way, did King Vidor in *Stella Dallas* (1937). Sturges undoubtedly had seen these movies; he saw everything—he was known as a movie addict. And at some point, whether before or after he wrote *Remember the Night,* Sturges accorded Barbara Stanwyck a special place in his imagination. Perhaps he felt close to her because she was an orphan in real life, and he was an orphan of sorts. In any case, Sturges was interested enough in the idea of a Stanwyck on the wrong side of the law to use her in this guise again, after he became a director.

WHEN STURGES GOT permission in 1940 from Paramount's then head of production, William Le Baron, to direct his own scripts, he acquired a fresh burst of energy. *The Great McGinty* (1940), his first project as both director and writer, poured forth such a flood of comic rhetoric, such a procession of inventive mugs and thugs, such a wild flurry of plot invention, that the public flocked to see it, even though it featured no big stars. The movie turned into an unexpected hit. The same was true of the second movie Sturges wrote and directed, *Christmas in July* (1940). It was in these two movies that Sturges, apparently at the suggestion of William Wyler, began creating a stock company of his own. He gathered a small crowd of eccentric and capable character actors, mostly male, of all ages and sizes, for whom he wrote specially tailored parts.

But on closer examination, Sturges's becoming a director didn't change the course of the career he had been building till then. It even backed him up a little, in terms of his central characters. Both *The Great McGinty* and *Christmas in July* were based on plays or treatments Sturges had written in the thirties. Both revolved around the familiar displaced Sturgean character, a man in these two cases, upon whom fortune suddenly smiles: in *McGinty* this character was a bum who suddenly got appointed to public office; in *Christmas* he was an office clerk who thought he had won an advertising-slogan contest. Both main characters, played by Brian Donlevy and Dick Powell respectively, were in some sense amiable blanks, who provided eyes of the storm for Sturges's swirl of designing rogues. Nothing happened *inside* them in the course of their movies.

But when Sturges got to his third project as a director, the one in which Paramount permitted him a big budget and big stars, he caught up to himself again. He had in readiness a romantic-comedy script that he had written for Claudette Colbert, around 1937, right after *Easy Living*. It was based on a short story by the English playwright Monckton Hoffe called "Two Bad Hats," and it concerned a pompous, though young and attractive, English lord who falls in love on shipboard with an exuberant American girl but rejects her as too "common" to marry. She gets her revenge by impersonating her own imaginary twin sister and acting well bred and distant with him. There was talk at Paramount of putting Carole Lombard into a movie of "Two Bad Hats," but the film never was made. When Sturges became a director, however, he rewrote this script for Barbara Stanwyck. What he actually did was place Stanwyck's criminal character from *Remember the Night* into the cross-class, shipboard romance of "Two Bad Hats," and rearrange accordingly. In this manner he began to mix the comic raucousness of movies like *Easy Living*, *The Great McGinty*, and *Christmas in July* with the romantic depth of *Remember the Night*. And in the process he added new complexity, new possibilities, and new problems to the romantic-comedy equation.

THE FACT THAT Stanwyck plays a thief again in *The Lady Eve* doesn't mean, at least not at first, that she is the impoverished and psychically wounded figure from *Remember the Night*. Instead, she's the elegant swindler and card shark Jean Harrington, daughter and ally of Colonel Harry—"Handsome Harry"—Harrington, played wonderfully by Charles Coburn. Sturges has promoted her in *The Lady Eve* to a top echelon of criminals. Father and daughter both display smart, worldly wardrobes and the sharpest wits seen in romantic comedy since Lubitsch's Gaston and Lily of *Trouble in Paradise* pickpocketed their way among the capitals of Europe. Professionally, they have staked out the territory of the transatlantic ocean liners. The movie first discovers them on such a ship, somewhere in the tropics, at the moment when the big liner rendezvous with a little boat to take on a passenger reputed to be a rich young man going home from a scientific expedition. The camera travels up the big white ship, past a line of people ogling the little boat, up to the top deck, where it finds Stanwyck and Coburn, arrayed in dazzling white sports clothes, noting the arrival of a prime victim. When Stanwyck protests that *she* shouldn't always be forced to do the romancing of victims—that she'd like to see her father "giving some old harpie the three-in-one"—Coburn gravely reprimands her. "Let us be crooked, but never common," he says, a line that signals the Irish lilt with which they go about their high-class thieving. As a final flourish to his introduction of Stanwyck, Sturges has her drop an apple onto the head of the tiny figure down below—the rich heir on the little boat. This Adam and Eve aren't going to meet mindlessly, in a slapstick situation, like most of their counterparts in romantic comedies. Sturges intends for her to go after him, like her biblical ancestress, and offer him the all-too-bitter fruit of knowledge.

One sees immediately that Jean Harrington is the apotheosis of her sister romantic-comedy heroines who were smarter than their paramours but couldn't make this too obvious within romantic comedy's conventions. Sturges has eliminated the ambivalence in earlier heroines—Stevens's and La Cava's street-smart but forgiving Ginger Rogers, McCarey's ingenious but submissive Irene Dunne, and, most of all, Capra's cynically witty but compulsively maternal Jean Arthur. Sturges's Stanwyck is smart enough to succeed in the business of outwitting people. She is a predator, in such a way as to forecast the forties, that decade in which any clever female in the movies was assumed to be duplicitous. But as aggressive as she is in her profession, Jean Harrington still belongs squarely to thirties romantic comedy, since her main task in the movie is to work out a viable relationship with the character played by her co-star, Henry Fonda. Fonda is Charles "Hopsie" Pike, son of the fabulously wealthy brewer of Pike's Pale ("The Ale That Won for Yale") and also a serious amateur ophiologist, a student of snakes. Chronologically, we meet Fonda's Hopsie even before we see Stanwyck's Jean—in the movie's very first scene, set on a desert island, where Fonda and his watchdog, Muggsy (William Demarest), are leaving the snake-hunting expedition to join the big liner. From the slightly bilious expression on Henry Fonda's face, from the way his Hopsie thanks the head scientist with earnest respect, we can tell what a chump he is.

Hopsie Pike, the inept and sheltered boy-child of great wealth and privilege, is even more of an exaggeration of the romantic-comedy hero than Stanwyck's Jean is of the heroine. His forebearers are all those charming but vague leading men who had preceded him—the politely opaque Fred Mac-Murray in *Alice Adams,* the mildly sadistic Fred Astaire in *Swing Time,* the emotionally impacted Cary Grant in *The Awful Truth,* the monstrously

Barbara
Stanwyck and
Henry Fonda
in *The Lady Eve*.

innocent Capra-Riskin characters played by Gary Cooper and Jimmy Stewart. Those movies hadn't spent much effort on clarifying their heroes'
psychology: the directors had concentrated on their "little man" heroines
and casually indulged the heroes. As a result, those heroes had gotten away
with potentially harmful degrees of rakish innocence. Sturges, however, put
his hero under relentlessly satiric scrutiny. Hopsie's innocence isn't indulged; it's mocked and deplored. Sturges spins out gag after gag about his
unpreparedness in the face of Stanwyck's feminine wiles. We watch the
Harringtons arrange to meet him. Hopsie is alone in the ship's dining
room, reading *Are Snakes Necessary?* and trying to avoid the eyes of passengers eager to socialize. Stanwyck has him under observation in her hand
mirror, and in this "movie within the mirror," narrated by her in a voice-
over, we see him get up from his table, walk toward the door, and—flash
of Stanwyck's shapely foot and leg—fall sprawling at their table. Having
tripped him, Jean proceeds to hook him on her female charms. She takes
him down to her cabin to help her find a new pair of shoes—he had knocked
a heel off one she was wearing. She lets him finger the shoes, put them on
her feet, and smell her perfume. It's too much for him, and Sturges jokes
about this by showing us a shot of Stanwyck blurred as if in Fonda's
swooning gaze. Then the Harringtons propose a card game, which Hopsie
joins like a true sucker. He even shows Coburn and Stanwyck how to palm
a card, with the words "Have you seen this one?"

Sturges's Hopsie Pike isn't just a caricature of youthful masculinity, he's
also an embodiment of Sturges's idea of excessive wealth. Earlier romantic-
comedy directors had been content merely to chastise the rich for their
narrow-mindedness, or mock them for their ridiculousness. Sturges takes a
rich character apart to see how he works. Fonda's Hopsie is a person who's
lived a good deal inside himself, who doesn't know how to listen, who has
no reflexes or instincts, whose generic good manners have anesthetized his
mind—and who is unacquainted with what romantic comedy considered
the prime tool for coping in the world: irony. Sturges had lived the life of
the rich enough to know at first hand how those automaton "good sons"
are formed. He himself, off and on, had played son to a wealthy father. One
can tell by the accuracy of Hopsie's characteristics that Sturges drew him
from firsthand knowledge. "Sir?" Fonda says when Coburn's Colonel Harrington gives him a fatherly warning, pointing to a "beware of professional
card sharks" sign. That "sir" precisely conveys the automatic, impersonal
subservience affected by good sons of the rich toward whomever they
thought was a father figure. In Hopsie, Sturges was holding a part of himself
up to mockery.

At the same time, there's something of Sturges in Jean Harrington, transmitted through the movie's obvious delight in her and her father's talents. The Harringtons impersonating wealthy people are much better at it than the actual wealthy: prettier and more seductive in the case of the daughter, more at ease with money in the case of the father. On the evening of Hopsie's arrival, Stanwyck as Jean looks keenly beautiful in a black se-quined décolleté dress, her midriff bared in forties fashion and her sharp, cynical little features softened by a forties topknot of curls. The Colonel at her side is reassuringly tweedy with his harumphs and his ready checks when he finds himself "losing" at cards. Observing the Harringtons and their routine, one thinks of young Preston and his rakish mother, Mary Desti, who together managed to catch a husband whenever they needed one. How many times did this mother-and-son team cross the ocean on a ship like this one? How close did they come, in their pursuit of the good life, to perpe-trating formal swindles like rigged card games? And how often did Preston play the perfect child in the manner of Stanwyck's Jean, charmingly dutiful yet a touch impudent?

IF *REMEMBER THE NIGHT* is Sturges's most vulnerable movie autobiogra-phy, *The Lady Eve* is his most inventive. He drew on both sides of his own divided life to contrast the *Eve* lovers: part of his experience went into Hopsie Pike, the other part into the Harringtons. But he also experimented wildly with the balance between the two worlds, and the two main charac-ters. Hopsie and Jean never quite reach the state of social equality that earlier romantic-comedy lovers had worked out: they're more like Mary and Johnny of *Easy Living,* always lurching from heights to depths as if on a seesaw with each other. At the beginning of *The Lady Eve* the Stanwyck character commands all the beauty, brains, worldliness, and ingenuity, while the Fonda character appears to have nothing going for him. But then she falls in love with him, partly because he has fallen so for her, and he learns from the ship's purser who and what she really is. The discovery causes Hopsie to seal himself off in the disdainful pose of his class, which sends Jean into despair. Their positions have been reversed: he is now self-righteous—and rich and respectable; she is humiliated and marginal. (She even thinks they've lost the money they made from him at cards, until the Colonel reveals that he has patched together the check he had "nobly" torn up after the card game.)

But Stanwyck eventually takes back the high seat. She and Harry meet an old confederate at the races, currently passing as Sir Alfred McGlennan-Keith, who has invented the scam of winning at bridge in the Connecticut "Bridge Belt," near the home of Hopsie Pike. Stanwyck decides to visit Sir

Alfred in the guise of his niece, the Lady Eve Sidwich. They go to a dinner given in her honor at the Pikes' house. Fonda's Hopsie doesn't consciously recognize her, but he is overcome with confusion in her presence, and humiliates himself in a series of extravagant pratfalls, tripping over couches, bringing down curtains, upending trays of coffee cups and whole roasts of beef on himself. Still, Eve agrees to marry him, but concocts a nymphomaniac past for her English character, which she confesses bit by bit on their wedding night on a train. It's a stormy night. In despair and disgust, Hopsie makes the train stop and gets off, sliding ignominiously into the mud. In the end, after we see Eve nobly refusing to accept any alimony from the Pikes, Hopsie goes off on a trip on the original ocean liner, where he finds her again, with her father, back in their old personae of Jean and the Colonel. He embraces them, orders champagne for the Colonel, proposes that they play "lots and lots of cards," then disappears into a stateroom with Jean, whom he still doesn't know is Eve.

As a comic drama about impersonators of rich people teaching real rich people a moral lesson, *The Lady Eve* is a triumph. The romantic-comedy equation appears to be worked out ingeniously: Hopsie is supposed to introduce Jean/Eve to true love; she is supposed to divest him of class bias and Victorian scruples. But as the story of a real romance flowering from a staged one, it doesn't work. Sturges gets too carried away with the comic spectacle of the unworldly Hopsie being made a constant fool of by the worldly Jean. The two seduction scenes seem more snide than romantic, especially their second trip to her cabin. In this tête-à-tête, Stanwyck holds Fonda's head in a sort of vise: she is curled up on a divan with her cheek against his, stroking his hair, as he huddles on the floor (he has fallen off the divan). Fonda runs through his gamut of sickish expressions and deathly smiles: he is so disturbed by close contact with her that he all but turns green on a black-and-white screen. And Stanwyck's flippancy, with its tones of resentment just beneath the surface, leaves a bad taste, a hint of sordidness we can't quite shake off when we see the two meet on the deck the next morning and act as if they're in love.

In giving in to his satiric impulses with the figure of Hopsie, Sturges has left Stanwyck's Jean/Eve to carry the human content of the movie by herself—a task that proves structurally impossible. After Stanwyck's Jean displays her prodigiously quick intelligence, she is then supposed to turn around and fall in love with this rich dodo, for no other reason than Sturges's cheeky notion of a Freudian time clock that goes off in young women when they become aware of the existence of snakes. The snake theme is woven cleverly through the movie, from the cartoon snake in the opening credits, with its derby and maracas, to Hopsie's scientific snake obsession. It signifies that Jean/Eve is ready to stop adoring her father and fall in love with someone her own age. But it doesn't have much to do with the dynamic between Hopsie and Jean. The real joke about the snakes is that Hopsie, who brings them into the story, is the least sexy person imaginable.

Nevertheless, Stanwyck does her best with her side of the love affair. Since her early-thirties collaboration with Capra, she had watched other actresses, accepted more than a few of their cast-off parts, and found ways to variously lighten and color what might have become a melodramatic acting style. One sees in this movie that she can summon, when needed, a breathlessness à la Carole Lombard ("My name's Eugenia—it's really Jean—c'mon," she says early on to Hopsie) or an aura of private amusement à la Irene Dunne or Katharine Hepburn ("My father," she tells Hopsie when he politely terms her father "uneven" at cards, is "sometimes more uneven than other times"). This kind of grace note enriches the movie's serious moments. Sturges wrote some surprisingly direct lines for Stanwyck's Jean in the scene when Hopsie finds out her real identity—lines in which she reveals her true feelings. She comes up behind him in the ship's bar. "Are you an adventuress?" he asks bitterly. "Of course I am," she says, realizing he's found her out. "All women are. We have to be. If we waited around for men to propose to us, we'd die of old-maidenhood. That's why I let you try on my slippers, and put my cheek against yours, and made you put your arm around me. . . . But then I fell in love with you," she adds softly. "And that wasn't in the cards."

In this scene, and in the short scene near the end of the movie when Jean/Eve tells her father that she regrets her revenge, Sturges endows her with finer manners than those of any of the other characters. She is able to speak clearly and gently to Hopsie about her own mistakes and his social blindness. She is even able to confess her grief at losing him. Letting the other characters, and also the audience, catch a glimpse of bottomless grief was what Stanwyck did best as an actress. "Please don't look so upset," she tells Fonda on the ship. "Maybe I wanted you to love me a little more too [before I told you who I was]." But the hard-edged cleverness Stanwyck must project when she goes after Hopsie, first as Jean and then as Eve, weakens the impact of these moments of vulnerability. She never gets a chance to knit her character together through technique. Nor does Sturges ever let Henry Fonda show Hopsie comprehending what Jean/Eve is up to, and so become worthy of her.

One feels Sturges's fierce pleasure in the comic inventions of this movie, and his genuine desire to connect these inventions to the deeper themes of love and loss. The connections are not properly made, though, because of what can only be called emotional inadequacy in the directing. The comedy in this movie originates, more than in any other Sturges movie, in events from Sturges's own life, blended with stock situations from earlier romantic comedies. The Harrington father and daughter are not only a reverse-gender evocation of himself and Mary Desti, they recall the pairs of high-class thieves from *Trouble in Paradise* as well as Capra's heiress and tycoon father from *It Happened One Night* (of which they are counterfeit fac-similes). Sturges deliberately evokes *It Happened One Night* with his shot of Stanwyck's foot and leg as she trips Hopsie in the dining room—a tribute to Claudette Colbert's immortal limb-that-stopped-the-car in Capra's movie. McCarey's *Love Affair* is present too, not only in the shipboard setting but also in some of McCarey's actual shots: Stanwyck coming into the ship's bar behind Fonda repeats the camera angles of Dunne and Boyer's similar encounter; Stanwyck and Coburn eyeing Fonda as the ship docks reprises Dunne and Boyer at their ship's railing. When we get to the ancestral seat of the Pike family in Connecticut, we find a nearly intact version of the Bullock household from *My Man Godfrey,* complete with frustrated, earthy father (played again by *Godfrey*'s Eugene Pallette) and social-butterfly mother. It's as if those earlier movies had shown Sturges a way to picture his own life. At the very least, they let him know that he needn't waste time inventing what already had been invented, that he could borrow angles, occasions, and settings from earlier movies and fill them with characters of his own.

But for all his obvious mastery of directing, Sturges let the emotions of *The Lady Eve* get out of control. He couldn't find a way to allow the counterfeit heiress and the actual heir to share the same state of mind long enough to establish the illusion of love. Perhaps he was still too confused about his own relation to wealth, and his position vis-à-vis his two heiress ex-wives. Perhaps he wanted to believe they were the ones who had seduced him, even though he must have known in his heart that he had all the seducing technique. So he reassured himself gender-wise, and gave the technique to the heroine and the sap role to the hero. But the strain in *The Lady Eve,* its tendency to jeer at romance, testifies to Sturges's ingrained habit of viewing his own person in bifurcated fashion—as seducer and seducee, as con man and victim, as master of strategy and child of nature, as poor card shark and rich waif. He brought this bifurcated vision of himself to a comic apotheosis in *The Lady Eve*. But in the process he lost the romance.

. . .

IN HIS FINAL ROMANTIC COMEDY, *The Palm Beach Story* (1942), made
a year after *The Lady Eve,* Sturges at last resolved his own romantic equation—that is, he found a way to offer his adventuress a true union with her
opposite. To accomplish this, he replaced the tough yet vulnerable Barbara
Stanwyck with the more playful and ironic Claudette Colbert—just what
Capra had done eight years earlier to lighten the directional tone. But
Sturges also altered the equation in another surprising way: he split his
by-now-stock hero, the rich man's son, into two people, one superwealthy
and the other not wealthy at all. A new figure thus entered the Sturgean
equation—a middle-class man, an inventor named Tom Jeffers, played by
Joel McCrea. Tom Jeffers is married to Claudette Colbert's Gerry Jeffers.
(The couple's first names came from the cartoon about the cat and the
mouse.) The Jefferses are behind in the rent on their Park Avenue apartment—Tom is more visionary than practical. So it's Colbert's Gerry, tired
of living in genteel poverty, who precipitates the drama of the movie. She
decides to leave Tom. One day she encounters a little old deaf millionaire,
the Wienie King, inventor of the Texas Wienie (Robert Dudley), being
shown the Jefferses' apartment by the building manager, who wants to rent
it out from under them. The little Wienie King, grasping Gerry's plight,
peels off seven hundred dollars from a fat bankroll and gives them to her,
no strings attached. She pays the rent, takes her husband out to dinner and
the theater, lets herself be seduced by him one more time, then flees the
next morning, with him vainly following, to the Palm Beach train and a
divorce.

Here is Sturges's ultimate adventuress, thrown out in the world, with no
money and no possessions. (Her suitcase had opened and spilled in her
flight, just like Astaire's in *Swing Time.*) She's not a criminal like the Stanwyck heroines, but she is equipped with plenty of charm and ingenuity, in
the manner of earlier Sturgean heroines such as Isabel Parry, and Colbert's
own movie characters from Ellie Andrews on. Using her charm, she gets
invited onto the train by the Ale and Quail Club, a group of "rich millionaires" going duck hunting down South. That night, when they get rowdy,
she finds an empty top berth in another car and, climbing into it, steps on
the face, in the lower berth, of the richest millionaire of all, J. D. Hackensacker (Rudy Vallee). Hackensacker falls for her, buys her breakfast on the
train and then a lavish wardrobe in Jacksonville, takes her on his yacht to
Palm Beach, invites her to stay at his sister's mansion, and proposes to her.
So far this chain of events merely escalates Sturges's own primal scenario—

the one from *Strictly Dishonorable, Easy Living,* and *The Lady Eve,* in which the adventuress gets showered with luck and money. (Gerry Jeffers has done nothing till now but trip over millionaires.)

But Sturges throws a wrench into the familiar works: he brings Gerry's husband, the middle-class man, back into the picture, so that Gerry is confronted with a tough choice between the two men. Tom Jeffers has been bankrolled by the little Wienie King to "fly down there in an aer-e-o-plane and meet her with a bunch of roses." Gerry, flustered, introduces Jeffers to Hackensacker as her brother, Captain McGloo. Hackensacker's sister, the Princess Centamillia, enters the scene. The much-married Princess goes after "the Captain" and invites him to stay at her mansion too. Sharing quarters, Gerry and Tom fall in love again. They confess their real relationship to their host and hostess, causing momentary dismay all around. The whole thing ends cheerfully, though, with Hackensacker resolving to help Jeffers build his visionary airport, the Princess rejoicing that she hasn't lost her marrying touch, and brother and sister discovering happily that both Tom and Gerry have identical twins. The movie's last image is a splendid expression of Sturges's special vision of ironic abundance—a triple wedding, with an extra McCrea and Colbert each marrying a Hackensacker, and the original McCrea and Colbert remarrying each other.

IN *THE PALM BEACH STORY,* Sturges all but recapitulated the entire history of romantic comedy. The movie reprises *It Happened One Night* (with Colbert making her Jacksonville–New York trip in reverse), then turns into a spoof of *The Awful Truth* (with Colbert and McCrea reenacting Dunne and Grant's sleight-of-hand mutual seduction). In short, it blends a mid-thirties boy-meets-girl romance with a later comedy of remarriage. And it clarifies a feature of the genre that most other directors had fudged—its attitude toward money. Sturges mocks the rich in *Palm Beach Story* more fatally than most other directors ever managed to do. The Wienie King is the only rich person who is at all human—and his quick sympathy and ready charity stem from his memory of an impoverished youth. The Ale and Quail Club, by contrast, is a bunch of rich louts—philistines. Sturges's character actors, usually scruffy guys in his movies, here read as flawless millionaires because of the inspired detail Sturges put into their portraits. He had them wear and carry a variety of ridiculous hunting gear—Tyrolean hats, rubber boots, guns, and hunting dogs. He and they imagined a whole range of drunk rich men's voices—from blissful speechlessness to slurred logic to belligerent confusion. And he pictured them all blearily following the herd, in situations ranging from a mass serenade of Claudette Colbert in her berth, to a mad "posse," with guns and dogs, that goes marauding through the train.

The character of J. D. Hackensacker III, however, is a more sorry specimen of humanity than all the Ales and Quails put together. Sturges had "discovered" Rudy Vallee during a slump in the latter's career, when Vallee was playing himself in a thin musical (*Time Out for Rhythm* [1941]) with Ann Miller and the Three Stooges. Delighted with his find, Sturges tailored the superwealthy Hackensacker to Vallee's constipated, flowery tone and bookish delivery. Hackensacker is even more cut off from life than Hopsie Pike. He even talks like an antique. When he discovers that Colbert's Gerry Jeffers has lost her clothes in the Ale and Quail car, he suggests that she "borrow some odd pieces here and there among the lady passengers." When Colbert saunters into breakfast in a turban and skirt made out of Pullman towels, he praises her domesticity, saying, "I like a woman who can cook and sew and clean." "And weave!" adds Colbert with her raised-eyebrow lilt. The quintessential distilled Colbert persona, the flower of urbanity, romantic comedy's supreme combination of gold digger and little man, finds herself sitting across the breakfast table from wealth that's beyond her wildest dreams. But it's wealth that's been so cloistered and puritanized that Hackensacker resembles a parsimonious old maid more than a man. His lines are absurd escalations of the anticonsumerist sentiment that the very rich used to foist on their children by way of compensation. Vallee compares the values of the twenty-five-cent breakfast and the seventy-five-cent one; he explains he's riding in an ordinary upper berth because "staterooms are un-American"; he tips the porter a paltry ten cents from New York to Jacksonville; he writes down all his purchases when he's buying Colbert clothes in the "little store" in Jacksonville. "I write them down but I never add them up," he says cheerfully, looking up from the hundreds of dollars of entries he is making in his notebook. It's the dismayed porter left with the tiny tip who best describes Hackensacker, when Tom Jeffers asks if his wife left the train alone: "She alone but she don't know it." Moreover, Sturges extends the brilliance of his Hackensacker critique to the person of his sister, the Princess (played by Mary Astor). If huge wealth has made Vallee's Hackensacker a Nonentity, it has turned the Princess into a Character. From the minute she meets Hackensacker's yacht, she doesn't stop parodying herself—gushing about anything that comes to mind with that irritating loudness of the female very rich.

Sturges doesn't go to these lengths to lambaste the rich just for the fun of it. He does it to educate his middle-class leading couple. It's their close contact with their rich suitors that makes them fall back in love—or, rather, makes Gerry fall back in love with Tom, since Tom never wavers in his feeling for Gerry. Passion is not stressed, though, in their reconciliation. The scene in which Gerry yields to Tom, saying "Darling, darling, darling!" to the strains of Vallee serenading her with "Good Night, Sweetheart," is almost perfunctory. Sturges didn't put his energy into picturing Tom and Gerry's restored romance; he put it into demonstrating to his corruptible heroine—and to his audience—that rich people are really so ridiculous, so maimed, so unnatural, and so tiresome that with all their money they still can't be endured. Gerry rejecting Hackensacker represents a big moment in Sturgean narrative development. No Sturges adventuress had ever renounced great wealth. She had always managed, in the Sturges structure, to have the "true love" and the wealth besides. But in *The Palm Beach Story* the adventuress comes to believe she must give up the wealth to have the love (even though Sturges relents at the end and brings the money into the family by means of the Jefferses' twins). The point is, though, that Colbert doesn't just return to her husband through a series of Sturgean comic accidents; she makes a conscious choice to renounce Hackensacker and choose Jeffers. When Vallee offers her an engagement ring with a "chip of the Hope diamond" on it, she sneaks a look, then covers her eyes and pushes the box away.

In theory, at least, the ending of *The Palm Beach Story* meant that Sturges had resolved his own ambivalent attitude toward big money. One can see this from the deliberate references—more deliberate than in any other Sturges movie—to his own past. The Tom Jeffers character, who's inventing an aerial airport, stretched "like a tennis racket" over the city, recalls Sturges himself, who spent his first married years inventing things. And Gerry Jeffers, the wife, is even more of a Sturges stand-in. She takes a train to Palm Beach and meets a millionaire on it, just as Sturges had taken the train to Palm Beach in 1930 and met Eleanor Post Hutton. This is the most explicit link yet between the real-life Sturges and one of his adventuress heroines. But this time the Sturgean adventuress doesn't marry the millionaire; she remarries the new Sturgean middle-class man. And when that happens, it's as if Sturges had finally put the temptation of great wealth behind him—somewhat ironically, of course, because it's still there in the final wedding tableau. Tom and Gerry returning to a married state is like Sturges reconciling the two parts of himself, the wily fortune hunter who went around marrying rich persons (the Gerry in him) and the pure-minded dreamer who invented things and disdained other people's money (the Tom part).

· · ·

IT'S FUNNY, though, what happens to this movie in one's mind. It's true that Colbert has given up the dream of big money that had lurked around the edges of romantic comedy ever since Capra invented it. She finally understands at the end why she, and therefore America, must reject rich people. She doesn't even rely on a deus ex machina from the Establishment to point it out to her, as Colbert's Ellie Andrews relied on her father in *It Happened One Night*, as Hepburn's Alice Adams relied on J. A. Lamb, as Lombard's Irene Bullock relied on Godfrey in *My Man Godfrey*. Nor is she forced to reinvent the aristocracy of wit that brought Dunne and Grant back together in McCarey's *The Awful Truth*—an "aristocracy" that was hard to distinguish from the ordinary money-conscious bourgeoisie. Instead, she's allowed to understand, in the course of prolonged contact with the Hackensackers, that "money" and "class" don't necessarily go together. It is the ideal kind of "class"—good manners, courtesy, and a sense of fun—that causes people to grow and true love to flourish, not money. In the end Colbert's Gerry chooses this kind of class, which most Americans in principle could aspire to, over the money, which they weren't going to get.

But what does Gerry Jeffers really have, once she's made her choice? The same marriage, the same lingering problem about money (once the airport is built)—the same husband. And that husband is a curiously static character. Joel McCrea was usually sympathetic on the screen; here he's monotonously grumpy in most of his scenes. This wasn't McCrea's fault; it was Sturges's. It's as if Sturges, who had turned rich young men inside out with consummate satire, had reserved no insight for the ordinary middle-class hero who was just as much a stand-in for him as they were. In the end, Tom Jeffers recalls the pre-Sturges romantic-comedy hero, the character who could get away with not apologizing for ill temper and not even communicating in a good temper. The audience at the time probably wasn't meant to notice that Tom Jeffers wasn't much fun to be around—that was just how American husbands were. But today we are struck by Jeffers's emotional blindness. He can't see that his own grumpiness caused his wife to leave him in the first place. Nor by the end has he learned anything about himself. If this movie displays an exemplary clarity about issues of money and class, it's missing that vision of growth shared by a man and a woman, of erotic-flavored companionship, that Capra had put on the screen in *It Happened One Night*. Capra's Colbert—the heroine, the adventuress, the Depression's revisionist new woman—turns up intact in Sturges's apocalyptic comedy; she's still a lot of fun, even if her refined Mae Westian innuendos sound mechanical sometimes. But the McCrea figure isn't anything like

Capra's Clark Gable, the revisionist hero. He's not mischievous or kind or dreamy—he's just a boorish, if attractive, husband. This movie, in which Sturges finally balanced the money and class in the romantic-comedy equation, stopped short when it came to gender.

The end of all Sturges's exploring of the comic love affair was to return to square one—the humdrum American marriage in which the wife does all the thinking about the emotions. It's not that Sturges didn't have the wit to figure out another solution; he might have done this, if he could have persisted with the genre. But the climate for figuring out the ethics of a romance had come and gone with the Depression. At the close of this movie, we can't help feeling that Tom and Gerry are settling for a stale compromise—life with each other. The forties are closing in. Tom doesn't even have to consider changing his manners the way earlier heroes had made a show of doing; Gerry doesn't once think of getting a job, which was how earlier heroines secured their identities. The national mood was veering away from the concept of a female's independence coexisting with a male's. Soon, after the war, would come the domestic comedies, in which the tensions of middle-class marriage would be both ignored and celebrated, in which the arena of the city would give way to the arena of the household, in which husband and wife alike would act restless and numb as a matter of course. Sturges, that consummate skeptic, bowed here to the atmosphere of diminished hope, of "business as usual," that had killed romantic comedy. He ended *The Palm Beach Story* as he began it, with a wedding tableau, albeit an ironic one. Out of the tableau loom big cloudy white letters, spelling out a formula, followed by a quintessential Sturgean question: AND THEY LIVED HAPPILY EVER AFTER . . . OR DID THEY?

Joel McCrea,
Claudette Colbert,
Rudy Vallee,
Claudette Colbert,
Joel McCrea, Mary
Astor, and Sig Arno
in the final tableau
of *The Palm Beach
Story*.

CONCLUSION

THE LADY EVE AND *THE PALM BEACH STORY* sum up a decade of intelligent examinations by Hollywood of the American idea of love and marriage. Sturges's brand of intelligence was not only sharp but wild and cynical as well. Other romantic-comedy authors also took refuge in comic cynicism in these last moments before the country's plunge into wartime. One might call the movies they made then the post-Depression romantic comedies: movies such as Garson Kanin's *Tom, Dick and Harry* (1940), Howard Hawks's *Ball of Fire* (1941), William Wellman's *Roxie Hart* and Billy Wilder's *The Major and the Minor* (both 1942), George Stevens's *The More the Merrier* (1943), and the one that tips a romantic comedy into the genre of film noir, Billy Wilder's *Double Indemnity* (1944). All of these movies display a relentless verbal wit, a machine-gun pace, a wildly satiric spirit, a ridiculousness of situation—and a somewhat sniggering approach to sex. For some of the thirties women stars—Stanwyck, Rogers, Arthur— these movies provided their last roles as funny, desirable, and bright leading ladies. Ginger Rogers, who had mostly hidden a wild, goofy streak in her persona, broke loose in this atmosphere: her comic scenes with Adolphe Menjou in *Roxie Hart* (a remake of Maurine Watkins's twenties play *Chicago*) display a marvelous control of pace and a demonic precision.

But when in early 1943 the war came and settled in, Hollywood dropped the comedies and answered the call of duty with a parade of movies about the women who stayed home, along with a flurry of surefire low-budget thrillers and light musicals. What could leisurely, farcical love have to offer in a war? Besides the abrupt switch in the national mood, there also had occurred a mass exodus of personnel. Anybody who called himself a man in Hollywood had enlisted promptly—not only leading men like James Stewart, Henry Fonda, and Clark Gable but directors such as George Stevens and Frank Capra. Capra went to work for the war ministry putting together information films, the "Why We Fight" series. Stevens joined an army unit of documentary photographers. Leo McCarey, disqualified from service for reasons of health, found his heart full of a moist mixture of music, religion, and patriotism, and out of this fashioned his biggest hit ever, *Going My Way* (1944), about cozily irreverent priests doing good deeds. Gregory La Cava, whose career was pretty much washed up by then, brooded his way through the war. Only Sturges took wartime culture fearlessly into his satiric universe, creating two great war comedies—*The Miracle of Morgan's Creek* (1944), about a GI's teenage bride who gives birth to sextuplets, and *Hail the Conquering Hero* (1944), about a guy who poses against his will as a decorated marine. Amazingly, the country bought them—especially the first one, which was immensely popular.

But when the war ended and the movie industry's soldiers came home, they discovered that America—and Hollywood—had changed irrevocably. A host of younger female stars had made their appearance in the early forties—Linda Darnell, Jeanne Crain, Gene Tierney, Jennifer Jones, Donna Reed, June Allyson, Cyd Charisse—most of them discovered and developed by middle-aged producers: Harry Cohn at Columbia, Darryl Zanuck at Fox, David O. Selznick at his own Selznick International, producers who were also shedding their first wives around this same time. And out beyond Hollywood lay a new country. A host of GIs and their child brides were putting up new houses and manufacturing babies. Very few of them could find the time, the money, or the inclination to buy flowers, to dress for dinner, to go to the theater, to listen to the words of popular songs, to savor one another with wit and irony. Accordingly, the movies stopped creating characters who were ambiguous, who blended wisdom and corruptibility, modesty and daring, in one personality. Now it was the good women or the bad, the maternal long-sufferers or the tawdry sex queens, the eager young husbands or the melancholy private eyes, the family epics or the reckless films noirs. Most striking of all was the projection onto movies of the postwar economic upswing. Collective memory had almost relinquished the Great Depression, that brutal time which once had forced the giant, profit-hungry entertainment industry to desist from picturing an endless parade of material appetites in favor of a comic exploration of the nature of those appetites, their effect on human nature, and their triviality in the face of romantic love. The phenomenon of a country looking at itself in the movies, in the graceful, unassuming, self-mocking, at times truly illusionless manner of Depression romantic comedies, has never been seen since.

SOURCES

This book was constructed from many sources, primary and secondary, which are cited below and in the Bibliography. The main source was, of course, the movies I watched for hours and hours at the Library of Congress and at the Museum of Modern Art. The most valuable nonmovie source was the RKO Archive, which used to reside in thousands of filing cabinets in a hangarlike building in Hollywood, and which I was lucky to explore before it was dispersed to UCLA and Ted Turner. Documents from this archive (letters, contracts, memos, telegrams, scripts, tables of profits and losses, etc.) form the bases of chapters 4, 5, 8, and 10, which deal with RKO movies. Material in this archive also gave me a sense of the questions I needed to ask and answer about the making of other studios' romantic comedies. In addition, the scrapbooks and the clipping files at the Drama Collection of the Performing Arts branch of the New York Public Library at Lincoln Center were an inexhaustible source for discovering facts and imagining atmospheres.

After research, the knitting together of information was accomplished by means of a constant cross-referencing of dates, personnel, and statistics. Several reference books were crucial here: Ephraim Katz's intelligent, trustworthy, and entertaining *The Film Encyclopedia* (Thomas Y. Crowell, 1979); Leslie Halliwell's *Halliwell's Film Guide* (Charles Scribner's Sons, 1979); Cobbett Steinberg's *Reel Facts* (Vintage, 1982); and the series of books published by Octopus Books Ltd. in London and Crown in New York which have been nicknamed "Chiclets" books (for the Chiclet-sized photographs) and which describe all of the movies produced by a studio—*The Universal Story* (by Clive Hirschhorn, 1983); *The Warner Bros. Story* (by Clive Hirschhorn, 1979); *The RKO Story* (by Richard B. Jewell and Vernon Harbin, 1982); *The MGM Story* (by John Douglas Eames, 1979); *The Paramount Story* (by John Douglas Eames, 1985). I frequently consulted back issues of *Variety* at the NYPL Drama Collection—especially year-end *Variety*s, which contain round-ups of the previous year in the movie industry.

NOTES

page ix Bow's career: David Stenn's fine biography of Clara Bow emerged just as this book was being finished and gave me a new perspective on the thirties comedies.

1. CAPRA AND STANWYCK:
LADIES OF LEISURE

9 Harry Cohn's purchase of *Ladies of Leisure* recorded in the Copyright Office, Library of Congress: correspondence with Neal Watson, Copyright Office.

10 Biographical information about Jo Swerling: Jo Swerling, Jr., to EK.

hit plays in the late twenties: Reviews and manuscripts in NYPL Theater Collection.

11 studio merger plans: *Upton Sinclair Presents William Fox* is exceptionally informative about the economics of the movie industry.

13 Some of the Stanwyck biographical material was gathered from Al DiOrio's *Barbara Stanwyck: A Biography;* more was taken from Ella Smith's labor of love, *Starring Miss Barbara Stanwyck,* and from the Drama Collection's clipping files. Paramount's *Dance of Life* (1929) essentially reproduces the play *Burlesque,* with Nancy Carroll in Stanwyck's role.

16 "Follies girl": See *The American Earthquake* by Edmund Wilson.

17 create a comic persona: See various biographies of silent comedy stars listed in the Bibliography, plus James Agee's great essay "Comedy's Greatest Era," in *Agee on Film,* volume 1.

Prévost's weight problem: Capra to EK.

18 Capra's transformation of Swerling's script: In Capra's shooting script for *Ladies of Leisure* in the Wesleyan archives, large portions of Swerling's dialogue are crossed out, with pungent substitutions written in Capra's hand. At the start of this scene Capra penciled in this command: "Close-up Kay to be taken for this section."

2. CAPRA AND COLBERT:
IT HAPPENED ONE NIGHT

29 early-thirties gangster movies: See Carlos Clarens's *Crime Movies,* especially chapter 2, "Nights of Chicago."

30 waning of undiluted gangster and weeper films: This point was gleaned from *Variety* and from counting examples of different genres in the Crown "Chiclet" books about the studios.

Capra's partial weepers: *Miracle Woman* was based on Robert Ryskind and John Meehan's play *Bless You Sister,* which had its premiere on Broadway in December 1927, and was itself based on the life of the Los Angeles preacher Aimee Semple McPherson. The play is more a crass exposé of the preaching racket than a love story, so one could say that the movie, in emphasizing the love story, all but transformed the events of the play. *Forbidden* was made from an "original" scenario by Capra himself. *The Bitter Tea of General Yen* was based on Grace Zaring Stone's 1930 novel of the same name, which is not a love story either but, rather, a sociologically flavored study of racial types colliding. What Capra did to all three properties was to inject, almost from scratch, his own brand of romance.

31 newsreels: See Raymond Fielding's *The American Newsreel, 1911–1967.*

34 Capra's non-Stanwycks at the box office: See *Variety.*

35 West as part-director of *She Done Him Wrong* and *I'm No Angel:* West claims this credit

in her autobiography, *Goodness Had Nothing to Do with It,* and she is borne out by the visual framing of the punch lines in these movies and by the amazing frequency of close-ups of her face.

Mae's West's box-office power: According to the very reliable *Variety.*

page 37 Barbara Hutton: C. David Heymann's biography *Poor Little Rich Girl.*

38 the single change of costume: Claudette Colbert made this point to EK.

Gable's effect on Colbert's decision: Colbert to EK.

39 Colbert on Broadway: See Colbert file at the Drama Collection.

Colbert's charm and willfulness: Both were experienced by EK in several lively and pleasurable encounters with Colbert in Barbados.

42 audience's confusion in 1934: The point was made by Ann Douglas.

47 "I've got a system . . .": The line is from *I'm No Angel.*

48 "private" act/"public" decision: The point was made by Stanley Cavell in his discussion of *It Happened One Night* in *Pursuits of Happiness* and pointed out to EK by William Rothman.

3. ROMANTIC COMEDY
SETTLES IN

55 Loy's early career: Her autobiography is grimly illuminating on the subject.

56 MGM and romantic comedy: This reading of MGM's—and Paramount's—relations with the romantic-comedy genre is mostly mine, not from any book; but it takes off from the spirit of Steven Harvey's innovative long-ago course at the New School "The Studio as Auteur."

58 Thalberg at MGM: Frances Marion in *Off With Their Heads* described the pains Thalberg took with scripts in the early thirties and acknowledged his respect for his writers' ideas.

62 the "new" attitude in Hollywood: My point came from reading a lot of biographies and autobiographies of movie scriptwriters. For me, the most revealing about this generation's attitudes were Donald Ogden Stewart's and Ben Hecht's.

63 "women of achievement": This idea about notorious twenties females comes from conversations with Ann Douglas and Margo Jefferson and from the course called "Parallel Modernisms" which they taught at Columbia, 1987–89.

64 the Code and the Breen office: The clearest, simplest explanation can be found in Cobbett Steinberg's *Reel Facts.* Further illumination of the Code can be found in Thomas Schatz's wonderful new book *The Genius of the System.*

4. STEVENS AND HEPBURN:
ALICE ADAMS

69 Hepburn on Broadway: See Hepburn clipping file in the NYPL Drama Collection.

71 Berman's mistake: This point came from noting the awed tone of Berman's and other RKO bosses' memos to Hepburn in the RKO Archive—indeed, this same overreverent tone surfaces in most contemporary articles and biographies of Hepburn.

73 Wyler was the safer choice: Pandro Berman to EK.

Hepburn deciding on Stevens: George Stevens, Jr., to EK.

74 Stevens's early life: Material for this sketch comes from Robert Hughes's 1967 interview with Stevens, from Leonard Maltin's 1970 interview with him, and from my conversations with George Stevens, Jr., and Stevens's first wife, Yvonne Stevens.

75 Stevens backstage at *A Tale of Two Cities:* From Leonard Maltin's 1970 interview.

Stevens peeping through the curtains: George Stevens, Jr., to EK.

Stevens . . . attended at least part of the ninth grade: Yvonne Stevens thought this was not so, but at the urging of her son, George junior, she found a faded textbook from Sonoma Valley Union High School stored with George senior's things.

76 Stevens's recollection of the first *Alice* meeting at Hepburn's house: This is in the Leonard Maltin material and was corroborated by Hepburn and Pandro Berman.

77 Hepburn and the story conferences: Hepburn to EK.

81 Stevens's use of the novel: One of the most wonderful items in the RKO Archive is Stevens's own copy of *Alice Adams,* with passages of dialogue—much of which got into the movie—underlined.

82 small towns during the Depression: See the Lynds' *Middletown in Transition.*

5. STEVENS AND ROGERS:
SWING TIME

93 The sections that describe Fred's and Ginger's arrivals at RKO—in fact, this whole chapter—was influenced by Arlene Croce's landmark study *The Fred Astaire and Ginger Rogers Book.*

94 the wealthy young cabaret crowd: For descriptions of this crowd's behavior, see Donald Ogden Stewart's autobiography, *By a Stroke of Luck.*

95 Astaire's artificiality: This point came clear in the Drama Collection's file of reviews of *The Gay Divorce.*

96 Astaire and Rogers as Chevalier and MacDonald: Arlene Croce's point.

97 "I always carried": 1936 interview with Lela Rogers in New York *World Telegram,* Ginger Rogers file, NYPL Drama Collection. Lela Rogers's personality was further illuminated by Lela's younger sister, Jean Owens Hayworth, in interviews with EK.

100 Rogers asking for Stevens: Arlene Croce's point.

The *Annie* script had come to him only partially completed: This was corroborated by Barbara Stanwyck.

106 "she would meet herself": Unidentifiable clipping in Ginger Rogers file in NYPL Drama Collection.

pattern of "Pick Yourself Up": Croce's point.

108 Astaire's inarticulateness: Hughes's and Maltin's interviews with Stevens reveal that as a young man he thought of *himself* as inarticulate.

111 Rogers and Stevens's affair: Corroborated by Pandro Berman.

112 *Swing Time* as poem to the city: It is interesting to note that Stevens, according to

Yvonne Stevens, made his first trip to New York just before he filmed *Swing Time.*

6. CAPRA AND ARTHUR:
MR. DEEDS GOES TO TOWN

117 Arthur's early life: Details came from the entry about her in *Current Biography.*

119 "to learn how to act": This statement comes from the Arthur file at the NYPL Drama Collection; the details of her Broadway career emerged from the Drama Collection's scrapbooks of yearly play reviews.

120 Cohn luring Arthur back: Joseph McBride kindly shared this part of his Capra research with me.

121 Capra's crisis: Capra describes all this in his autobiography, *The Name Above the Title.*

122 Cohn's bad mistake: This too comes from Capra's autobiography.

7. LA CAVA AND LOMBARD:
MY MAN GODFREY

137 The sketch of Lombard's life owes much to her biography by Larry Swindell and to *Current Biography.*

139 Lombard's verbal toughness: Lombard's legendary penchant for swift, deadpan swearing is corroborated (wonderfully!) in the Lombard edition of a video series called "Power Profiles: The Legendary Ladies," produced by VidAmerica (New York, 1987).

142 Universal and the Depression: See *The Story of Universal.*

143 The details of La Cava's childhood and career all came from files and scrapbooks in the collection of his son, William.

144 La Cava at the Chicago Art Institute: Correspondence between EK and the Art Institute, which found La Cava's registration in its back files.

145 Beryl Morse and Lewis Mumford: Tom Bender caught the discussion of Beryl in Mumford's book *Sketches from Life.*

149 the ashcans and socialism: See *John Sloan* by Bruce St. John (Praeger, 1971). The cultural populism of the Depression can be seen in part

as a revival and an expansion of the radical "bohemian" spirit that had prevailed among a certain cadre of pre–World War I American artists (Stephen Crane, Theodore Dreiser, Isadora Duncan, John Reed, D. W. Griffith, the ashcans, etc.).

8. LA CAVA, ROGERS, AND HEPBURN: *STAGE DOOR*

page 161 *Stage Door*'s history was pieced together from material in the RKO Archives, William La Cava's collection, and interviews with Pandro Berman, Katharine Hepburn, Andrea Leeds, and Morrie Ryskind.

173 Rogers playing Jean's ambivalence: This point was worked out in conversation with Arlene Croce.

177 "The calla lilies . . .": The original *The Lake* was rewritten in part for Broadway and Hepburn, to make it suitable for American audiences; this line does not appear in the English play.

9. MCCAREY AND DUNNE: *THE AWFUL TRUTH*

185 Dunne's early life and career were reconstructed from *Current Biography* and from clippings in the NYPL Drama Collection.

188 McCarey's background was gathered from *Current Biography;* from McCarey's "oral history" on file at the American Film Institute library; from interviews with his wife, Mrs. Stella McCarey; his sister, Gertrude McCarey Tietzel; his daughter, Mary Virginia McCarey Washburn; and his onetime employer the late Hal Roach; and from the lengthy interview with him that appeared in *Cahiers du Cinéma* no. 163 (1965), pp. 11–21.

189 McCarey matching Laurel with Hardy: See especially Peter Bogdanovich's interview with McCarey in *Esquire,* February 1972.

190 He had noticed the success of his former colleagues: This is my assumption, based on the evidence.

191 McCarey wanted to be a Depression comedy auteur: Something like this point was made by Charles Silver in his lovely article on

McCarey in *Film Comment* (vol. 9, no. 5, September 3, 1973).

193 Zukor's visits to the set: McCarey interview in '65 *Cahiers du Cinéma.*

194 Dunne and McCarey's rapport: Dunne to EK.

195 preparing *The Awful Truth* for filming: By a wonderful fluke—a query by RKO to Columbia in the midst of the filming of *Love Affair*—copies of the records of *The Awful Truth*'s preparation were sent to RKO in 1939 and so ended up in the RKO Archive.

196 Dunne and Grant remembering filming: Dunne and Grant to EK.

the Delmars' conditions: Viña Delmar in a letter to EK. The description of working with McCarey also is quoted from her letter.

197 Dunne's response to McCarey's personality: Dunne to EK.

McCarey unnerving Grant: Mentioned by Bellamy in *When the Smoke Hit the Fan* and corroborated by Grant in an interview with EK.

198 Grant's background was gathered from Grant biography by Jerry Vermilye (New York: Galahad, 1973).

199 Lubitsch's world: I am indebted to James Harvey's *Romantic Comedy* for a lyrical and provocative discussion of Lubitsch.

206 Dunne at her most infectiously funny: Also in this scene, Dunne accuses Mrs. Vance of sitting on her handkerchief. Dunne told me that she thought at the time that this was too bold a gesture and said so to McCarey. McCarey reassured her that it would "play," and during the first preview of *The Awful Truth* she caught his eye to let him know she conceded the point.

207 All this hysteria: It helped to watch this movie with Laurie Stone, who has a nose for "classism."

10. MCCAREY, STEVENS, AND DUNNE: *LOVE AFFAIR* AND *PENNY SERENADE*

213 McCarey being wooed: From McCarey's contract and other directors' in the RKO Archive.

214 Lombard and Selznick: From Ron Haver's *David O. Selznick's Hollywood*. Information on other actors' contracts from *Variety*.

"Ginger was on her way up": Hepburn to EK.

Hollywood restructuring itself: This trend culminated briefly *after* the war in such projects as Frank Capra, George Stevens, and William Wyler's short-lived producing organization, Liberty Films.

"Middletown": The Lynds' *Middletown in Transition*.

movie attendance in 1936: Cobbett Steinberg's *Reel Facts*.

215 Both directors and players were now removed in time: This is my impression, culled from biographies and from the interviews with this book's personnel.

217 last-minute reunions: Impression received from *Variety*.

Bluebeard's Eighth Wife: Cooper's trial, for instance, is essentially a restaging of his trial in *Mr. Deeds*.

218 McCarey and the approaching war in Europe: This idea was suggested to me by Stella McCarey.

the casting of Dunne: Actually, Stella McCarey told me, *she* was the one who decided Dunne should be cast.

European revenue from American movies: *Variety*.

219 McCarey shutting down the set: Dunne to EK.

220 Dunne's hair and costumes: Dunne confirmed, when I asked her, that McCarey was very clear how he wanted her characters to dress and style themselves in his movies.

223 a world heading toward war: The disembodied nature, for Americans, of the menace of war in Europe can also be sensed while watching 1939 "March of Time" newsreels.

226 no less than seven writers: RKO Archive.

229 Stevens exceeding budget on *Gunga Din:* Pandro Berman to EK.

11. STURGES, STANWYCK, AND COLBERT: *THE LADY EVE* AND *THE PALM BEACH STORY*

237 My sketch of Sturges's life is based largely on James Curtis's biography of Sturges, *Between Flops*. My view of Mary Desti is based on *her* book, *The Untold Story: The Life of Isadora Duncan, 1921–27,* and on my own knowledge of "Isadoraiana," gathered for my 1979 book about the beginnings of modern dance, *Where She Danced*.

244 *Remember the Night:* I saw this movie long after I had encountered most of Sturges's oeuvre; its melancholy changed my reading of Sturges.

246 Stanwyck's special place in Sturges's imagination: When Stanwyck talked to me about Sturges, her voice, usually distant and dutiful, grew warm with conviviality, which to my mind corroborates this point.

247 genesis of *The Lady Eve:* Diane Jacobs, a Sturges scholar, kindly shared with me a long letter (dated January 17, 1939) from producer Albert Lewin to Sturges, which expresses his guarded approval of Sturges's transforming "Two Bad Hats" into *The Lady Eve*.

250 "movie within the mirror": This insight is from Stanley Cavell's *Pursuits of Happiness,* the chapter on *The Lady Eve*.

253 significance of snake theme: Also Cavell's point.

BIBLIOGRAPHY

Agee, James. *Agee on Film.* New York: Grosset & Dunlap, 1969.

Allen, Frederick Lewis. *The Big Change.* New York: Harper and Row, 1952.

Barnouw, Eric. *A Tower in Babel: A History of Broadcasting in the United States.* New York: Oxford University Press, 1966.

Barr, Charles. *Laurel and Hardy.* Berkeley: University of California Press, 1968.

Beard, Charles A. and Mary R. *America in Midpassage.* New York: Macmillan, 1939.

Bellamy, Ralph. *When the Smoke Hit the Fan.* Garden City: Doubleday, 1979.

Blesh, Rudi. *Keaton.* New York: Macmillan, 1966.

Capra, Frank. *The Name Above the Title.* New York: Macmillan, 1971.

Cavell, Stanley. *Pursuits of Happiness.* Cambridge: Harvard University Press, 1981.

Chaplin, Charles. *My Autobiography.* New York: Simon and Schuster, 1964.

Chierichetti, David. *Hollywood Costume Design.* New York: Harmony Books, 1976.

Clarens, Carlos. *Crime Movies.* New York: Norton, 1980.

Congdon, Don, ed. *The Thirties: A Time to Remember.* New York: Simon and Schuster, 1962.

Croce, Arlene. *The Fred Astaire and Ginger Rogers Book.* New York: Galahad Books, 1972.

Curtis, James. *Between Flops: A Biography of Preston Sturges.* New York: Harcourt Brace Jovanovich, 1982.

Dardis, Tom. *Keaton, the Man Who Wouldn't Lie Down.* New York: Limelight, 1979.

De Mille, William C. *Hollywood Saga.* New York: E. P. Dutton, 1939.

Dickens, Homer. *The Films of Katharine Hepburn.* Secaucus: Citadel Press, 1971.

——. *The Films of Ginger Rogers.* Secaucus: Citadel Press, 1975.

DiOrio, Al. *Barbara Stanwyck: A Biography.* New York: Berkeley Books, 1984.

Ferguson, Otis. *The Film Criticism of Otis Ferguson.* Edited by Robert Wilson. Philadelphia: Temple University Press, 1971.

Fielding, Raymond. *The American Newsreel, 1911–1967.* Norman: University of Oklahoma Press, 1972.

Fitzgerald, F. Scott. *The Crack-up.* New York: New Directions, 1956.

Gebhard, David, and Von Breton, Harriette. *L.A. in the Thirties.* Los Angeles: Peregrine Smith, Inc., 1975.

Gish, Lillian, with Ann Pinchot. *The Movies, Mr. Griffith, and Me.* Englewood Cliffs: Prentice-Hall, 1969.

Harvey, James. *Romantic Comedy in Hollywood from Lubitsch to Sturges.* New York: Knopf, 1987.

Haskell, Molly. *From Reverence To Rape.* New York: Penguin, 1974.

Haver, Ronald. *David O. Selznick's Hollywood.* New York: Knopf, 1980.

Hecht, Ben. *A Child of the Century.* New York: Simon & Schuster, 1954; repr. Donald I. Fine, 1986.

Heymann, C. David. *Poor Little Rich Girl: The Life and Legend of Barbara Hutton.* New York: Simon and Schuster, 1986.

Higham, Charles. *Kate: The Life of Katharine Hepburn.* New York: Signet, 1975.

Kael, Pauline. *The Citizen Kane Book.* New York: Bantam Books, 1971.

——. *When the Lights Go Down.* New York: Holt, Rinehart and Winston, 1975.

Kendall, Elizabeth. *Where She Danced*. New York: Knopf, 1979.

Lasky, Betty. *RKO: The Biggest Little Major of Them All*. Englewood Cliffs: Prentice-Hall, 1984.

Lloyd, Harold. *An American Comedy*. New York: Longman Green & Co., 1928.

Loy, Myrna, and Kotsilibas-Davis, James. *Myrna Loy: Being and Becoming*. New York: Knopf, 1987.

Lynd, Robert S., and Helen Merrell. *Middletown in Transition*. New York: Harcourt Brace Jovanovich, 1965.

Maltin, Leonard. *Of Mice and Magic*. New York: New American Library, 1980.

Marion, Frances. *Off With Their Heads*. New York: Macmillan, 1972.

Meltzer, Milton. *Brother, Can You Spare a Dime?* New York: Knopf, 1969.

Menjou, Adolphe. *It Took Nine Tailors*. Sampson Low, Marston & Col, London, 1950.

Mumford, Lewis. *Sketches from Life*. New York: Dial Press, 1982.

Ott, Frederick W. *The Films of Carole Lombard*. Secaucus: Citadel Press, 1972.

Robinson, David. *Buster Keaton*. Bloomington: Indiana University Press 1970.

———. *The Great Funnies*. London: Studio Vista Ltd., 1969.

Rosen, Marjorie. *Popcorn Venus: Women, Movies and the American Dream*. New York: Avon, 1973.

Schatz, Thomas. *The Genius of the System*. New York: Pantheon, 1988.

———. *Hollywood Genres: Formulas, Filmmaking, and the Studio System*. New York: Random House, 1981.

Schulberg, Budd. *Moving Pictures: Memories of a Hollywood Prince*. Briarcliff Manor: Stein & Day, 1981.

Scott, Evelyn F. *Hollywood When Silents Were Golden*. New York: McGraw-Hill, 1972.

Sinclair, Upton. *Upton Sinclair Presents William Fox*. Los Angeles: Sinclair (published by author), 1933.

Sklar, Robert. *Movie-Made America*. New York: Vintage, 1975.

Smith, Ella. *Starring Miss Barbara Stanwyck*. New York: Crown, 1985.

Smith, Gene. *The Shattered Dream: Herbert Hoover and the Great Depression*. New York: William Morrow, 1970.

Stenn, David. *Clara Bow: Runnin' Wild*. New York: Doubleday, 1988.

Stewart, Donald Ogden. *By a Stroke of Luck*. Paddington Press, 1975.

Swindell, Larry. *Screwball: The Life of Carole Lombard*. New York: Morrow, 1975.

Thomas, Bob. *Thalberg: Life and Legend*. New York: Bantam, 1969.

———. *King Cohn*. New York: G. P. Putnam, 1967.

Walker, Alexander. *The Shattered Silents*. New York: William Morrow, 1979.

Weinberg, Herman G. *The Lubitsch Touch*. New York: Dover, 1968.

West, Mae. *Goodness Had Nothing to Do with It*. New York: Belvedere Publishers, 1981.

Wilson, Edmund. *The American Earthquake*. Garden City: Anchor Books, 1964.

INDEX

Italicized page numbers refer to photographs

A NOTE ON THE TYPE

This book was set in a film version of Galliard, a typeface originally drawn by Matthew Carter for the Merganthaler Linotype Company in 1978. Carter, one of the foremost type designers of the twentieth century, studied and worked with historic hand-cut punches before designing typefaces for linotype, film, and digital composition. He based his Galliard design on sixteenth-century types by Robert Granjon. Galliard has the classic feel of the old Granjon types as well as a vibrant, dashing quality which marks it as a contemporary typeface and makes its name so apt.

Composed by The Haddon Craftsmen, Inc.,
Scranton, Pennsylvania

Designed by Iris Weinstein